WORLD TOUR

OF

EVANGELISM

by

Henry Clay Morrison

First Fruits Press
Wilmore, Kentucky
c2012

ISBN: 9781621710370

World Tour of Evangelism, by H.C. Morrison.
First Fruits Press, © 2012
Originally published by the Pentecostal Publishing Company, ©1911

Digital version at http://place.asburyseminary.edu/firstfruitsheritagematerial/20

First Fruits Press
B.L. Fisher Library
Asbury Theological Seminary
204 N. Lexington Ave.
Wilmore, KY 40390
http://place.asburyseminary.edu/firstfruits

Morrison, H. C. (Henry Clay), 1857-1942
    World tour of evangelism / by H.C. Morrison.
    Wilmore, Ky. : First Fruits Press, c2012.
    3rd ed.
    280 p., [27] leaves of plates : ill., ports. : 21 cm
    Reprint. Previously published: Louisville, Ky. : Pentecostal Publishing
    Company, c1911.
    ISBN: 9781621710370 (pbk.)
    1. Morrison, H. C. (Henry Clay), 1857-1942 -- Travel. 2. Methodist
    Church -- Missions -- Asia. 3. Methodist Church – Clergy – Biography. 4.
    Evangelists – Biography. I. Title.
    BV3705 .M75 A3 2012

Cover design by Haley Hill

asburyseminary.edu
800.2ASBURY
204 North Lexington Avenue
Wilmore, Kentucky 40390

First Fruits
THE ACADEMIC OPEN PRESS OF ASBURY SEMINARY

Henry Clay Morrison.

World Tour of Evangelism

BY

Rev. H. C. Morrison, D. D.

Author of "The Baptism with the Holy Ghost," "Two Lawyers," "Life Sketches and Sermons," Etc., Etc.

THIRD EDITION

PENTECOSTAL PUBLISHING COMPANY,
LOUISVILLE, KY.

This book is affectionately dedicated

to

Rev. T. F. Taliaferro and Wife,

who were my steadfast friends in the early days of my conflict with poverty and ignorance while preparing for the ministry.

CONTENTS.

Chapters.   Page.
1. Why I made the World Tour............7
2. Steaming Down the St. Lawrence........13
3. A Run through England and Scotland......18
4. A Visit to Sacred Shrines.............30
5. A Short Visit to Paris.................34
6. A Sabbath in Ancient Rome............37
7. Quail to Feed the Multitudes...........44
8. Going up to Jerusalem.................48
9. Within the Holy City.................53
10. Round About Jerusalem................58
11. Many Days Upon the Deep.............70
12. Opening the Campaign in India..........78
13. The Historic City of Lucknow...........85
14. On the Mountains with the Missionaries....96
15. Evangelizing in Bombay...............105
16. A Gracious Revival...................114
17. Pentecostal Meetings at an Annual Conference
                                        122
18. Going into Southern India.............131
19. The Great Work of Ramabai...........140
20. A Day in Delhi 148
21. Baptizing Converts 158
22. A Beautiful Monument 168
23. Methodism in India.................176
24. The Unrest in India.................185
25. Down the Straits to Singapore..........194
26. Evangelizing in Manila...............203
27. Our Campaign in China..............214
28. Korea's Turning to the Lord...........227
29. Salvation Scenes in Japan.............249
30. The Highest Duty of the Hour.........269
31. The Tobacco Fiend 274
32. The Hand of God in History 277

LIST OF ILLUSTRATIONS.

Rev. H. C. Morrison, taken in India.

Rev. J. L. Piercy.

Graduates from the Kindergarten in Japan.

Methodist Conference in Jubbalpure, India.

Rev. Mr. Hill and Family, Supt. of Bombay District

Group Japanese Evangelists.

Japanese Bible Woman.

Chinese Bible Woman.

Indian School Children.

Dr. Felt and Group of Young Indian Preachers.

The Temple Site in Jerusalem.

Methodist Missionaries at the Great Meeting in Lucknow, India.

Street scene in Songdo, Korea.

The Taj Mahl of India.   The Magnificent Tomb of a beautiful queen.

Scene in Woman's Hospital at Soochow, China.

South Gate in Songdo, Korea.

Korean Women Washing at the river bank.

Japanese Girls.

Korean Country Woman.

Mango Tree in India.

Group of Missionaries and Native Christians at Nagasaki, Japan.

Indian Conference at Bareilly, India.

Korean Methodist Preachers at Seoul, many of them sanctified during the revival.

Entrance to the Old Fort, Agra, India.

British Soldiers, most of whom were converted or sanctified in Bombay meeting.

Group of Southern Methodist Missionaries in Kobe.

East Gate in Songdo.

INTRODUCTION.

When the scientist goes 'round the world, the scientists are glad to hear him expound the scenes and events of his journey; so the report of the technical historian interests a class, and so the scholastic philosopher sees things at an angle peculiar to himself; but the writer of these pages is one of the people; a chief man among the brethren. He writes as a plain, comprehensive thinker, a discerning preacher, and a Christian to whom the kingdom of God is bigger than all other kingdoms combined. He sees things as an ordinary man would see them, and allows himself to be very human in the details of his observation and in his style of putting his impressions. As a mighty preacher, whose presence and ministry naturally bring to the surface situations which would remain hidden under ordinary conditions, the reader of these pages may expect some rare side lights upon national life and upon the life of humanity in general among the leading peoples of civilization and heathenism, on all sides of this great round world.

JOHN PAUL.

CHAPTER I.

WHY I MADE THE TOUR.

In the fall of 1904 a number of devout Christians of various denominations, representing the South and Southwest, met in the city of Memphis, Tenn., for prayer, consultation, and organization, looking to the conservation and general spread of the revival of Scriptural holiness. It was their special desire to preserve so far as possible this great movement of the Holy Spirit from fanaticism, and to keep it free from the narrow channels of sectarianism. It was far from their thought to organize a new church; they rather desired as far as possible, to unite the Spirit-filled people of various denominations into a union of hearts, seeking a great revival of spiritual life in all churches. They hoped also to be able to combine their efforts for pentecostal revival work in various foreign mission fields.

To this convention, which was held in one of the large halls of the city, came about one hundred delegates from many of the Southern states. The local attendance was large. There was a beautiful spirit of harmony and brotherly love, and the Holy Ghost was present in revival power, convicting sinners, converting penitents, reclaiming backsliders, and sanctifying believers.

An organization was perfected and called the *"Holiness Union."* Officers were elected, and by unanimous consent it was determined that the convention should meet some time in the month of October each year. Meridian, Miss., was selected as the place for the first annual meeting. Accordingly the Holiness Union met in Meridian, Miss., October 21-25, 1905. At this convention a Missionary Board was elected to collect money and assist in the support of several full salvation missionaries in various foreign fields. The Holy Ghost manifested Himself graciously at the Meridian convention, saving and sanctifying many souls. The magnitude of these conventions has continued to increase each year.

It was the unanimous decision of this Board of Missions that we should not undertake the organization of churches, or the establishment of independent missions or schools in any of the foreign fields, but that our work should be evangelistic and that we should send out evangelists to travel in the various mission fields, assisting the missionaries of existing churches in promoting revivals of religion. It would be the special work of such evangelists to seek to bring missionaries and native Christians into the experience of entire sanctification. The great desire and purpose of the Holiness Union is to assist in promoting a world-wide revival of full salvation, to help, so far as in them lies, to carry to the ends of the earth the glad news that Christ Jesus is able to save all men from all sin.

It was in accordance with these purposes that this writer was appointed by the Board of Missions of the "Holiness Union," in the fall of 1908 to make an evangelistic tour around the world preaching full salvation, assisting missionaries in revival meetings, making careful note of the spiritual state of the church, and gathering such information as would be of general use to the Board in future efforts to promote the doctrine and experience of entire sanctification in the various mission fields of the world.

Having provided a comfortable home for my family, on the campus of Asbury College, Wilmore, Ky., in the midst of devoted Christian friends, and the Board having provided for their support during my absence, and for my traveling expenses, I left home for my missionary tour of the world, Monday morning, July 19, 1909. For some days as I approached the time of separation from family and native land, I had a feeling not untinged with sadness, a deep, solemn sense of humility. I felt as if I were closing up one of the volumes of my life and opening a new one.

I praise God that He gave me a place in the *holiness movement*, and that it has been my privilege to preach and witness to the mighty power of Christ to save from sin.

For years I have believed moral and spiritual conditions to be far worse than is generally supposed, and that an insidious unbelief, which is destined to affect the whole moral and social life, of our nation, has been working away in our schools, universites, and pulpits; and I have believed that as the fearful results of these conditions begin to manifest themselves, the holiness people, could they be held to the Lord and held together, would prove a powerful agency in the maintenance and propagation of the saving truths of the Bible.

Those of us who have followed the main line of Scriptural teaching blazed out by John Wesley, have no occasion for regrets or apologies on this account. While the Bible lasts and a lost race needs a Redeemer, and we preach the great doctrines of the natural depravity and sinfulness of mankind, the *new birth*, the remains of the carnal nature, the cleansing away of that carnal nature by the blood of Christ through the baptism with the Holy Ghost, and the growth in grace of the sanctified, we will see the power of God manifested in the salvation of souls, and there will be life and action resulting from our ministry.

After two busy days in Louisville, I left for Des Plaines camp meeting, near Chicago, stopping off there for ten days to lead the daily Pentecostal services. This is one of the greatest Methodist gathering places this side of Ocean Grove.

The famous evangelist, Dr. Biederwolf, preached every night during the camp. He is a Presbyterian; full of zeal, uses the altar of prayer, and strikes at sin with a directness and severity rarely surpassed by any preacher I have heard. He is a man of tender heart and a great pleader for souls. Socially, he is a most genial, sweet-spirited man, but never dissipating the spirit of devotion. He carries a burden for souls and plans large things for the advancement of the kingdom of Christ.

I had never heard Bishop Quayle preach before. He is one of the most remarkable pulpit men on the continent. His Sabbath morning sermon from the text, *"He is able to do,"* moved and shook the people. It was like gathering clouds, with deep thunder and lightnings, and a great downpour of rain upon the thirsty earth, with the winds rocking the trees; then the clouds passed, the sun broke out, the raindrops sparkling like pearls upon the leaves, grass, and flowers, with the birds singing everywhere.

This was the fiftieth anniversary of the camp and many of the old veterans told of the great victories of the past in the days of Inskip, McDonald, and other men of precious memory who have passed to eternal rest and blessed reward.

The daily Pentecostal service was attended by thousands, and we never had sweeter liberty preaching full salvation. The altar was filled many times with earnest souls seeking cleansing from all sin. I think after some sermons, not less than two hundred held up their hands requesting prayer for their entire sanctification. Quite a number claimed the blessing of perfect love and I believe that thousands were stirred up with deep desires and strong prayers to be saved from all sin and filled with the Spirit. The people of this camp manifested much interest in our missionary tour of evangelism, and offered many prayers for us, bidding us God-speed.

From the Des Plaines camp meeting we went direct to Mooers, N. Y., stopping off one day to enjoy the beauty and grandeur of Niagara Falls. This camp is situated on the banks of the beautiful Chazy River, only three miles from the Canadian border. It seemed providential that my summer camp meeting campaign should bring me to within forty-four miles of Montreal, the point from which we sail. I am profoundly grateful to the camp meeting committees of Des Plaines and Mooers for making it possible for wife and children to attend me thus far on my journey.

Rev. J. L. Piercy, my traveling companion, joined me at the Mooers camp meeting and spent a number of days with us in altar work and testimony for the Lord. Our readers will want to know something about Bro.

Piercy. He was born and reared in Barren county, near Glasgow, Ky. Early in the history of our Pentecostal Park camp meeting an arrow of conviction struck him deep in the heart. He went West for one year, carrying this arrow, came back to Kentucky, and while attending a revival near his father's house, was powerfully converted, returning to the state of Iowa, he graduated from the *Agricultural College* at Ames, took a position as foreman at a good salary on a large farm, and while thus engaged received his call to the ministry. He gave up his position, sought and obtained full salvation, and went at once into the work of soul winning. The Lord has blessed him with a meek and humble spirit and a great love for souls.

Mooers camp meeting is run strictly on holiness lines, and has the largest annual gathering of any meeting of the kind in this region. There was a large number of workers present; among them Bro. Henderson, president of the Young Men's Holiness League; Evangelist Scobie, a redeemed prize fighter from Canada and a wonderful preacher of the gospel. A long chapter could be written of this meeting, but time and space forbid.

We closed the Mooers camp meeting Sabbath evening, August 15. I had a quiet day with my family Monday on the deserted camp ground, and Tuesday afternoon said good-bye to wife and the four children at Mooers Junction, N. Y., put them on the train facing South, and a little later boarded a northbound train for Montreal, Canada. This parting was one of the most trying moments of my life, and as the oceans and months sweep between, I commit them all to God, trusting His divine mercy for our preservation and reunion.

CHATER II.

STEAMING DOWN THE ST. LAWRENCE RIVER.

The population of Montreal is largely French, hence Catholicism is the predominating religion of the city. One church in the city, *Notre Dame*, cost more than three millions of dollars, and there are a number of vast churches besides a great cathedral which cost into the millions.   There are also many large schools, but there are saloons and dramshops in every direction, while thousands of women and children show the pinched hunger and destitution which must exist among them, where the liquor traffic flourishes, and the hard earnings of the people go into vast church buildings with images and pictures that cost untold thousands.   We were told that French Catholics held practically every political office in the city.   The sturdy English have charge of much of the great business and financial affairs.

Who would have thought that one could go almost one-third of the way from Montreal to Europe on the St. Lawrence river, yet such is the fact.   From Montreal to the mouth of the St. Lawrence is about nine hundred miles. We steamed out of the harbor at Montreal, Saturday morning, August 21, about thirty minutes past five.   The weather was calm and the sun shining brightly.   Our ship being a swift steamer passed quite a number of vessels which had gone out ahead of us, bound for foreign ports, and as we swept down the river we waved a welcome to other ships com-

ing into port after their long voyages at sea. The one
hundred and thirty miles to Quebec is through a beautiful region of farming land, pastures and villages clus-
tered along the shore, with tall church steeples pointing
to the sky. The river is sometimes two or three miles
in width, blue and clear, with ships going and coming,
busy tugboats hurrying here and there, and small sailing vessels spreading their white sails, beautiful in the
sunlight, to the gentle breeze which had sprung up.

With a spyglass we swept the shores on either side
with their lighthouses, meadows and harvest fields, and
people moving about their employment, all looking as
peaceful and happy as if the millennium had already
begun. Our ship stopped for four hours at Quebec,
giving the passengers an opportunity to see that old historic city. We went at once on a trolley car to the
Heights of Abraham, where the English and French
contended for the mastery of this new world, and stood
on the spot where General Wolfe, the commander of
the English troops, fell and held onto life until one of
his officers hastened to him crying out, "'They run, they
run." "Who run?" asked Wolfe. "The French,"
was his reply. "Then God be praised, I die happy,"
said the brave commander, and he fell back and ex-
pired.

It was one of the decisive battles of history. It
meant the English tongue, religious liberty, the open
Bible and Protestantism, instead of the French language, religious tyranny, the closed Bible, and Catholic
superstition.

Bro. Piercy and I strolled over the old battlefield
where a score of young Englishmen were playing crick-
et in almost dignified silence. We could but note and

comment on the absence of noise and hubbub heard on an American playground. A great fortification stands here on a high promontory overlooking the river and holding the gateway to the interior of Canada. The city has narrow streets and many quaint old buildings, with not a few modern structures springing up and over-shadowing the humbler buildings of the centuries past.

We steamed away from Quebec down the broad river which widened into five miles in width and then into the broad, beautiful Gulf of St. Lawrence. At Father Point the pilot left us, taking the mail back, and we had broken the last link in the farewell to native land. The Sabbath was a beautiful day. The only public religious service was the Church of England conducted by the ship's doctor in the saloon (dining room) at 11 o'clock. Before night we were passing the Island of Anicosti on our north, and Monday evening late we could see the dim bleak shores of the coast of Labrador. We were now in the region of the iceberg and the air was chill and damp like a December day. In the twilight we saw an iceberg looming up to the northern side and felt his cold breath sweeping over the deck.

We were passing through the straits of Belle Isle, Labrador to the north, and New Foundland to the south. When we took our walk on deck just before retiring, we could see an electric light blinking from a point on the New Foundland coast and bade farewell to the St. Lawrence, plowing out into the deep blue of the Atlantic Ocean, with nine hundred miles of our voyage behind us and sixteen hundred miles before us. The warm winds on the icebergs produce a mist or fog and that with the night makes it a passage not without

danger through this home of the iceberg, worst enemy
of the mariner. Only two weeks ago a ship in this region crashed into one of these mountains of ice, floating
in the open sea, and smashed her prow, but a warship
was near to render help, and no one was lost, the ship
being brought safely into port.

The fog is thick, the night is dark, but faithful men
are on the bridge, the hand of God is over us, Bro.
Piercy reads the second chapter of Paul's second epis-
tle to Timothy, we say our prayers and crawl to our little shelf beds, about twenty inches wide, and sleep as
sweetly as on the shore, until daylight finds us safely
and steadily sailing the main in a heavy fog, our steam
whistle sounding a long, loud note of warning every
minute, lest we should crash into some other ship in
the darkness. The waves were rolling high and our
good ship rocking heavily in the sea. We ate a meagre breakfast, but a little was that much too much,
and concluding that an empty house was better than a
bad tenant, we yielded to the inevitable and cast up
the breakfast, to our great relief. Almost every passenger on board was seasick for the day. Piercy and
myself lay close to our berths and suffered but little.
The day was rough on deck, with rain, raw wind, and
not a wink of sunshine. The following day the sea
was much better, the clouds had lifted somewhat, the
sun broke out frequently, our seasickness had passed
away, and we trod the deck like old sailors.

With morning and evening prayers in our stateroom,
our Bibles and plenty of good books to read, three
meals a day and a good tramp on deck after each
meal, with another walk just before retiring, the time
passed rapidly enough, and before we could realize it,

we looked out into the dark night,Saturday night, August 28, and saw the flash lights from a lighthouse on the coast of Ireland.   Sabbath morning we arose early while our ship was passing the rugged shore of the Isle of Man, a small island off the English coast ten miles long and six to eight miles wide.

At breakfast I announced that we would have a prayer of thanksgiving in the ladies' reading room and a few of us gathered there.   We read the 19th Psalm and Bro. Piercy and myself each led in prayer, and the Spirit of the Lord was graciously with us.   After prayers all hands were on deck gazing at the shores of England looming up in the distance.   Soon the ocean was enlivened by steamers and sailing vessels going and coming in every direction.   A pilot came on board to conduct our ship up the river and the towers and steeples of Liverpool arose out of the smoke and mist before us.   A great multitude of people had gathered on the dock to welcome our ship and many were watching with anxious faces for expected friends.   Of course no one was looking out for us, but somehow we had no feeling of being strangers and went on shore glad to feel the solid earth again, after eight days and a half of swaying deck beneath our feet.

CHAPTER III.

A RUN THROUGH ENGLAND AND SCOTLAND.

We had secured the name of the Mona, a modest temperance hotel, and after a few moments delay at the customhouse where the officer asked, "Have you any spirits, tobacco, or perfume?" to which of course we could answer "none," our baggage was marked and passed before we could get it open for inspection, and in less than ten minutes after we left the ship we were bag and baggage in a cab dashing away for our hotel, which we found to be a clean, modest, comfortable place.   Dinner was not served until half past one, and after we were shown our room, eager to get out after more than a week pent up on board ship, we walked out to stretch ourselves.   We found a small park near our hotel, and strolling around in it, we saw a mass of men gathered at the foot of a monument listening to a man in a red shirt who was delivering a fierce harangue on social conditions.   We stood long enough to hear him scream out, "If any Christian says there is a hell, he is a liar," at which the motley crowd broke into laughter.   He was especially bitter against Gen. Booth and made many statements utterly false, representing the grand old man as selfish and indifferent to the suffering conditions of the poor.   The speaker himself was a bad looking specimen of humanity, but was mixing in some sad and startling truths about the hunger and starvation of the poor masses in his jargon of falsehoods and abuse.

After dinner we walked down a street for a few blocks and turned into a large mission hall where we saw men gathering. In fact a man on the street handing out cards, had asked us in. Soon a goodly number of men had gathered, and led by a man at the organ, in fine voice, they broke out singing, "There's not a friend like the lowly Jesus." How sweet and homelike it sounded. For some reason the leader called on this writer to lead the prayer and from the hearty "amens" I judged there were some fully saved men in the audience. The evangelist, a stout Scotchman, preached a lively sermon against intemperance, bristling with sharp points and striking illustrations and offered a Christ mighty to save from the drink demon.

When we came out it was raining gently and coming back to our hotel we came to the monument and the man in red shirt was still bawling away, having put on his coat and cap, and the mass of men had tightened up about him listening with close attention, apparently indifferent to the shower. He was by this time so hoarse that he spoke with much difficulty.

In the evening we went to Central Hall, a magnificent down town Methodist Church, built to catch the masses. It cost two hundred and forty thousand dollars. The auditorium seats two thousand and three hundred people, and notwithstanding the rain, it seemed to be full to the top gallery. There was a band of violins and horns, with a monster pipe organ and a great choir; besides, all the people sang and the music was inspiring. They sang, "Abide With Me, Fast Falls the Evening Tide;" "My Faith Looks up to Thee;" "I Will Sing the Wondrous Story," and "I Could not do Without Thee, O Savior of the Lost." Every

word good poetry and good doctrine, with tunes the
angels might sing in heaven. It was almost worth the
trip over to hear those two thousand people sing. The
regular preacher was not present and a young man from
London preached. The sermon was short and very
suggestive, but not much fire or power. Quite a number remained for the after service, which consisted of
several songs and two prayers, and we were out by
half past eight. The streets were literally full of people.

We walked up to where a great multitude
was gathered about a blind woman singing
beautiful gospel hymns and scores of the people were
joining in. They sang one hymn after another and
an old man passed a box for pennies. Starting home
a block further down we found a young man—a handsome, clean fellow, playing an instrument something
like an accordion and singing, keeping time to the music
with a graceful swing of his entire body. His voice
was remarkably mellow and while he did not seem to
sing loud, he could be easily heard more than a block
away. The passers-by stopped in a circle about twenty or thirty feet from him and almost every one joined
in the singing. Well-dressed people, men and women,
stopped and picked up the tune; common fellows of
the street and dirty urchins joined in. The quiet was
like the sanctuary, no word was spoken; now and then
some one would leave the circle and go over and whisper to the leader. He would nod his head, going right
on and directly would break into the song asked for.
There was a dirty one-eyed boy in an old coat, much
too large for him, sitting on top of a garbage can smoking a cigarette. He flung his cigarette away and joined

in the song with a marvelously sweet voice, rising and falling with an elasticity and mellowness that called for an effort to keep from weeping while we listened. They sang "Lead Kindly Light," "A Little Talk With Jesus," "Why not To-night," and on and on from one beautiful song to another until the great silent buildings seemed to listen in reverence, and the air about us was burdened with hope and love.

From Liverpool we went to Glasgow, Scotland, and from that city we ran over some forty or fifty miles to Edinburgh. The scenery through England and Scotland at this time of the year is beautiful. The harvesters were in the fields gathering in wheat, oats and hay. We saw modern binders, the old scythe and cradle, and the reap hook or sickle, all in use in the fields.

Much of the land is in grass and covered over with flocks of sheep and herds of cattle. The pastures were intensely green and dotted here and there with clumps of beautiful trees. It would be difficult to exaggerate the beauty of an English landscape. There is scarcely a weed to be seen anywhere, and almost every foot of earth is covered with grass, vegetables or flowers. Frequently we saw rows of potatoes growing outside the field enclosures, along the railway track. The beauty of the landscape is enhanced very much with well trimmed hedges or compact stone walls. There are no rail fences and we noticed but one short string of wire fence. The highland pastures of Scotland were beautifully green and dotted over with great flocks of as fine sheep as one could wish to see. These islands surrounded by the ocean are kept cool and moist; they rarely suffer from drought and the verdure

everywhere is of rich growth and dark healthy green.
We were struck with the perfection of the country
roads. They are as smooth and firm as the streets of
a well kept town, and much cleaner.

Edinburgh is a famous old city, with a population,
as near as we could learn, of something near four hundred thousand. The places of chief interest to us were
the Castle, the Cathedral and the Old Palace. The
Castle stands upon a great hill, or small mountain,
which lifts itself abruptly from the plain, about the center of the city. It was a great natural stronghold in
the days of clubs, bows and arrows, swords and
spears, and even the old time fire arms were powerless
against its impregnable rocky sides. Massive stone
walls run around at the crest of the bluff, and there is
only one way of approach, and here an enemy would
meet with huge walls and vast gates of heavy wood
and iron.

Of course the modern guns would pulverize the masonry, but in the olden time the invaders looked on from
afar and turned away from the hopeless task of capturing the Castle. It is now a barracks for soldiers, kept
in perfect order, with quite a warlike appearance.
There are stairways and passages worn with the tramp-
ing feet of the centuries; prisons and dungeons from
which the weary captives gazed out upon the sweet
freedom of the valleys far below; parapets and towers
from which the sturdy watchers have swept the horizon
for more than a thousand years.

At the highest point in the Castle is a
stone chapel in which kings and queens used
to pray in times of sore distress, and at
another point is a vast banqueting hall, with ceil-

ing as high as a church, in which they held their feasts.
This hall is now a museum in which one may see the
armor and weapons of the olden times—swords and
helmets, spears and shields, battle-axes, coats of mail,
and shirts made of small rings of steel.   Here also is
the gun carriage upon which the body of the late beloved Queen Victoria was conveyed to its final resting
place.

Parts of several famous Scottish regiments are stationed in the Castle, among them the "*Black Watch*" and
"*Seaforths.*"   They are great sturdy Scotchmen with
white leggings, plaid pants, and blood-red coats. When
in full dress uniform they wear kilts, with bare knees
and Scottish caps and feathers dancing in the air, while
they stride about as if they owned the earth. A Scotchman of the Black Watch arrayed in his brilliant uniform with his bagpipe in full cry is about the most
picturesque spectacle to be seen in the Castle.

One of the most interesting places to visit in Edinburgh is Giles Cathedral.   It was built in the eleventh
century; has suffered from fire and been added to many
times, but much of the original structure has defied the
gnawing tooth of time and stands firmly awaiting coming events, and will no doubt be here when Christ appears with His saints. Much history clusters about this
place.   It was here that John Knox thundered out the
truth, fearless of kings, queens, men, or devils.   There
are many memorial tablets and windows in this church,
commemorating the devotion of Christians and the he-
roism of soldiers.

In the Old Palace we saw the life-size portraits of
many kings, the reception rooms, bedchambers, with
the beds falling to pieces with age, the dressing rooms,

and winding stairways. We were shown the little
room where Mary, Queen of Scots, sat eating supper
with her false lover when Lord Darnley, her drunken
husband, came in with a party of men, dragged the
fawning favorite from the Queen's presence, and while
a brawny Scotchman stood over her with a sword in
hand, the men carried her screaming lover into another
room, and a brass tablet marks the spot where they
stabbed him to death. The Queen afterward contrived
the death of her husband, married the nobleman who
arranged the murder, wound up with many years in
prison, and finally her beautiful head was chopped off
on the executioner's block. We left the place with a
mingled feeling of sadness and disgust.

The trains of this country and the engines that draw
them look like playthings compared with our trains and
locomotives in the states, but they make good time with
not one-tenth the fuss about it. I have believed for
years that all of our bedlam of screeching whistles in
the United States was useless. Now I know it. The
trains here whistle but little, and then not one-tenth so
loud as ours.

Glasgow is not nearly so interesting a city to the
traveler as Edinburgh. It is much larger, being a great
shipping port, manufacturing and commercial center.
We spent one night in Glasgow with the hospitable family of Rev. George Sharp. He was a Congregational
pastor until a few years ago, when he and his people
were turned out of the church because they had received
and proclaimed the experience of entire sanctification
through the blood of Christ. They organized a Pentecostal Church and have erected an excellent stone
structure, and the Lord is prospering them. Within

REV. J. L. PIERCY.

about three years they have grown into five congregations and it now looks as if they would grow rapidly and accomplish a great work in Scotland. The need is great beyond words to describe. I preached to them one evening. A great congregation had gathered, filling the floor and almost every seat in the gallery. The singing was marvelous and the Lord was in the place. Four persons came to the altar; two professed to find peace and two purity.

I was profoundly impressed with the looks and feeling of the people. It was exactly like it is on our side of the ocean. The holiness people are baptized by one Spirit into one body. May the Holy Ghost abide with and lead Bro. Sharp and his people.

While in Edinburgh some one pointed out a tablet on the wall of an upstairs room where Burns once lived for a time. Underneath this room was a saloon, "*The Bobby Burns,*" and lying in a heap on the street with her head against the wall of the saloon was an old woman beastly drunk. A couple of frowzy-looking women came out of the saloon, dragged her to her feet, and hustled her away to save her from the police and thirty days in prison. It was the saddest sight we have seen since landing on these shores.

We made the trip from Glasgow, Scotland, to London, England, about three hundred and ninety miles, in a little less than ten hours. When the little vehicle in which we rode to our hotel pulled out into the streets we were caught in the turbulent stream and roar of traffic and borne forward like a chunk on a swollen river. There are but few street cars in London. The people travel in two-story omnibuses, almost as large as street cars, about one-half of them drawn by horses, and the

others, great mammoth automobiles, propelled by gas-
oline.   The number of these vehicles is so great that at
times you will see five or six of them going each way
in one block, with wagons, carriages, carts and
cabs all mixed in between.   They move rapidly, every
fellow trying to get ahead, and how they keep from
killing scores of people we could not tell.   In fact,
there are many accidents in the streets.   We have seen
no place either at home or abroad where there are such
rivers of human beings flowing in the streets as in
London.

For a penny (a two-cent piece) you may ride quite a
distance on top of one of the great automobiles and
look down upon the multitudes below you.   As our
time was short we selected the places of most historic
value and visited them, getting a good view of the people, and stores and shops, as we went from place to
place.   Of course Wesley's old chapel was full of interest to us.   There it stands some twenty or thirty
yards back from the street where John Wesley built
it, and where he preached to the throngs who crowded
to hear him.   The great multitudes heard him in the
open air.   In Wesley's day the church seated fifteen
hundred people; now the seats are larger and more
comfortable and will accommodate twelve hundred.
The old wooden columns that supported the gallery
have been removed and replaced with marble pillars,
representing the various Methodist bodies of the world.
There was one for the M. E. and one for the M. E.
Church, South.   We sat a moment in John Fletcher's
chair and stood up in Wesley's pulpit, and Bro. Piercy
the old sexton and myself had a season of prayer at the
altar rail.   On Sabbath morning we heard a poor

sermon in this church, and at night we went to hear an energetic young Methodist preacher who delivered a good sermon, to a great audience in the Lyceum Theatre, from the text, "*What think ye of Christ?*" He sometimes has four thousand people to hear him, but had been away on his vacation and this was his first evening service after his return, so the audience was smaller, I should say two thousand. A pleasant gentleman gave us seats in a private box where we could look down on the audience and it seemed that every one sang. The beautiful old hymns were printed on folders and these were passed to everybody. There was a large orchestra. The advertisement of the meeting said sixty instruments. The singing in England charmed and thrilled us. They do not hollow and bawl, but sing with marvelous sweetness.

London is dotted over with great monuments; England has produced a host of great men and she will never forget them. The monuments to Nelson and Wellington tower above all others. They are now building a monument to Queen Victoria in front of the palace; it will be one of the most beautiful in the world; it deserves to be taller than the trees and whiter than the snow.

We visited Westminster Abbey and walked among the monuments, and tablets, and tombs of kings, statesmen, soldiers, missionaries, and ministers of the gospel. The most interesting to me was the tablet to the Wesleys, the bust of Chinese Gordon, and the grave of Livingstone. There is a tablet to the memory of Haverlock, but in the wilderness of tombs and monuments we failed to find it. One of the most interesting objects

in this old Abbey was the throne chair in which the
kings and queens of England have been crowned for
many centuries.   Fastened underneath the seat of this
chair is the *stone of destiny*.   It is eight or ten inches
thick and some twenty inches long.   Our guide said,
"Under the seat of this throne chair you will see the
stone of destiny.   It is supposed to have been Jacob's
pillow.   It was brought to Ireland in ancient times and
from there to Scotland where it was kept by the kings
for five hundred years, then captured by one of the
kings of England and placed many centuries ago where
you now see it."

It is eighty miles from London to Dover, at which
point we took ship for France.   Our train ran
right up to the ship's side and there was a
great scramble to get on board.   The ship
started at once.   I left Bro. Piercy to guard
the baggage while I looked for our quarters.   The
wind was blowing a gale and the spray leaped high,
and by the time I had gotten back to Piercy our ship
was out to sea.   We got our luggage and made a run for
our quarters.   The ship curved and a gust of wind
pitched me across the deck and blew my hat off, which
I caught just as I was brought up against the guards,
which kept me from going overboard.   Piercy was
thrown to his knees several times, but we had a good
laugh and got inside just before the waves commenced
sweeping over our deck.   We crawled up into our berths
and watched the mad waters through the bull's eyes,
heavy round glass windows, about the size of a large
dinner plate, fastened in the steel sides of the ship.
The wind was terrific, but we lay still and neither of
us was sick a moment; and in a little more than an

hour we were gliding safely into the port at Calais, France.

The thing that saddened our hearts in England and Scotland was the widespread evidence of intemperance. Not that all of the people drink, not that there is not a considerable element of abstainers; but drinking is very general and drunkenness is shockingly common.

England, as well as our own country, is in great need of a religious awakening. May God send it. The English home and the English court stand for much that is good and great, and all along through the years England has produced men like Haverlock, Gordon, and Gladstone, who have not only towered up as statesmen and soldiers, but have shone brightly as true disciples of our Lord Christ. It has been almost a century since our last war with England and the time has fully come when American children should not be taught to hate the *"red coats."* The people who speak the English tongue should be taught to love and respect each other and should stand together for mutual protection, the advancement of civilization, the peace and evangelization of the world.

CHAPTER IV.

A VISIT TO SACRED SHRINES.

The British Isles have given the world a number of distinguished Christian heroes. During our brief stay in England and Scotland it was our privilege to uncover our heads at the graves of Wesley, Bunyan and Livingstone, and to look upon several monuments that commemorate the lives and deeds of men whose names are revered throughout civilization. The remains of John Wesley and John Bunyan sleep close together. Wesley's grave is in a small burying ground in the rear of Wesley Chapel. Just in front of the chapel across the street is a small cemetery, and in it lies all that is mortal of the great dreamer, Bunyan, only a few hundred feet from Wesley's grave. What mighty men they were! How unselfish, how fearless, and how faithful! Standing at the simple monument that marks the spot where Wesley sleeps, what a procession of memories came trooping before us. The humble beginning, the ridicule and persecution, the steadfast devotion, the ceaseless labor and the great victory. I believe all men of all creeds and those of no creed honor that faithful, loving, fearless soul and look upon his life as one of the most laborious and unselfish spent in the service of his Master for the salvation of men since the days of St. Paul.

John Bunyan's tomb is a modest block of masonry a few feet high with the bronze figure of the great preacher lying at full length upon it facing up toward the "celestial city." On one side of the masonry is a man with a huge burden upon his shoulders, with head bowed in sorrow for his sins. On the other side the same man with the burden fallen off and his face lifted in joy for the forgiveness of his sins. Nothing could be more appropriate. We stood there, hat off, thinking of the time when his persecutors offered to release him from prison if he would pledge himself to preach no more and the immortal hero of the cross answered them: "I will remain in prison until the moss be grown upon my forehead like my eyebrows; but if you release me to-day, I will preach Jesus to-morrow." Think of such a man turning back or hesitating to preach to the perishing multitudes because some pompous, indolent ecclesiastic forbade his doing so. Unthinkable.

Dr. Livingstone lies buried in one of the naves of Westminster Abbey. There is a slab in the stone floor the full length of his grave and on it his earnest appeal for Africa and his prayer for the blessing of God upon all who may help to heal "this open sore of the world." Reflecting on his life of self-denial and unceasing toil and his death upon his knees in the far away dark continent, without relative or friend, save his faithful black men, to comfort his dying moments, we could readily believe that in that great day the Master could say to him, "Well done, thou good and faithful servant." But, reader, can the Master speak thus to us who have done and suffered so little for Him and the lost souls for whom He died?

There is only a small bust of Chinese Gordon in Westminster Abbey, but in St. Paul's Cathedral as if in peaceful sleep there is a beautiful life-size reclining marble figure of the great soldier and saint. It was a sacred spot at which to stand and meditate.   I visited it twice during our short stay in London and longed to go back again.   He was a fearless soldier, a wise ruler, and a meek and lowly disciple of Christ.   I could but think of the time when he gave the great gold medal conferred upon him by the Chinese government for signal services, to relieve famine sufferers.   He finally lost his life trying to save the lives of others.   He saved others, himself he could not save; and this is the strange and beautiful philosophy of our holy religion.   No man can save the lives of others until he is willing to give up his own life. Deep surrender, constant surrender, crucifixion of self, consecration of self, forgetfulness of self, lifts the flood gates of power into the soul for glorious service.

In one of the squares of London there is a beautiful monument to Sir Henry Haverlock, the brave soldier and devout Christian who led the mere handful of British soldiers against the countless hosts to the relief of the beleaguered residency in Lucknow, India, during the great mutiny. He was a small, wiry man, past sixty years of age when he accomplished that almost superhuman feat.   It is said that during those awful days of marching and fighting under the burning sun of India he spent two hours on his knees every morning before taking the saddle at the head of his dauntless little army.   He seemed to wear a charmed life.   No doubt the hand of the Lord was over him until his work was done.   He rode untouched amidst many a storm of bullets, but when those for whom he so bravely fought were saved, he sickened and laid him down in quiet rest, fell on sleep, and awoke, I doubt not, in the presence of the Christ he so deeply loved.

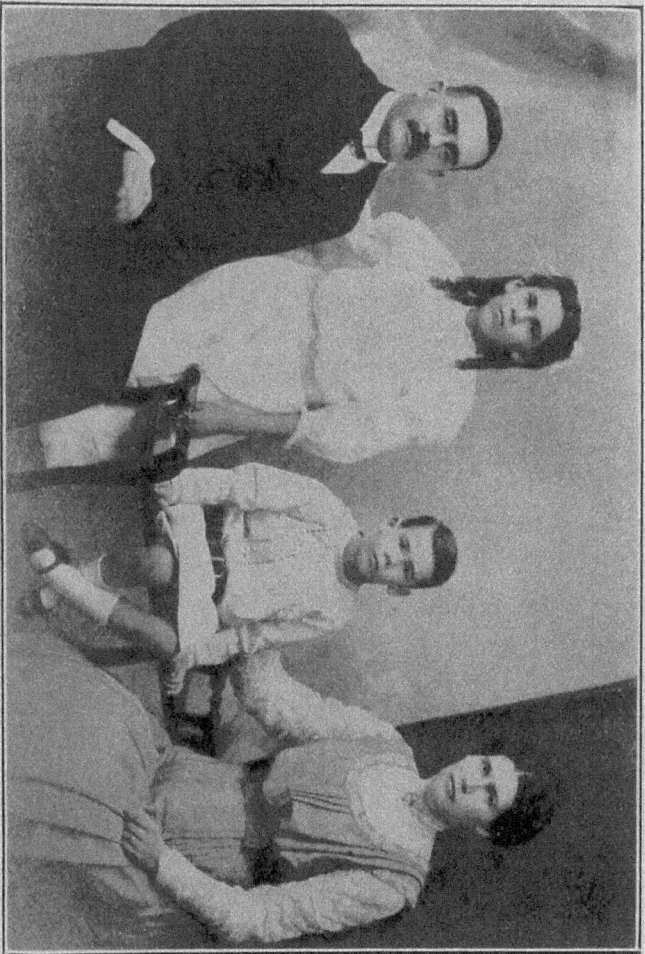

Rev. Mr. Hill and Family, Supt. of Bombay District M. E. Church.

No such thrill tingled through my entire being since I left my native land as that which swept over me while standing at the foot of a bronze statue of John Knox, in the old kirk at Edinburgh. There were two sayings chasing each other through my mind. The first fell from the lips of Knox and the other from the lips of an Englishman standing at Knox's grave. The former: *"Give me Scotland or I die."* The latter: *"There lies a man who never feared the face of man."* My soul caught fire and I could have wept and shouted. For the moment my soul rose within me, and I felt as if I loved all men, feared no man, and longed to preach to all the mighty power of Christ to save and sanctify from all sin.

I am sure I do not worship living men, much less dead ones, but it was an inestimable privilege to stand by the graves or monuments of these great souls for a few moments and reflect and pray and gird up one's own soul for the battle. Men may so live that they cannot die. Their bodies crumble into dust, their immortal souls ascend to God, but their lives, words, and actions, seem to linger, an invisible, hallowed presence to bless the world.

CHAPTER V.

A SHORT VISIT IN PARIS.

Paris is reckoned to be the most beautiful city in the world. It abounds in splendid buildings, wide streets, beautiful parks, and magnificent columns, arches, and monuments. Their principal art gallery has no rival. Its magnificence dazzles the beholder as he passes from one great hall to another, looking upon the productions of the old masters. The pictures in this great gallery representing the various scenes in the life of Christ, from the nativity to the ascension, would alone fill a large gallery. As artists and architects the French are not surpassed. Their aesthetical nature is highly developed and their very bodies and slender, delicate hands seem to be formed for the mastery of the fine arts.

Catholicism has been the blight of France. After centuries of worship of the virgin, the pope, the bones of saints, and all sorts of relics, the people have turned against the church and drifted into infidelity, spiritual death and moral waste and degradation pitiful to contemplate. The French people worship the *Beautiful.* Splendid architecture, great paintings, gold-covered ceilings, rose-tinted walls, sparkling jewelry, exquisite form, elaborate drapery and graceful manners are the god of France. Paris is a whited sepulchre with the white dropping off in great flakes, revealing her moral decay for which she seems to feel no conviction, but which she treats as a matter of course.

One may cross the channel which separates the British Isles from France in a little more than an hour's time, but measured by moral and religious conditions one has traveled fifty years, if not a century.   It is the wide difference of civilization with a Bible and a civilization without a Bible; of a people worshiping the Lord and a people worshiping a virgin.   Protestantism has made the English the great civilizers and evangelizers of the world, while Catholicism has made the French a nation of unbelievers, incapable of helping themselves or any one else into moral and spiritual light. Could a John Wesley have appeared among the French one hundred and fifty years ago what a different France we should have today.   But Rome locks the door against the light of truth and stumbles on with her degraded people into darkness.

What France needs is the gospel.   Would God some mighty Frenchman would arise, some Napoleon of grace, or some Gambetta of spiritual power, and sweep the beautiful land of France with a tornado of gospel truth.   A great field preacher would attract multitudes of hearers in this land of moral night, and I doubt not turn thousands to our Lord.   Some very aggressive movement ought to be set on foot to give the gospel and the Bible to the French people.

The most beautiful and impressive sight in Paris is Napoleon's tomb.   His ashes rest under the great dome of the chapel of the Invaledes (or Old Soldiers Home).   Entering the front door you walk forward to a circular marble railing and leaning over you look down some twenty feet into a vast circle, surrounded by angels carved from marble white as snow, all facing the great block of brown marble in which, in a golden coffin, the Emperor sleeps.   Some twenty yards further on is a vast altar with four large columns supporting a magnificent capping wrought in gold, upon which falls a mellow light from windows on either side typifying the love of the French people.   Back of the altar is a huge cross and on it a bronze, life-size figure of the Christ.

We spent two days and two nights in Paris, and were glad to get away.   Her grandeur and beauty could not charm us as we thought of her moral depravity and spiritual death.   If we had had the time we would have been glad to have stopped at Milan, Venice, and Florence, but as our time was limited and our hearts yearning for the field of battle, we hurried forward to Rome, stopping for a part of a day and one night in Geneva,Switzerland,landing in Rome Saturday at noon, tired, hungry, and dusty. We had not had our clothing off, nor our heads on a pillow but once from Tuesday night to Saturday night.   We went forward in the second-class cars amidst the dust and smoke of cigars and cigarettes, getting off now and then for fruit or lunch.   I thought often of Paul's far more rugged journey to that famous city almost two thousand years ago, and again and again the words of the inspired writer passed through my mind.   In describing the storm and tempests and hardships, he says, "And so we went toward Rome."

CHAPTER VI.

A SABBATH IN ANCIENT ROME.

We arrived in the ancient city at noon on Saturday, and after taking a bath and something to eat, we took a cab and were driven to many places of interest. From a hilltop overlooking the city the driver pointed out to us Ancient Rome, Modern Rome, and Catholic Rome. The view was splendid. There lay spread before us the most renowned ancient city in the world, except Jerusalem. There were the ruins of palaces, forums and mausoleums that had been erected long before the birth of Christ. Every great stone and broken column, and worn tower, and stately archway is burdened beneath a weight of tragic history. St. Peter's Cathedral and the Vatican stand very near each other, great piles of masonry, gray with age. There is nothing attractive in the outside of these structures except their immense size and the great forest of huge stone columns which support the porticos.

The Vatican was not open to visitors on the day we were there. We stood at the door and looked into the vast hall at the armed guards of the Pope as they paced to and fro. St. Peters within is magnificently beautiful beyond anything we had ever seen or dreamed. The vast pillars, arches, columns, altars, tombs, statues, and carvings with splendid mosaics and paintings and great sweeps of lofty ceilings overlaid with pure gold representing millions of dollars fairly dazzle the beholder. I have no doubt but the money which

has been raked together from the four quarters of the
globe and put into mere ornamentation in St. Peters and
the Vatican, if rightly used, would have been sufficient
to have evangelized the heathen world.   It would at
least have planted mission churches and schools
throughout the world.   We did not stay long in the
place.   I wanted to get out into God's fresh air and
breathe freely.

We went to the Methodist Church Sabbath morning; we arrived at the church more than a half hour
before preaching, and while waiting stepped into a
small Catholic Church. I sat in a chair near the door,
and without moving from the seat counted forty odd
pieces of statuary, images of angels and supposed saints,
carved from snow-white marble.   The cost of these
figures was something enormous.   It was very
restful to get into the Methodist Church after
looking on so much gorgeous and idolatrous display.   The Methodist Church is substantial in its simple beauty, and well adapted to the work for which it
is intended.   The preacher for the day asked me to
preach.   I declined, but offered to exhort after him,
which I did, and so had an opportunity to bear witness
to the sanctifying power of Christ's blood in Rome.

After the service we bought some cakes and fruit
and went down to the Coliseum; and finding a comfortable place in the shade on a great broken stone, we sat
and rested, and ate our dinner, looking out over the
great arena on which so much tragedy had been enacted, and up into the vast galleries from which eighty
thousands of spectators looked down upon those
scenes of blood and slaughter.   Out there in
that arena five thousand wild beasts were slain

in one hundred days, when the Coliseum was first opened for the entertainment of the public. There gladiators have fought land and naval battles for the gratification of a people who delighted in the excitement of human conflict and bloodshed. There a multitude of Christians have given up their lives for their faith in the world's Redeemer.

We ate slowly of our simple lunch, and divided it with an humble priest who sat near us gazing thoughtfully upon the vast ruins which surrounded us. After the luncheon, we crept under an arch near to one of the prisons in which the Christians were kept and in which they offered their last prayers before going to the arena to be torn in pieces by wild beasts. There we offered up prayers and thanks to our Christ who has led his church on through the conflict of the centuries. We took a walk out the Appian Way which made us think of the long ago when the great Apostle Paul, in clanking chains, walked over the same stretch of highway when he came a prisoner to Rome. As we walked back to our hotel in the cool of the afternoon, and the sun went down, the churches were closed, the bands played gay music in the squares, and tens of thousands of the people poured into the streets and gathered about the cafes to eat and chatter and drink wine while the silent stars, which have shone over the city for thousands of years, came out and looked down upon these vast multitudes of members of the Catholic Church who seem to have scarcely any knowledge of the Bible or of practical piety. Without doubt, Rome is badly sunken in idolatry, superstition, and sin.

Monday morning after a visit to the ancient broken gateway, through which Paul is said to have entered

Rome, and the Catacombs, the underground city near Rome in which the ancients buried their dead, and in which the Christians used to hide in times of persecution, we took the train at noon for Naples, reached there a little after dark, and after supper walked out to get a glimpse of the city under electric light. It is the habit of the people in southern Europe to keep close during the heat of the day and to pour forth in multitudes in their best clothing after sun down, to listen to music, chat about in the little parks, eat ices and drink wine. Bands were playing in various places and great throngs were gathered about the cafes, seated at tables, while men and women sang on raised platforms for their entertainment, and the multitude cheered over their wine glasses.

Next morning we went to Cook's office and got our mail. How delightful to get good news and loving words from the far-off homeland. After an early lunch we set forth with three other young Americans, to see grim old Vesuvius. One of our companions was a New York business man, the other two were young professors of Johns Hopkins University, at Baltimore. From the city we saw the volcano with a wreath of smoke drifting from the top of its great fire-scorched cone. We rode on a trolley some distance, then up a grade in a buss. Then we took an incline car up the mountain side. Each side of the track was lined with vineyards, the vines burdened with great clusters of grapes that looked delicious.

One of the recent eruptions had swept away a large portion of the railway track, from which point we had to foot it. When we left the car we got off in the midst of

as motley a gang of Italians as you could well imagine.
They rushed at us with offers of scrubby little horses
and chairs on poles to assist us up the mountain side, all
of which we refused.   The lazy soldiers fell down in
the shade and left the chattering mob to follow us,
which they did with most vehement insistence that we
should employ them. "Has anyone a revolver?" asked
one of the young professors as we wound up the ascend-
ing path.   "There are six of them and only five of us."
Gradually the men dropped behind and turned back,
but one stout fellow with a heavy leather strap wound
about him walked just a little in front of me.   When
we came to the foot of the cone and started almost
straight up the climbing was laborious.   At every step
the soft ashes and cinders would give way and the foot
would slip back half the distance of the step.   I was
carrying from fifteen to twenty years more of hard work
up that cone than any other member of the group, and
every one of those years seemed to weigh a ton.   The
beating sun was blinding hot.   With the fearful glare
of light and the sinking cinders I was staggering about,
laughing to keep my courage up, when my friend who
had walked in front of me darted back and applied the
leather strap and up the hill I went.   Don't think
the good fellow beat me.   No, he slipped a stirrup on
the end of his strap into my hand, and throwing the other end over his shoulder, leaned forward and
pulled me up, a part of the time one of the
guides whom we met, pushing me in the small
of the back, fortunately placing his hand on
the very spot that was aching intensely at the moment.
Piercy pushed ahead and longed for a snapshot to send
home to my boy, and so we climbed to the rim of the

great crater and looked down into the yawning depths from which has leaped out so much destruction and death. The yellow sulphurous smoke was rising slowly up while the invisible fires crackled and rumbled in the depth of the mountain.

Going down was easy, but as I sat on a rock and pulled off my shoes and beat the cinders out of them I bade Vesuvius good-bye and promised myself to climb its rugged sides no more, which promise I am fully persuaded I will faithfully keep.

The next morning we found we could drive out the ten or fifteen miles to Pompeii cheaper in a little hack than we could go with Cook's party on the train, so we secured one of the little vehicles and drove out through the city into the suburbs, then a town, and through many villages, giving us a busy street most of the way, with a stretch of garden or vineyard here and there. We met hundreds of every conceivable sort of vehicles hurrying pell-mell into the city market with their various products, while the streets were lined with stalls and walking peddlers with a hundred different fruits or articles for sale.

The evidences of abject poverty were on every hand. And dirty! It would seem impossible for human beings to get so dirty even if they devoted their time to industrious effort to that one purpose.

Pompeii, the reader will remember, was a populous city standing on the plain near the foot of Vesuvius, and many years ago was buried by a volcanic eruption. It seems that first a poisonous gas swept over the city in an instant asphyxiating the people in a horrible death grip, and then the falling ashes and lava turned the whole into one vast cemetery. For centuries the city slept in unknown silence, but some years ago the work of exhuming it was begun. About one-half the city has been uncovered and the work is still going on.

As one tramps through the streets of Pompeii once teeming with life, now empty and silent as the grave, he thinks again and again of the truthfulness of that Scripture statement, *"The wages of sin is death."*

CHAPTER VII.

QUAIL TO FEED THE MULTITUDES.

From Naples to Port Said, a voyage of near four days, we had beautiful weather and a comparatively smooth sea. Neither Bro. Piercy nor myself was seasick for a moment. As we passed out of the strait of Sicily, at the southern point of Italy, we had a very good view of Messina, the city so recently wrecked by the earthquake which swept into eternity one hundred thousand souls. Our ship rode into the harbor at the mouth of the Suez Canal at Port Said, at two o'clock Sabbath afternoon. We went ashore in a perfect bedlam of humanity. The stores were wide open and hundreds of people were in the streets with various articles of trade in trays, in their hands, swung over their shoulders, and crying out for customers. There were Turks, Egyptians, Arabs, Africans, French, Italians, and every sort of mixture of blood conceivable, mingled in one chattering mob of frenzied humanity striving to make a franc or a penny.

We walked for hours in the burning heat trying to find the Peniel Mission. Had we asked for the "American School for Girls" any one could could have told us where to find it. When we finally located the place we were given a most hearty welcome and I was comforted to find that Sister Richardson, the head of the mission and principal of the girls' school, had been sanctified and prepared for this good work in a revival I conducted in the Southern Methodist Church in

Woodland, California, some fifteen years ago. The school, which is supported by Sister Manie Payne Ferguson, of Los Angeles, Cal., stands in the midst of Arabtown, an oasis of prayer in a desert of sin. I preached at night at the *Seaman's Rest,* a little chapel kept open by Rev. Locke, a faithful man who has stood at this trying post for twenty years. Dwight L. Moody, the great evangelist, and Gen. Booth, preached at this place when passing through. I preached in this chapel four nights in succession and the Lord was with us. A number asked for prayer and others testified to great uplift of soul.

We found three groups of faithful souls here. The American School for Girls, the Seaman's Rest, and Rev. Bro. Hope, a faithful Scotchman, with two helpers who has charge of the British Bible Society work. It is their business to distribute Bibles on the various ships that come through the canal. Most ships coal here, spending some hours, sometimes several days, and it gives these men a good opportunity to go on board and sell copies of the Scriptures. Last year they sold seventeen thousand copies of the Bible or Gospels. This widespread distribution of the Scriptures in all languages is a great work and must bring untold good to the race. The French ships buy the least number of Bibles, and laugh at the men who go on board to sell them. The Italian ships are buying many copies. The Bible men who speak many languages, told me that a colored regiment of our nation coming home from the Philippines bought more Bibles than any other ship. They go on board, pile up their books and go among the sailors, cooks, firemen, and all conditions of

men and offer Bibles for sale.   Sometimes their books
are stolen.   But, they said, our colored soldiers bought
books, took care of the books they left on deck and did
not steal one.   The Lord bless old "blackey."   The
men spoke so well of these soldiers not stealing Bibles
that we were quite pleased.

We were surprised when we landed at Port Said to
see people about the streets with live quails in their
hands.   Monday we saw great quantities of quail in
ccops in the market.   Children had bunches of them
tied with strings.   People were picking quails on the
sidewalk and their feathers were blowing about the
streets.   We had quail served at the table, and upon
inquiring were told in a matter of fact way, "this is the
time of year that the quail come over."   It is a remarkable fact that hundreds of thousands of quail fly
across the Mediterranean Sea from southern Europe to
Egypt.   It is a full thousand miles across.   They alight
in Port Said where the people eat them in great numbers.   Many are dressed and shipped back in cold
storage to Paris and London.   Bro. Locke, the missionary, told us that he once sailed west from here on
a French steamer which carried alive in coops one hundred and fifteen thousand quails.   They erected poles
about as high as telephone poles along the beach and
stretched great nets on them. Birds come over in flocks
something like wild pigeons used to fly in the South
and are entangled in these nets by the thousand.   It is
a common thing for them to fly in the windows of the
houses and to light on the house tops.   When they fall
they are very tired and it is easy to catch them.   They
look quite like our partridge at home, but are smaller.
In Numbers 11:31 we read: "And there went forth a

wind from the Lord, and brought quails from the sea, and let them fall in the camp." These birds were coming over from southern Europe, as the custom is, just as our blackbirds go South in winter. They would have fallen by the seashore, but God sent a strong wind and bore them on into the wilderness to the camp of the Hebrews. Bob Ingersoll used to make great fun of this Bible account of the feeding the Hebrews with quail. Had he been in Port Said, Egypt, some time when these migratory quails were falling along the sea-shore by the hundred thousand, he would have dropped that item of ridicule from his blasphemous speeches.

We closed our meeting in Port Said Wednesday evening, September 22, and after the benediction was pronounced some one came forward and said that Bubonic plague had broken out in the city and we would perhaps not be permitted to go to Jerusalem. But next day we went before the proper health officer, he passed us and we went on board a Russian ship bound for Joppa. Our ship was a dirty little craft with a variety of horrible odors, but we had a restful night and next morning we arrived in Joppa with a yellow flag at our mast, which notified the health officers that we had come from a plague-stricken city.

CHAPTER VIII.

GOING UP TO JERUSALEM.

We waited for the health officer to come on board the ship at Joppa and grant us permission to land. We were kept waiting - but a short time, and the doctor was generous, and we all passed the examination without trouble. Then there was a scramble for the dozen boats that had come out to take us to land. The landing at Joppa is a notoriously rough one and ships stop out some hundreds of yards from the shore and you are brought to shore in small boats, with ten or a dozen strong men at the oars and a pilot who knows how to take advantage of the waves and shoot you in between the great rocks. Once on shore we found ourselves in a perfect rabble of men, donkeys, and camels. The streets are narrow and filthy, with fruit and vegetable peddlers sitting in haphazard fashion on the pavements or out in the streets.

After dinner we had time to visit the Russian Church which is supposed to stand on the spot where Peter raised Dorcas from the dead. We also visited the house reputed to be the one upon which Peter had his vision of the four-cornered sheet. We went on to the flat stone roof and had a fine view of the sea over which Peter doubtless gazed and meditated on his vision after he had slept and dreamed.

We took second class in the dirty little train that leaves Joppa for Jerusalem at 2 o'clock in the afternoon and clattered away past groves of orange trees, with fig and olive trees growing in luxury on either hand.

The Temple Site in Jerusalem.

Just out of the city we saw a village of good stone houses in course of construction, homes for a thousand of the returning Jews. We crossed a broad, fertile plain with herds of goats, flocks of sheep, bunches of camels, and now and then a large number of cattle, grazing in the harvest fields from which the wheat had been gathered. We were surprised at the appearance of thrift and plenty spread before us in this beautiful valley. The valley passed, we were going up a narrow gorge between barren rocky mountains towering up on either hand. We could plainly see the marks of the old terraces that once reached the mountain tops when their sides were covered with vineyards and fig and olive orchards. This is now a barren waste. Just before reaching Jerusalem we passed through a narrow valley of beautiful vegetable gardens and terraced hillsides with grapevines growing luxuriantly.

"As the mountains are round about Jerusalem, so the Lord is round about His people from henceforth even forever." Jerusalem is so surrounded by mountains that you can not see the city till you get quite near it. The city is on a hill surrounded by a rim of mountain ranges, like the rim of a huge bowl. There is the narrow outlet for the brook Kidron. The railroad station is quite out of the city, and we hurried from the train into a carriage, and coming around the curve of the road the city burst upon us with its great, gray walls, towers, spires and domes. The road leads over a fill built across the valley of Gehenna, and as you drive over it and turn toward the Joppa gate the tower of David looms up at your right, only the deep, wide moat separating you from the huge grim walls which have stood there through the centuries. The

lower part of these walls no doubt date back to the
days of Solomon, but the upper portion, built by Cru-
saders and Turks, is of a much more recent date.

We were in a hotel just across the street from the
tower of David where a detachment of Turkish troops
are stationed.   At 3 o'clock in the morning the crash
of a cannon jarred and shook our windows and I called
out to Bro. Piercy, "Jerusalem shall be trodden under
foot of the Gentiles until the time of the Gentiles be
ended."   The contempt and scorn of the Mohammedan for Jews and Christians amounts to a bitter hatred.   I see that a traveler who has recently visited
Jerusalem and the East speaks of the decadence of
the Mohammedan religion.   As a proof of his statement he says that he saw but a few of them at prayer.
A Mohammedan might write the same of Christianity
from St. Louis.   Suppose a Mohammedan should
spend Monday and Tuesday visiting the churches of
St. Louis and write home that he had visited a hundred
large churches in that city, and that they were all
empty; no one seen at prayer, and that therefore he
was fully convinced that Christianity was fast passing
away.   We would calmly smile at his credulity.   I
visited a Mosque in Port Said during worship, and it
was packed with devotees.   I saw thousands of Mohammedans on the streets with their strand of prayer
beads in their hands, counting them and often moving
their lips in prayer as they went about their daily avo-
cations.   In Jerusalem there is a Mohammedan temple
near the Mosque of Omar that will hold several thous-
and people, but cannot accommodate the throngs
who gather there for worship on special days of prayer;
when the temple is filled large numbers of people bow

in the streets in front of the temple. Let no man for a moment suppose that Mohammedism is in a state of decay.

Jerusalem is the great center about which religious thought crystallizes. Jew, Christian and Musselman come here to worship, and, wide apart as they are in their views of God, to them all, Jerusalem is a sacred city and they cling tenaciously to the revelations and traditions clustering about these ancient hills. It would seem as if the compassionate God of all men had made Jerusalem a powerful magnet to hold the different sections of divided and embittered families of mankind together, and here through the centuries they have met and quarreled and fought, no one set of believers able to drive any other away, but all alike clinging with tenacity to the sacred spot where God has so wondrously revealed Himself to men.

The next morning after our arrival we were walking up the street, and looking across, I saw four well-dressed men, who looked like our sort of people, and I called out, "Speak English?" "Yes," was the answer as they started over to meet us, asking, "Is this Morrison? We were expecting you and want you to come up and stop with us at the Hughes Hotel." Our group of new friends turned out to be four young professors of Beirut College, who have spent their vacation in the holy land and in and about Jerusalem, traveling and studying. We were soon quartered at the Hughes Hotel, and were delighted to find Bro. Forder, a faithful and fearless Englishman and missionary to the Arabs, whom we met in the United States a few years ago, with his wife, in temporary charge of the hotel during the absence of the proprietor, Mr. Hughes. We were quite at home with these friends, and before the day passed had seen Rev. Mr. Thompson, the pastor of the American Church and head of the "Christian Missionary Alliance School" for boys and girls. It was arranged that I should preach Sabbath morning and evening and each evening during the week, closing on Friday night, October 1. Our young professors had arranged to leave Monday, but becoming interested in the meetings, decided to remain through the week and attend the services. During the day they rendered us most valuable service, showing us the places of interest about the city. At night they attended the meetings, two of them frequently at the altar seeking full salvation from sin. The thing about Jerusalem that powerfully impresses the thoughtful mind is the fact that the life and customs of the people are the same today that they were in the times of the writing of the Scriptures.

As God shut up the Old Testament in the Hebrew language, and the New Testament in the Greek language, so He has shut up this land of the Bible in the hands of a non-progressive people, and they have held and kept it as it was in the days of Christ and the ancient Hebrew kings. Had some progressive Christian people had control of the land it would long ago have chaged its customs and habits, and would today be quite unlike the Palestine of the Old and New Testaments. But it has pleased the Lord to preserve it as it was when His word was given—a powerful witness of the inspiration and unchanging truth of the Bible.

CHAPTER IX.

WITHIN THE HOLY CITY.

The streets within the walls of Jerusalem are very narrow. The principal business streets in the old city are never used for wheeled vehicles. Many of them are more of an arcade than a street, arched over much of the way with stone masonry, with large openings at the top to admit the light. The little booths fronting on the streets are from ten to sixteen feet wide and run back ten, twenty, or thirty feet deep, and are packed with articles of trade. The entire front is the counter, and when you trade you do not go into the store, but stand in the street and the eager merchant lays out his wares for your examination on the counter. During business hours there is a busy throng pressing, shouldering and pushing by each other in these streets. The smallest and stoutest little donkeys pass along with great sacks of grain or bolts of cloth or baskets of fruit strapped on each side, or a heap of raw sheep skins contributing their part to the fearful odors.

Here is a woman, thin, sun-baked, and miserably clad, crouched up against the wall with three little chickens for sale; another has green pepper pods in a basket; another a tray of green olives; another some sort of greens, and still another with dry shelled beans. An old man in white silk robes, with grey beard and of most dignified bearing, rides by on a well groomed and finely saddled donkey; two Turkish soldiers walk rapidly through the throng, women with veiled faces and noiseless feet move along; Hebrew priests, in rich velvet robes almost touching the ground, walk past for the synagogue; sisters of charity in white bonnets, monks with great woolen garments tied about the waist with a rope, young Turks in long Prince-Albert coats and red feze caps with walking cane, and groups of dusty Bedouins from the far away plains with sheets once white drawn over the shoulders, belted at the waist and tucked up until the lower part strikes the knees, with sockless feet thrust in broad, low, rough, homemade shoes, with heads high in the air, and searching eyes and fearless tread, move through the chattering, bawling throng.

In trading, the people gesticulate and shout at each other as if they were hot with anger; the price is "all I can get," with the merchant and "the least I can pay," with the purchaser. The trade made, our friends who seemed a moment ago ready to leap upon each other, are all smiles and bows and compliments.

Down in the market you will see great heaps of watermelons, small ones that were pulled a long while ago; piles of pomegranates, fresh, juicy and delicious; figs in plenty, and grapes everywhere in large bunches, and almost as sweet as sugar. A half franc, equal to our dime, will get as many grapes as two men should eat at one sitting.

The temple area is one of the most interesting spots to visit in Jerusalem. This place is especially sacred to Jew and Mohammedan. Abraham is the father of the host of Ishmaelites, who swarm over the plains, and all Mohammedans, I believe, claim that Mohammed ascended to heaven from the rock on top of Mount Moriah, where Abraham offered Isaac. The magnificent Mosque of Omar is built on the spot where Solomon's temple is supposed to have stood with the great natural stone altar under the center of the dome. The court of the Gentiles is a vast space large enough for regiments of soldiers to drill in. On the higher court directly around the temple there is space for standing room for tens of thousands of people. The Mosque standing in the center of this space is reckoned by architects and artists to be one of the most perfect buildings in its proportions and one of the most beautiful in its decorations in all the world. Near the Mosque at one side of the court of the Gentiles is a vast Mohammedan temple. Let those who suppose that Mohammedanism is dead go there some morning when people have met for worship and listen to the harangues of their priests. Thousands of people can stand or squat within the temple, but it will not begin to accommodate the worshipers on special occasions, and great throngs gather without, bowing in reverence and kissing the stones.

The saddest place in all Jerusalem is the "Jewish wailing place." When we visited the spot, a section of the old wall of vast stones laid by Solomon's masons, a number of Jews, men and women, were present crying aloud for the coming of the Messiah. Many of them had their faces covered and their hands pressed against the rocks, chanting out in wearied voice their grief and sad longings. There hath stood One among them whom they knew not, who was rejected and slain, and now they wait and weep and plead in vain for the coming of their Messiah, whom their fathers crucified. The Mohammedans are a powerful, insolent, fierce people—Turks, Egyptians, Arabs and Indians.

When the old Sultan's power was departing, who was recently superseded by the *Young Turks' administration*, he, in a rage of hate and bloodthirstiness, ordered Christians slain in every direction. Perhaps fifty thousand Christians were murdered only last April in the most cruel manner. Women and children never met with more cruel treatment at the hands of wild barbarians than the poor defenseless creatures who fell into the hands of these Mohammedan human monsters. An order was sent to Jerusalem and many other places for the slaughter of all the Christians. Had it been carried out these delightful Christian brothers and sisters we have met and worshiped with would have met a fate no less cruel than that of those who perished.

There is much unfavorable comment on the fact that there was no American warship in the Mediterranean Sea at the time of the slaughter of the Christians. No, there is no excuse whatever. It was criminal stupidity and indifference. The President knows, the cabinet knows, the diplomats, consuls, war and navy department know, that the situation in the East is delicate and dangerous all the time. Any day or night, at any hour, the Mohammedans are likely to rise and murder Christians. They have done so always under any sort of pretext and will continue to do so. England, Germany, France, and the United States ought to keep at least one well equipped warship on this coast all the time on police duty for the protection of Christian people. The *Young Turks* saved the multitudes from slaughter and have hung up by the neck a large number of those who participated in the bloody butchery. There are reasons to hope for better days for a time at least, under the present administration. Our people are heavily taxed for the support of the navy, so why should the officers and men not be in those places where there is likely to be most serious need of them? Besides, if the ships were here these butchers would express their devotions by some other method than that of murdering Christians. There was never uttered or penned a more unphilosophical statement than that of Col. Roosevelt, that a man's belief had nothing to do with his fitness for office, the administration of the government of the people, etc., etc. A man's faith has everything to do with him—the molding of his character, the illumination of his mind, the warming of his heart and the steadying and strengthening of his hand. "As a man thinketh in his heart, so is he." With a full appreciation of his relations to God, man may come to understand his relations to man and properly adjust himself to life's labors.

A Mohammedan or Unitarian may have many good qualities and strong points of character, but the men who refuse to believe in the Christ get a narrow and false view of life and its full meaning, and are unfit to rule, direct, and administer for their fellow men of this dispensation. The true men, the men fit to lead the nations to intellectual development and high moral planes of living, are men who delight to sing,

"All hail the power of Jesus' name!
  Let angels prostrate fall:
Bring forth the royal diadem,
  And crown Him Lord of all."

CHAPTER X.

ROUND ABOUT JERUSALEM.

It will be interesting to our readers to know that there are many great Christian institutions in Jerusalem. The Mohammedans are losing ground in the Sacred City. Both Hebrew and Christian are buying and building at a marvelous rate in the new part of the city outside the walls which encompass the old city as it stood in the days of Christ. That the restoration of the Jews promised of God through the ancient prophets has begun in earnest, there can be no doubt. We were powerfully impressed with this fact throughout our short visit to Palestine.

But the prophecy of the city without walls is so literally fulfilled that our hearts were made glad to look upon it. In Zechariah 2:1-5 we read: "I lifted up mine eyes again, and looked, and behold a man with a measuring line in his hand. Then said I, Whither goest thou? and he said unto me, to measure Jerusalem, to see what is the breadth thereof, and what is the length thereof. And, behold, the angel that talked with me went forth, and another angel went out to meet him, and said unto him, Run, speak to this young man, saying, Jerusalem shall be inhabited as towns without walls for the multitude of men and cattle therein: For I, saith the Lord, will be unto her a wall of fire around about, and will be the glory in the midst of her." Standing in the great tower of the Russian Church on the Mount of Olives, we looked with a field glass over the new part of the city spreading far beyond the walls with many buildings now going up.

In Jeremiah 31:38, 39, you may read: "Behold, the days come, saith the Lord, that the city shall be built to the Lord from the tower of Hananeel unto the gate of the corner. And the measuring line shall yet go forth over against it upon the hill Gareb, and shall compass about Goath." I stood upon and walked over the hill supposed to be Gareb, and the measuring line has gone over it. Bro. Piercy and myself, with a friend, walked over the ground and it is covered with a beautiful new village containing more than a thousand Jews who have returned here within the past twenty-four months. The buildings are excellent one-story stone structures, with foundations and walls arranged to add another story later on. The people had moved into some of these houses before their completion and here and there a gable was closed up temporarily with sheet iron. Looking into the open doors as we passed along the new streets yet unfinished, we could see the homes were well-furnished, neat and clean.

The young Turkish Government will no doubt be much more generous toward the Hebrew people, and within the next few years tens of thousands of them will come flocking home to the *promised land*. Is it not remarkable that after two thousand years of exile these people have preserved their identity and their blood as pure as that which flowed in the veins of Jacob or Solomon, and that they should be coming back to their old city from the ends of the earth? The old Romans are gone. The old Egyptian is no more. The old master and conqueror have passed away, but here is your Jew, indestructible as the eternal hills he loves,

wearing the same garments, reading the same Scriptures, keeping the same feasts, chanting the same Psalms,
clinging tenaciously with unwavering faith to the same
promises which animated his heart nearly three thousand
years ago.   You cannot get rid of, or away from the
Jew.   In the everlasting toughness and tenacity of his
nature he survives all the conflicts of the centuries,
comes back from all of his wide wanderings over all
lands, and walks the streets of his ancient city with calm
consciousness of his power among the multitude, with a
patient faith in his God that is melting away the prejudice and winning the admiration of the nations of the
earth.   God bless the Jew.   Now that he has been a
living witness to all nations of the invariable truth of
God's word, he is coming home to rest.   We believe
the darkest days in Jewish history have passed and the
day of restoration, peace and power is dawning upon
this chosen people.   The time of the Gentiles will soon
draw to a close and a new and glorious dispensation
will be ushered in.

The Christian churches are getting a strong foothold
in Jerusalem.   The German Emperor had large influence with the old Sultan, who has just been set aside,
and secured many favors in Jerusalem.   The Germans
have a fine large colony, a sort of suburb of the city, of
excellent buildings and clean, beautiful surroundings,
with three or four hundred population.   There is a
magnificent German Lutheran Church situated in the
midst of the old walled city not far from the Church
of the Holy Sepulchre.   The German Catholics are
now building a church on Mount Zion near the tower
of David, outside the walls, which will cost not less
than five hundred thousand dollars.   It is the most con-

spicuous building in Jerusalem, towering high above the Mosque of Omar.

A German gentleman has a large industrial school of about four hundred boys. A stately building with ample grounds and several work-shops where many useful trades are taught. The man in charge is evangelical and said to be most devout in spirit and life. He has many blind children in his institution. There is also a large German hospital where the natives are treated with great skill for various diseases. They are just completing a large and beautiful Hospice, a sort of hotel, for the use of German pilgrims who come up to Jerusalem to worship. One of the German Emperor's sons is coming soon with a large retinue of prominent officials and influential people to the dedication of the great Catholic Church on Mount Zion.

The Russians also have large holdings in Jerusalem. On rising ground to the north of the walled city they have a tract of some twenty-five acres of land under a massive stone wall with heavy iron gates which are closed and locked at night. Within this enclosure they have many great buildings—the Russian Consulate, a beautiful church, a large Hospice, and other great buildings all of hewn stone. We attended service in the Russian Church one Sabbath afternoon and heard the male choir pour forth a great torrent of sacred music. This Russian quarter is a veritable stronghold, well supplied with guns and ammunition. If the Mohammedans should rise against the Christians they would flee into this enclosure and make a determined stand until help could come. There is a guard of giant Russians with big pistols stuck in their belts walking about within these walls. At certain seasons of the year there are at one time as many as fifteen thousand Russian pilgrims in Jerusalem. They are all entertained in the Russian quarters.

The French and Italian Catholics have large churches and schools in and about the city. The English have two large Episcopal churches and a resident Bishop, a hospital, some schools, a Bible depository, a house of industry, and a house of inquiry for converts. America has but little. There is what is called the *American colony*, with some one hundred and fifty residents, most of whom, I am told, are Swedes. The *Christian Missionary Alliance* with headquarters in New York, has a faithful man here in the person of Pastor Thompson. He has charge of what is called the *American Church*, and also a Boys' and Girls' School. It was in this church that the writer preached while in Jerusalem. Here a pure, evangelical gospel is proclaimed and a devout group of our people and natives meet here. Bro. Thompson is now erecting a large stone building for church and school purposes. He would greatly appreciate a dollar to help in its completion. I doubt not there are truly devout hearts among all of these different sects who, whatever their name or method of worship, center their faith and love about one common Christ.

Some one expressed surprise that England and America, the two most evangelical countries, should have such small holdings in Jerusalem, while the Catholics and Greeks have so many large churches and splendid buildings, and at once I answered in the language of Christ when the woman at the well said to him, "Our fathers worship in this mountain; and ye say, that in Jerusalem is the place where men ought to wor-

ship." Jesus said unto her * * * "Neither in this
mountain nor yet in Jerusalem * * * God is a
Spirit: and they that worship Him must worship Him
in spirit and in truth." Christ is universal. The devout heart can find Him anywhere. It might prove a
means of grace and a confirming of the faith to go up
to Jerusalem, but such a pilgrimage is by no means necessary. The Holy Ghost has come to reveal our Lord
in His beauty and power in all places to them who desire Him. Years ago when plowing corn in Barren
county, Kentucky, I used to hitch my horse at the end
of the row and creep into the fence corner to pray, and
there I found Christ just as consciously to the joy of my
heart as I found Him in the most sacred places in Jerusalem. It is not a matter of geography or location, but
of Christ abiding in the hearts of the people.

One morning in company with three of our young
college professors and another gentleman and several
ladies, we mounted our horses, with a mule and two
donkeys in the cavalcade, and clattered out of the city
for the village of Mizpah. Solomon, a crow-black lad
in white shirt, ran along with us to take care of the
animals. When a short distance out of the city we
found ourselves riding through an old cemetery with
many ruined vaults and sepulchres cut into the solid
rock. There was no sign of human remains; this place of
burial may have been discarded a thousand years ago.
We dismounted to examine one of these sepulchres,
called the tomb of the Judges. By stooping low we
entered a door hewn into the face of the solid rock;
once in, by striking a match we could see about us a
room cut out of the solid limestone, perhaps twelve feet
each way and eight or nine feet high. From this main

room there were two others leading off through a very small door into which the bodies of the dead were thrust, and I suppose the opening cemented up.

From this on the road was very rough, and we proceeded in single file over a pathway among the stones that could be traversed only by animals accustomed to such a rugged country. We arrived at Mizpah in time for dinner with which we were provided. We climbed into the tower of the Mohammedan Mosque from which we had a splendid view of the vast expanse of country, taking in the home of the old judge, Samuel, and the Mediterranean Sea, forty-five miles away. We spread our blanket on the hillside under the shade of some olive trees, laid out our dinner and ate it overlooking the broad valley in which Joshua fought and conquered the five kings while the sun halted on Gibeon and the moon stood still in the valley of Ajalon.

The villagers were living in dirt and squalor and the thin little children who gathered about us seized eagerly with lean fingers the food we offered them. Nearby was an old man driving two cows around on a threshing floor on a small heap of straw. The grain had been threshed from it and he was now grinding it up for food for camels.

From here we rode away to Emmaus the village to which two of his disciples walked with burning hearts while Christ, unknown to them, expounded the Scriptures concerning Himself, not only illuminating their minds, but also putting His endorsement upon the Old Testament. At Emmaus we were kindly entertained by a German Catholic father of manly bearing and radiant face who assisted his servant in setting the table and poured the tea into our cups with his own hands.

Dr. Felt and Group of Young Indian Preachers.

He was so handsome and genial I could but wish he had a beautiful wife to love him, and children about his knee. But I need not worry about the matter; he seemed content and happy. Life at best is short and human loves are changing and uncertain, but Christ can never fail. Be faithful, dear brother priest, and may I press, one day in the eternal city, the hand which poured me a cup of tea in the name of a disciple in the restful village of Emmaus.

But the day is passing rapidly and we must start on the homeward journey, for I am to preach in Jerusalem at eight o'clock in the evening. A short mile out from Emmaus we were attracted by weird music and guns firing, and turning off some hundred yards from the road we found an Arab wedding feast in full blast. The women were dancing and singing while the men, some twenty of them having guns, were shooting at a target. They were poor marksmen and I dismounted and took one of the guns, believing I could hit the stone they had set up on the wall, but after examining it I was afraid it would burst and gave it back to its grinning owner. We lost some time at this wedding and when we got away one of our young college professors was detailed to hurry forward with Bro. Piercy and myself. The professor took a short cut for the Joppa carriage road plunging down a rocky mountain side where it would seem almost impossible for a horse to keep his feet. After a long, hard ride pitching down and scrambling up and loping across we came out upon the Joppa road about eight miles from Jerusalem. We cantered by the village where John the Baptist is supposed to have been born and climbed the hill beyond,

the mountain towering up on our right with a deep
valley on our left.

People, until quite recently, traveled through this
region with an armed escort. Only a few nights ago
a man was shot dead and robbed not far out from Joppa gate. "Professor, are there not robbers in this region?" I asked in a cheerful off-hand tone. "Oh, yes,
an occasional robbery," said he, "but no danger much.
If any of these fellows we meet should take your horse
by the bridle and say *Bach Shesh*, just kick him in the
stomach and lay whip to your horse, and we will gallop
off." Certainly, what could be simpler. But I have
conscientious scruples about doing a man bodily harm,
so it occurred to me it would be just as well to gallop
ahead before the fellow took my horse by the bridle.
It is now deep dusk. Preaching at *eight*. We are
all mounted on Arabian stallions and we Kentucky
boys know how to ride, so off we go. Piercy had no
curb on his bit and every time we struck a gallop his
fiery steed ran away. It was funny to see him dart by
us, feet braced in the stirrups, coat tail in the air, saying
"whoa" at every jump; but the horse was an Arab and
could not understand English, and on he went. The
only way to stop him was for the professor and myself
to slow up and the runaway would stop for the sake of
company.

We tumbled off of our horses in front of the Hughes
Hotel in time to eat a bite, wash, say a prayer, and get
to church while the introductory prayer was in progress.
I preached with considerable fever. We had a good
meeting, but I came home sick and sore after this strenuous day in the saddle, the first one in twenty years.

We enjoyed our visit to Bethlehem and Bethany,

the Mount of Olives, and other points of interest, but the tenderest spot in all the environs of the sacred city is *Gethsemane*, a beautiful little garden with high stone wall about it and well kept flowers blooming in it and old, old olive trees, and quiet monks with serene faces and kindly manner to unlock the iron gate of the inner fence and let you in. With uncovered head and melted heart I sat upon a little stool and prayed to Him who suffered here for us all.

"Oh suffering Man of Galilee!
Oh submissive Lamb of Gethsemane!
Oh, glorious Christ of Calvary!
Oh, risen King of all the universe!
Reign in our hearts forevermore!"

During our meetings quite a number of persons were at the altar; some for full salvation and some for the forgiveness of their sins. Among the sinners seeking grace, there were, I was told, one or more Mohammedans. I preached about half of the time through an interpreter in Arabic; the other half to the English, with a number of natives present; quite a few of them could understand. We closed our meetings Friday night, October 1. Many people professed to be greatly blessed and we believe there will be permanent results; we hope an evangelist and a missionary.

One of the most interesting sights we saw in Jerusalem was a Catholic procession which met and formed in Pilate's court and proposed to march over the road Christ traveled from that place to the crucifixion. We went to Pilate's court. It is now a barracks for Turkish soldiers. We saw a large company of priests and monks, with devout lay people, men and women, kneeling upon the stones, after which one of the priests stood upon an elevation and delivered a short sermon. They then marched out and laid a huge wooden cross upon the shoulders of fifteen or twenty priests and took up the march for the spot where they believe Christ was crucified, stopping at a number of stations where some incident occurred in his progress to Calvary, to pray and preach a short sermon. We followed them as far as the fourth station. Turkish officers went along with sword and pistols buckled on them and whips in their hands to keep order among the Mohammedans. In spite of them a group of Bedouins coming in through the Damascus gate leading their Arabian steeds strode through the company of priests, making so much noise that the speaker stopped for a moment. I caught the picture fully. It would have been a study for an artist, full of history and conflicting ideas and prejudices. The elevated priest with uplifted hand and impatient silence, the meek, surprised look of devout monks at such startling sacrilege; the Turkish officers making a show of displeasure at their people which they did not feel; the curious women and children looking on in ignorant wonder at the solemn sight which they could not comprehend, and tall, sinewy, sunburnt, erect Bedouins, contemptuous alike for soldiers and for priest. Their keen eyes glittered defiance at all men as they strode past, leading their beautiful horses, with luggage bound neatly to the saddle and empty stirrups swinging . I would the picture could be put upon canvas just as I saw it, and caught for the moment its profound and far-reaching significance.

The last service of our meetings was full of grace and tenderness. Several friends walked with us to the hotel and bade us a real Christian good-bye. When will we again meet with four such young men as our college professors from Beyroot? Fine young Christian athletes. They have galloped over Palestine this summer with their rifles on their backs and their Bibles in their saddle pockets studying out the land and handing out tracts. Two of them were frequently at the altar and told us before we left that they had planned a prayer meeting in their rooms every morning before school hours, to which all might come who would. One of them who went with us to the train as we left Jerusalem slipped in the car and said, "If you find a place in the mission field open for me, let me know."

CHAPTER XI.

MANY DAYS UPON THE DEEP.

Some of the priests who were in the procession of the cross in Jerusalem, were on the train on which we went to Joppa, and I am sorry to say, were smoking cigars and drinking whiskey. They took the bottle all around at least twice in the fifty-four miles from Jerusalem to Joppa. We shipped from Joppa to Port Said on an Austrian ship. We were tossed on the big waves in our row boat as we went to our ship off shore, the ten oarsmen keeping time with their oars to a chant of "God help us," in Arabic. We were stored away below decks in a little stateroom with seven berths in it, a man for every berth, the front windows opening out on a lower deck with a great mass of poor, dirty humanity sweltering in the heat. Men, women and children piled about in heaps of soiled luggage. You will remember that we were second-class passengers. It is a wonder contagion does not break out and sweep them all away.

I heard a noise directly after midnight, pulled my curtain aside and saw Piercy dressing. "I have enough of this and intend to go on deck," he said. I soon followed with my big Scotch blanket, wrapped it about me, snuggled into a reclining chair and gazed into the beautiful sky with the great blazing stars which appeared to be trying to tell me some marvelous thing and seemed surprised and saddened that I could not understand. I thought long into the silent night of the loved ones at home, of the preachers who are brothers in the Lord, of the holiness movement, and what a step forward would have been taken in the Southland if the Holy Ghost had been given free course. Then I slept until Piercy called my attention to the revolving light flashing from the tower at Port Said.

We landed Sabbath morning at six o'clock and found that I was announced to preach at nine a. m., when a goodly company gathered. I preached again at seven thirty in the evening, and at nine a boat load of brothers and sisters went with us out to our ship and went on board for a final good-bye. At ten they clambered down the ladder to their boat and rowed away under the moonlight, sweetly singing as far as we could hear them, "We'll never say good-bye in heaven." The sailors at the forecastle cheered them and the song came up faintly from the distance, "We'll never say good-bye in heaven." At twelve o'clock at night our piston rods leaped forward, our screws cut the water, and we were off for half a long month before our feet should press the sunny shores of India.

We entered the great canal from the Mediterranean at Port Said and issued from it into the Red Sea, or the Gulf of Suez, at Suez. Ships pass through the big ditch very slowly, lest the waves wash down the banks and result in a cave-in, filling up the canal. I believe six miles an hour is the speed limit. There are places at intervals for a ship to slip into an enlarged space that other ships may pass. At one point we stood in one of these pockets and six ships passed us in stately line. One of the ships passing was of the same line of the one we were on and a group of our sailors made up a band of a cornet and accordion, with the bottom of a metal bucket or tub, for a drum, and gave them a lively tune as they passed; while the lads on the other ship tied their dish cloths to mop handles and waved us their good wishes.

We lay for full twenty-four hours at the mouth of the canal discharging freight and repairing machinery about our ship.   The canal is ninety miles in length and is simply a vast ditch through a flat plain of sand. Its construction did not call for genius, but hard work. It is no great engineering feat, but a monument to the muscle of the sons of toil.

The father of Rameses the Great cut a canal fifty-seven miles long here nearly three thousand years before Christ, from one of the branches of the Nile to the bitter lakes.   These lakes are now a part of the Suez Canal.   The sands of the desert gradually filled up this canal.   Other rulers of later dates undertook the cutting of a canal, but for various reasons gave up the enterprise.   Napoleon contemplated such a canal, but abandoned the project when his engineers assured him that the level of the Mediterranean was thirty feet below that of the Red Sea. Their estimates were false.

The English own most of the shares of the canal while the French hold the principal offices.   The tolls for ships passing through amount to more than one million dollars per month the year round.   It is said that as a result of the arduous work of digging the great ditch, under the burning sun, thousands of poor Egyptians lie buried inthe great sand dump along the sides of the canal.   The death rate was so great that England interfered and put a stop to the horrible loss of life in the early processes of the work.

A poor native ran alongside our ship in the sand and

eagerly snatched up the hard biscuit which were thrown to him from our deck. That reminds me that I have been wishing for a target rifle. I should like to throw one of these biscuit overboard and shoot at it. I am curious to study the impression of a bullet on one of them. I would cheerfully give a half dollar at this moment for three of those corndodgers one gets at Benedict's on Fourth Avenue in Louisville. Our people at home do not know how to appreciate the many good things they have to eat and the bountiful supply they have of them.

As we came down the narrow portion of the Red Sea they pointed out to us the high peaks of a mountain, seen very plainly from our deck, called "Mount Sinai," and the captain told me of a shallow place called the "Shoals of Israel," extending from shore to shore, in many places not more than three fathoms deep, with two narrow deep passages for the ships. This is doubtless where Moses crossed with Israel in the flight from Egypt.

We are traveling on a very slow ship, and have been four full days on the Red Sea with more than a day yet before we pass out into the gulf. The heat is terrific. We go from one side of the ship to the other searching for a cool breeze. We go to bed moist all over with perspiration. We awake in the night with great drops of sweat rolling from face and neck, pillow, nightshirt collar, sheet all about the shoulders, wet with perspiration. It is difficult to pull our clothing on in the morning over our oozing bodies. We have on thin white suits, but we perspire all day long. Notwithstanding all this, we are having a good time, and promise keen enjoyment of the better things when they come.

We left five new cases of bubonic plague in Port Said and an Englishman on board has been telling us interesting stories of smallpox, bubonic and cholera in Bombay, but assures us that care and courage will take us safely through and we have no uneasiness.

Bubonic plague is carried by rats. The rat has the disease and dies; the fleas which covered his body scatter and bite men. First they have fever, then the glands begin to swell in their groins, under their arms, and under the jaws. They suffer great agony and die soon. If the people would kill off the rats the disease would disappear, but the Indians will not kill the rats; the result is, they are swept away by the plague. A couple of fleas got on me in Port Said, or it may have been a fine point of vivid imagination. At any rate I went after the supposed little animals as if they had been snakes in my boots. I found no fleas, but the mental relief was full compensation for my trouble.

We had a bit of interesting pastime yesterday. A half dozen little swallows came aboard our ship, tired out by their long flight. A tender-hearted English girl, the sister of a young officer who has been home on leave and is now going back to his regiment in India, accompanied by said sister, took great interest in our little visitors, and with various helps caught several of the birds and gave them water. Directly a hawk, bent on mischief, swooped down into the rigging, frightening our little friends into a great flutter of distress. Our captain had a target rifle handy and kept a keen eye on the hawk, and when he alighted on a rope to survey the situation and lay his plans for a grand coup of the swallows, the captain, with a well-aimed shot dropped the intruder to the deck. The ship's doctor was in too much of a hurry to pick it up and got one of his fingers lacerated by a sharp claw of the dying bird.

We have on board two British army officers, one officer in theAustrian army, an Italian, a traveling man from Germany, a Hollander and his wife, three young Englishmen who are in business in India, four English women, a gentleman and his sisters from Persia, a very dark man from Arabia, several others of what race I do not know, three Americans, including Piercy and myself, and quite a number of Indians going home to native land.

Looking upon the degraded women of the lands where the Mohammedan religion is prevalent I am strongly impressed with the debt of gratitude our women owe to our glorious Christ for the rich heritage they enjoy. No wonder our women love Jesus. The sad wonder is that any of them should fail to love Him. I am sure if our Christian women at home could see with their own eyes the dirt, disease, degradation and sufferings of their Mohammedan sisters over here and see how little is being done to help them they would put even more zeal into missionary work.

As I see these commercial men, soldiers, officers and sailors of the ship going out to foreign lands leaving their loved ones behind them, facing storms, battle and contagion, without a fear or a murmur, I am made to feel it would be pitiful indeed for the soldier of the Cross to hesitate or complain at the call of his Commander to go out to the ends of the earth seeking for the lost sheep of the Father's fold.

At the point where the Red Sea empties into the Arabian Sea, stands crouched at the foot of the mountains the little city of Aden. Our ship stopped here

for some hours to discharge and take on cargo and Bro.
Piercy and myself went on shore for a couple of hours
to stretch our limbs and feel the solid earth again.   The
natives of this place are black, not so large as our ne-
groes at home, but a lithe, nimble lot of fellows swarming about the ship and shore eager to sell you fruit or
trinkets of some sort.   Most of them had no clothing
except a loin cloth about them, but seemed indifferent
to the burning sun which poured its fierce heat upon
their naked bodies.   They looked peaceable enough
but we were told that a white man could go. but a
short distance from the town without protection.   The
English are strongly fortified here and several men of
war lay in the harbor.

We found a good breeze in the Arabian Sea.   The
heat was not so intense and all on board were happy
over the change.   Looking about a lower deck we
espied a lean old steer with a branch of blood flowing
from his kidneys and looking utterly unfit to live or to
be butchered.   Most of the passengers got a look at
the poor animal and when his hide was found neatly
folded up in his stall and fresh beef appeared at the
table, the passengers sat back and said, "No, I thank
you."   The cook fixed him up in every possible style,
but the people with few exceptions let him pass by.   It
greatly crippled our bill of fare, but we fell back on
sardines and pulled through fairly well, as they gave
us chicken once a day.

Our captain was a big Austrian, over six feet,
and a most genial, jovial man with the passengers,
with a savage, carnal nature handy for use with the
sailors.   He cheerfully granted me the use of the cabin
for preaching on Sabbath morning.   The steward put

it in neat order.   I announced the meeting at the breakfast hour and most all of the passengers came.   We had present a Turkish governor and his secretary, a Jewish doctor, two Greek merchants, two English officers, an Austrian army officer going out to hunt tigers, a group of Germans, and a number of English gentlemen and ladies.   The Lord gave unction and I have never preached to a more attentive and serious looking audience.   May the Lord bless the seed and make it fruitful.

For a number of days our ship rode a great swell, that rocked us from side to side with almost clock-like regularity, but we kept our feet like old sailors and responded promptly to every call of the dinner bell.

At break of day on the morning of October 19, we could plainly see land ahead.   A little after sun up our faithful ship rode into the great harbor of Bombay. The boats swarmed about us and several letters of welcome and direction were handed me, which warmed our hearts and made us feel somewhat at home in this far-away, strange land.

Say what you will of your unions, societies, and fraternities, but there isn't anything that so unites and binds men together in this world as true brotherhood in Jesus Christ.   All men who love Jesus with fervent heart love all other men who truly love their Lord.   If you do not love the brethren you do not love the Lord.

CHAPTER XII.

OPENING THE CAMPAIGN IN INDIA.

When we landed in Bombay the temperature was not less than 110 in the sun and we were for sometime walking about in the sunshine arranging for our journey to Lucknow, not knowing of the danger of exposure in the tropical sun. We soon became quite exhausted with a dull pain about the head and a general relaxation of energy. We went into a little park, and, seeking a shade, stripped off hat, coat and vest, and took a long rest. We afterwards learned that a European, especially a newcomer, must protect his head from the sun with a heavy cork, or pith hat, and if convenient an umbrella also. If one should expose his head uncovered in the sunshine for one minute, he would be quite uncomfortable for sometime afterward. To stand with bare head in the sunshine at any time from ten to three o'clock, for ten or twenty minutes, would in all probability result in severe sickness at the stomach and violent headache for many hours.

On coming to the grave of Sir Henry Lawrence, who was killed in the defense of the Residency at Lucknow, I instinctively removed my hat. We were standing in the full glare of the sun. A friend said, "You had better keep your hat on your head," but I stood I suppose a minute with bared head, and as a result had a dull pain for some hours afterward in the side of my head which was exposed to the sun. But this was after the intense heat of the summer was passed, in the cooler days of October, when the temperature was not more than ninety-five in the shade. Think what it must be in June before the summer rains begin falling, when the temperature is often one hundred and twenty in the shade.

The missionary who stands faithfully to his or her post in such a climate through decades of toil and stress, with multitudes of people dying all about them from the bite of venemous reptiles, and the scourge of small-pox, cholera, malarial fever and blackdeath, deserves not only the hearty and substantial support of the church at home, but her tenderest sympathy and most earnest prayers.

We left Bombay at three o'clock in the afternoon on the Punjab Mail train for Lucknow. These trains are like those of Europe, not large coaches like we have in America, but small carriages, not much larger than an old omnibus, holding only a few persons. Bro. Piercy and myself were shut into one of these carriages with the president of a mechanical school for natives in Bombay, who was on his way to the mountains to shoot big game during his vacation, and one of the big horse racers of India, a polite old gentleman in his way. They were both bound for Lucknow and for the 880 miles they puffed tobacco smoke, first from rank cigars and then from horribly strong old pipes. It was a nice thing to adjust the blinds so as to keep the glare of the sun out and yet ventilate so as to let the smoke out.

We had twenty-seven hours of it. I believe we were kind; I am sure we suffered long. They pull down a little shelf for one to sleep on in these carriages, but you must furnish your own bed clothing. We had been forwarned and had provided ourselves with big

Scotch blankets while in London. A missionary brought
me up a pillow and our college president who had two,
insisted on Bro. Piercy taking one of his, so with blanket and pillow we climbed up to our little shelves.   It
was quite cold, for we were now high up in the mountains and I put in one of the most uncomfortable nights
of my life.   In spite of it all there was some rest, and
our traveling companions, both Britons, had, for a long
while, been residents of India and were full of information, and in the cloud of tobacco smoke poured out
a volume of talk with an occasional oath to give emphasis to their views of the situation.   The profanity
was dropped after Piercy and myself knelt in prayer before climbing to our shelves at night.

The "Deshara Meetings" is a great gathering of
Methodists, both missionaries and native workers, at
Lucknow.   They have come together every fall for
some twenty years in this city.   In these meetings much
business is transacted, plans are laid, enterprises set on
foot, and there is a general touching of elbows and
intermingling of missionary and native Christian life,
but the chief object of these meetings is the deepening
of personal piety and the enlargement of spiritual life.
It is a time for the preaching of the higher truths of His
grace, for prayer and testimony.   For a year these missionaries have been separated widely apart.   They
have been surrounded by heathenism, the very air has
been heavy with superstition and diabolical influences.
They have had to look upon sin in its most gross and
hideous forms.   They have been giving out from the
pulpit, from the street meeting, from the school platform, in the destitute homes of filth and disease, to the
hungry hearted inquirers after Christ, who came to them.

Every faculty of the mind, every sympathy of the heart and every muscle and nerve of the body has been called upon to do its part in the strenuous conflict. Having somewhat emptied themselves they come together for a refilling of Christ's grace and Spirit. Some missionaries came on the same train with us from Bombay, others got on at the stations along the route, and by the time we got to Lucknow we had quite a goodly company, and every train was bringing in missionaries and native workers from every direction, until something like four hundred and fifty workers had gathered for the great yearly convocation; about one hundred and fifty of them our missionaries, and about three hundred of them native preachers. The services were held in the large hall of the Isabella Thoburn College for young ladies, and in the large native M. E. Church. We had three services a day in the college hall and the others in the native church.

We had preaching every morning at 8:30 and evening at 5:30. It was my privilege to preach at all of these morning and evening services. The congregations were large and responsive and the altar well filled at the close of every service; sometimes all the space about the altar was filled and many souls were blessed. Missionaries, Indians, and broad-shouldered artillerymen from a British battery and a man in the red coat and plaid pants of a Scotch regiment, were all crowding about one common mercy seat. Some were converted, some reclaimed, some sanctified, and others greatly renewed in grace and refreshed in love. Bishops Oldham and Warne "amened" the truth and worked faithfully in the altar. I doubt if two more apostolic men can be found in the mission field of the wide world than these two bishops, greatly beloved by the people among whom they move with the simple dignity and the tender sympathy of fathers or elder brethren.

Bishop Oldham gave a searching and instructive talk to workers each afternoon at two o'clock, which sent us to our knees in prayer. At four o'clock Bishop Warne or Bishop Oldham preached at the native M. E. Church to the three hundred native preachers and the great congregations which gathered to hear the message. Their theme was full salvation, and the Spirit was present to bless. One afternoon I heard Bishop Oldham preach to the native Christians on the *Canaan life.* He had one of the brethren read the story of the spies and the fruits they brought back from Eshcol. He preached to the three hundred native preachers and the great audience a plain, powerful sermon on entire sanctification and the blessed fruits of perfect love. While Bishop Oldham preached, Bishop Warne slipped out of his chair and got upon his knees in prayer and remained there through most of the sermon. As I looked upon this scene, the one Bishop preaching full salvation, the other Bishop on his knees in prayer, and three hundred native preachers still as death giving rapt attention to the truth, I got a hopeful outlook for the future of Methodism in India.

In the course of his sermon, Bishop Oldham related how that before he obtained the experience of perfect love he had been somewhat annoyed at a certain camp meeting in Michigan by the shouts and praises of the people under the leadership of an earnest preacher. He said later he saw that same preacher stand the test when he brought his daughter to New York City to send her away to the foreign mission field. He said, "Bro. Ruth stood there telling his daughter good-bye, weeping and praising God." When it broke upon me who he was talking about—our Ruth and his daughter, to whom I have preached often in St. Louis, I could not hold in any longer. I had to pour out my heart in tears and praise.

At the close of the Bishop's sermon a large company of native preachers came weeping to the altar and there was a time of great refreshing. Among those who came to the altar at the college hall and were greatly blessed, sanctified, or refreshed with a renewal of grace, were some of the strongest and most influential men and women among our white missionaries in India. Calls came in and invitations were given for meetings in almost every part of India.

In the midst of our meetings one of our brethren was suddenly taken down violently ill, having every symptom of cholera. I saw him at midnight on Saturday as I came out of the chapel where they were having an all-night prayer meeting. He looked perfectly well. In a few minutes the sickness came upon him; all the remainder of the night he was in agony of vomiting and purging, just as is the case in cholera. Sabbath morning, when I called to see him, six hours from the time of his taking down, I would not have known him. He was shrunken and white, shriveled it seemed to one-third less than his size the evening before. He looked as if he could scarcely live till noon; he was removed from the parsonage in which many of us were stopping. When I called to see him at noon he was resting somewhat better, and a few hours later his physician thought he was past the danger line. A few nights later his nurse was suddenly taken down as he had been and suffered fearfully for a few hours, but the physician got to him, and gave him a powerful cholera treatment, and soon had him improving. Both of the brethren are now well; one of them has gone to his home, and the other one will be able to travel in a few days.

The thing that impressed me was the quiet, matter-of-fact way in which the incident was treated. No missionary fled or seemed in the least excited. They prayed earnestly, administered the remedies and went about their affairs as if nothing had happened. This is an heroic band with their lives in the hands of God, and their treasures laid up in heaven.

CHAPTER XIII.

THE HISTORIC CITY OF LUCKNOW.

Many of the missionaries who attended the Deshera, or Pentecostal meetings at Lucknow, came over a thousand miles. Several gave interesting accounts of how the Lord gave them the means for the journey. Others who were somewhat cold in their experience, told of how they made up their minds not to come and after concluding to come, determined not to go to the altar, but were among the first at the altar and among those most graciously blessed.

At the close of the convention on Sabbath night, November 24, we moved the meetings across the street to the English speaking M. E. Church, Rev. E. Stanley Jones, an old Asbury College boy, pastor. The many friends of Bro. Jones' school days, and those who enjoyed his ministry during vacations while he was at Asbury, will be glad to know that the Lord is graciously using him in India. He is pastor of the English speaking church in one of the most important centers of Methodism in this great country, is much beloved by his people and respected by the community. He has conducted a number of successful revivals in other English-speaking churches and his services are in great demand. He preaches full salvation without objection or hindrance. From all I saw and heard at this convention, entire sanctification had right of way.

In one of his addresses to workers, Bishop Oldham said, "Bro. Morrison, you may tell the church at home that we cannot get on without holiness out here in the mission field." It would seem that there is no need for independent movements here for the spread of holiness, while the M. E. Church is loyal to the doctrine and experience. There is the greatest need of a revival of the experience among the people, and there are hopeful signs of its coming. I have nothing to say against the independent movements. The harvest is so great and the laborers so few compared with the vast multitudes of India, we bid all Godspeed who are proclaiming the gospel of Christ in this land. But it were a pity to waste effort.

If Bishop Taylor had worked on independent lines out here, his work would largely have disappeared ere this, but he worked with the church, organized the church as he went, and laid foundations on which the church has built; thus the great work he did in his evangelistic tour has been conserved, and enlarged. Be it known I would not silence one voice lifted for our Lord in India, and I am sure he is greatly blessing various groups of workers, but if I were coming to India to work I would cast in my lot with the M. E. Church.

In Lucknow, the Methodists have a large church property and excellent parsonage, with adequate and beautifully shaded grounds. There is also a large and well appointed deaconess home. The Isabella Thoburn College, for young ladies, with several excellent buildings and large grounds for the rapidly growing school, is located here, under the efficient management of Miss Ruth E. Robinson, a daughter of Bishop Robinson. It was my privilege to preach many times at the morning chapel service to the young ladies of this school and see many of them converted at the evening meetings in the church. Miss Robinson told me at the close of the revival that all of her girls had professed salvation except one. I was impressed with the intelligence and culture of these Indian maidens and have no doubt some of them will make useful women in the work of the Lord.

Reid Christian College, for young men, is also located in Lucknow. This school has a large tract of valuable land and some five or six handsome buildings. I believe boys and men all told, they have something over five hundred students. Rev. C. L. Bare, D. D., the president of the college, a man of fine character and spirit, had me address his students in their large chapel. It was an interesting sight and a fine audience to speak to—Christians, Hindus, and Mohammedans. Some of these young men were saved in our meetings. This school needs a great revival of God's saving grace.

There is also a large Methodist publishing house in this city. It makes one of the handsomest blocks on the main business street and works a small army of men under the efficient management of Bro. Meek, of West Virginia, who has been in the mission field for a number of years, but entered the experience of full salvation only a few months ago, and with his fine business capacity combines a spirit of cheerfulness that keeps sunshine in his quarters all the time.

There is also a large native Methodist Church here, with a devout and able native pastor. I preached once in this church through an interpreter and a number came to the altar seeking perfect love. I also spoke on temperance one night down at the barracks, in the Kings Theatre, to the British soldiers, and had a good time. So speaking in these several places I reached many peo-

ple in Lucknow, and saw a number of souls saved or
sanctified, and praise God for so auspicious a beginning of our work in this country.   Bro. Piercy spoke
to the Sabbath school and to the Good Templars, and
worked faithfully in the altar throughout the meetings.

Lucknow has a population of about three hundred
thousand people.   Before this country came under the
rule of England, Lucknow was the capital of the kingdom of Oudh.   Here the old kings lived in splendor.
The city in those days had a population of about seven
hundred thousand people.   The palaces and tombs of
these kings are yet standing; the palaces are used for
government and city club purposes.   We were driven
through the grounds, surrounded by long rows of handsome buildings in which lived the three hundred wives
of the last king of Oudh.

The most interesting place in Lucknow is the Residency, the historic spot where during the Seapoy rebellion a comparatively small number of English soldiers and citizens, with a number of women and children and a few faithful natives, remained shut up in
poorly constructed defenses, for several months sustain-
ing one of the most famous sieges in all the history of
war.   I want to write quite at length, later on, of this
heroic struggle and of the courageous Christian men
who acted their part so well in this bloody and tragic
chapter of English and Indian history.

The place is now a sort of government park with the
old buildings in which the people fought and suffered
so faithfully, standing in eloquent ruins with ten thous-
and battle scars upon them.   A white tablet in the wall
marks the place where Sir Henry Lawrence received
the wound from a fragment of a bursting shell from

Methodist Missionaries at the Great Meeting in Lucknow, India.

which he died a few days later.   He was borne
away a short distance from the Residency to the house
of the doctor. The stretcher upon which he was carried
was put down upon the portico of the physician's home,
and upon Sir Henry being told that he could live but a
short time, he asked the chaplain to administer the sacrament of the Lord's supper.   A group of soldiers
gathered about him with uncovered heads and under a
heavy fire of musketry, with cannon balls crashing into
the buildings about them, those immortal Britons cele-
brated the death and coming of the Lord.   At the close
of the sacred ceremony Sir Henry was carried into the
house.   No one had been touched during the admin-
istering of the holy sacrament but almost immediately
after it had closed an officer and private soldier were
shot down upon the spot where the stretcher had rested.

A marble slab marks the place where Sir Henry
died, and not far away his last resting place may be
seen with this inscription on the stone slab which covers
his grave:

Here lies

HENRY LAWRENCE,

who tried to do his duty.

May the Lord have mercy on his soul.

My heart has seldom been so stirred with memories
of the past as it was while we walked about this famous
little battlefield, and stood by the graves of the heroes
who fell here.   There were several acres of land and
five or six houses within the enclosure.   Some faithful
old Indian soldiers who fought through the siege, carrying medals of honor on their breasts, showed us about
the place.

"In this basement one hundred and fifty women and children spent five awful months of the siege." "The large hole up yonder is where a cannon ball came through into the cellar and this huge dent in this pillar is where it stopped." "In that little room Jessie Brown lay sick upon the floor when all at once she leaped to her feet and declared that she heard the bagpipes of the Highland Brigade." "Here is where fifty women and children were kept." "There is where the wounded were treated." "At this point the wall was blown up by a mine which was run under us from the outside." "There stood a battery." "The portico of this building was cut down by cannon balls and when it fell it made a strong breastwork behind which the English leaped and fought, each with the strength of ten men, for the women and children." "It was up this way that the kilted Scotchmen charged with fixed bayonets, when Haverlock broke through the dense human wall with deliverance to the little band of hungry, bleeding, smoke begrimed heroes." I wanted to lie down on the ground and weep. It was worth a hundred lifetimes to charge up that little hill and save those famishing battle-smitten people. But no more of the mutiny now.

There were several interesting incidents in the Lucknow meetings. I was profoundly impressed with the cool, Christian courage of Rev. W. D. Schermerhorn. He came out from Kansas some years ago and has been greatly blessed in his labors. He is a picture of robust health. When Rev. J. N. Garden was smitten with cholera Bro. Schermerhorn, who has ridden *third class* for more than a thousand miles to get to the convention, was in the

room with him and waited on him; when he was removed to another place he went with him and stood by
him day and night. I slipped in and had prayer with
them, these brothers in the Lord. Garden looked like
a corpse and Schermerhorn stout as a giant nursing him
as tenderly as a baby, with no thought of personal danger. After a few days and nights Schermerhorn was
taken down with all symptoms of the dread disease,
but at once was drenched with medicine and after a few
hours was much better, and a little later was on his feet,
but somewhat robbed of the ruddy glow of health in
his face. A few mornings later he was buttoned up in
a plain suit of dust colored clothing and off for his
thousand miles in a third-class car to save expenses.
When the missionary collection plate comes around to
you Methodists out in Kansas, remember this man
Schermerhorn and a goodly bunch of Kansans out here
just as brave and true as he is.

Bro. Stanley Jones was greatly rejoiced over the
sanctification of one of his stewards, a man high up in
railway position, with some thousands of employees under him. Bishop Warne's heart was made happy over
the bright conversion of his daughter, an accomplished
young lady just returned to her home in Lucknow, after
a four years' course in Syracuse University, N. Y.

As we passed through Bombay we met an elderly
and devout Methodist, Bro. Bishop, who said, "I have
a son in the army, now stationed at Lucknow. I am
praying for him and want you brethren to get hold of
him and see that he is converted during your meetings."
Bro. Piercy took his name and the number of his battery, and we set our hearts to see him saved. While
preaching the first night in the Lucknow meetings I saw

in the audience a big, handsome soldier, and as soon as I made the altar call walked back to him, clapped him on the shoulder and asked him to come to the altar. He came at once and after coming the second evening was blessedly saved and stood faithfully by us during the meetings. He was Bro. Bishop's son.

We closed Sabbath evening, and I was to go to Cawnpore Monday at noon, only fifty miles, look over the tragic grounds of the mutiny, preach in the Methodist Church at night, and go on to begin our meetings at Allahabad on Tuesday night. But Sabbath night about one thirty I was taken violently sick and had a strenuous time of it until daylight. Bro. Jones dosed me with cholera medicine and sent for good Dr. Mackey, who prescribed for me, and I was soon better. I got out of bed a half dozen times to get ready for the train for Cawnpore, but each time became so sick that I had to tumble back. It had been a long while since sickness kept me out of the pulpit, but I had to give it up and telegraph, canceling the visit to Cawnpore. A good rest Monday night put me in fine shape, and Tuesday we ran over to Allahabad, 144 miles, and commenced with Bro. Guthrie, pastor of the M. E. Church, and superintendent of the district, made up of about forty native preachers who had come up to attend district conference. We remained with these friends for nine days, preaching twice each day. On the Sabbath, I preached twice to the English congregation, once through an interpreter to the natives, and made a short address at the Y. M. C. A.

The Episcopal Church was having a convention in the city with eight of their bishops present, and our congregations were small, but we had a gracious work of grace. Several were sanctified, among them Miss Bessie F. Crow, who is in charge of the native girls' school at Allahabad. Several were converted, and first and last quite a number were at the altar. Many led in prayer and gave a good testimony who had heretofore been silent. Some of the Indian brethren were greatly blessed. One English gentleman of considerable prominence was brightly converted and gave promise of making a fine worker in the church. Bro. Guthrie and his wife, who is a devout woman and a worthy helpmeet, are doing a great work. He pastors two English speaking congregations and travels through this large district looking after these forty ministers and their many members. He is one of the hardest worked men in the great Methodist army, he and Sister Guthrie raising by private correspondence much of the money for the support of this mission. They are from Iowa and have often attended the holiness camp meetings at Des Moines. Bro. Guthrie grew up at the knee of a sanctified mother. There is no way to estimate what the holiness movement has been worth to the great cause of missions. Out from the holiness camp meetings, conventions, and revivals, an army of missionaries has gone to the ends of the earth with the tidings of free and full salvation for all men from all sin.

Allahabad is a city of some two hundred and fifty thousand. The English-speaking part of the city is very beautiful. The native portion is crowded and there is much poverty, but many of the natives are wealthy and prosperous people.

A large cobra, one of the most poisonous reptiles of India, caught a frog within about forty feet of our door; one of the servants saw the snake, but let him get away

Bro. Guthrie told us to put our shoes on a chair at our bedside and not to get out of bed in the night without slipping our shoes on, so that if we should step on a serpent or scorpion we would be somewhat protected. He did not have to tell us but once. We were assured that there was but little danger. True in the second bungalow below us a man was recently bit by a cobra and only a few thousand people died last year in India from snake bites, but it was well enough to be careful. "Yes, thank you, we will put our shoes on a chair; there is no harm in such precautions even though there is but little danger."

At Allahabad I met with Dr. Lucas, pastor of the native Presbyterian Church in that city,, who is a delightful and consecrated Christian gentleman, and I judge a successful and much loved missionary. He was born, reared, educated, and ordained in Danville, Ky. I knew his brothers well when I was pastor of the Methodist Church in that town. He knew the Durhams, my mother's people. We traveled some distance on the train together and had an interesting conversation. He graduated in the same class with Rev. Ben Helm, and spoke of him with Christian affection.

When our train stopped for a few moments at a station as we came from Allahabad to Lanowli, a man put his head in our carriage window and called out, "Hello! this looks like Louisville, Ky." It was F. J. Michel, who was a Y. M. C. A. secretary in Louisville for sometime. He is now just closing out five years Y. M. C. A. work in India, and has started home to Harrodsburg, Ky. I went down the train to speak to his wife and when she told me who her mother was, I asked, "What kin are you to Mr. Will Rue, who recently died in Danville?" "He was my own uncle," she replied. "Yes, and he married my cousin, Miss Durahm." Well, well, and the world is not so large after all.

We traveled, in going from Allahabad to Lanowli, from twelve M. Wednesday till three P. M. Thursday. We were in a second class carriage or compartment, supposed to accommodate five people. There were three seats below and two shelves above upon which a man could stretch himself full length. Piercy and myself had each a comfort, a sheet and a little cotton stuffed pillow, and a scotch blanket. We made down our beds and retired early. A dear old Yankee, many years over from Boston, took the center berth, but had to leave at ten o'clock at night and I awoke to tell him good-bye, and we promised to meet if no more down here, when the general roll is called up yonder. Then a big Scotchman took the center berth, but he had to leave at three o'clock in the morning, and I awoke again for friendly words at parting. Then a big Indian appropriated the shelf and winding up head and heels in a quilt, held it until daylight.

At every change coolies came in with boxes, bags and trunks, and there was a great chattering and much noise. Soldiers came in rattling their accoutrements, peering around for a place to lie down, and there was profanity and cigarette smoke. Yet there are people who will tell you that "travel is much more pleasant in India than in the United States." There is no accounting for taste. But we got through, made our connections, and reached the camp ground in time for me to preach to a good congregation Thursday evening.

CHAPTER XIV.

ON THE MOUNTAINS WITH THE MISSIONARIES.

Epworth Heights is a beautiful place situated some eighty miles from Bombay on the mountains, at an altitude of two thousand feet above sea level.   Here the people can escape for a short time from the parching heat of the plains and recuperate their physical energies as well as deepen the spiritual life.   This is the third annual convention at Epworth Heights.   The Methodists have purchased some twenty acres of land and built a beautiful tabernacle, large dining room and kitchen, and a number of bungalows.   They have been able to rent several buildings contiguous to the grounds, but this year they were unable to accommodate the people and had to refuse some who wrote for lodgings. It is their purpose to erect two large dormitories, one for women and one for men, with ample accommodations for all who may wish to attend the meetings.   The dining room also must be enlarged; this year only a little over one-half of those in attendance could get into the dining room at once.

The gathering is entirely interdenominational.   This year a large number of missionaries and native pastors, college professors, and religious workers were present— Methodists, Presbyterians, Episcopalians, Wesleyans, Free Methodists, members of The Christian and Missionary Alliance, with headquarters at New York, and members of the Pentecostal Mission, with headquarters at Nashville, Tenn.   There was also a group of soldiers

Mango Tree in India.

from the British army who had gotten leave of absence and come up from Bombay to attend the meetings. Everybody was welcome and everybody seemed to feel perfectly at home. There was no sort of sectarian prejudice in the air. The Methodists have shown a beautiful spirit of Christian fraternity by throwing open this place for the tired bodies and hungry hearts of all Christians.

The preachers for this convention were Rev. T. Walker, of the Episcopal Church, Rev. P. Jones, of the Presbyterian Church, and this writer, of the Methodist Church. Walker gave a Bible reading from the book of Acts at 8:30 a. m., Jones preached at 11:30 a. m., Morrison preached at 8:30 in the evening, and this was the regular order of the meeting for the five days of the convention.

Rev. Mr. Walker is a low church Episcopalian and an Englishman, once a rector in London. He came out to India in mission work twenty-five years ago and has been a most faithful and devout servant of Christ. He is now devoting his time visiting the Indian churches and striving to lead them into the deeper things of divine life. His services are in great demand. I am told that he sometimes preaches to twenty thousand Indians at once, with six or more interpreters standing out in the audience to pass the word along. He is a man of gentle spirit and much prayer, and has the love and confidence of all who know him. His Bible readings from Acts were luminous, full of warning and exhortation and promise of the abundant grace of God. On Sabbath he preached a very clear sermon on holiness in the Episcopal Church of Lanowli, the village near the camp ground. He was clear on the second

coming of Christ, saying that faith in His speedy coming was a great stimulus to zealous service, and there is
no time to be lost by those who believe that Christ is
coming soon.

Rev. Mr. Jones, the Presbyterian, preached each
day from one of the letters to the seven churches, found
in Revelation. While his messages were given in the
spirit of Christian love, they were very searching and
pressed home with great earnestness. He is a Welch-
man and has been in this mission field for more than
twenty years. He is a man of deep piety and great
zeal for Christ and the salvation of souls, much loved
by the people of all churches.

I was pleased with the earnestness with which both
of these ministers contended for the inspiration of the
Scriptures, the Deity of Christ, and the all-sufficient
atonement in His blood. I have not been associated
with ministers of the gospel in a long while who spent
more time in prayer.

The services conducted by the writer in the evening
were evangelistic, in which the supreme object was the
conversion of sinners and the sanctification of believers.
The altar was filled with seekers for pardon or purity
almost every evening and quite a number of earnest
hearts were graciously blessed. If there was any opposition to the doctrine and experience of full salvation
from sin, I did not hear of it. This would not prove
that it might not exist, but if present, such prejudices
were very quiet.

It was modestly suggested that the breeze and rush
of the Western spirit was not suitable to India. Of
this I am not so sure. I believe that a strong gust from
the West would have a good effect upon the dead calm

of Indian conservatism. At any rate, I preached loud and lively and the Lord blessed the message in the conversion of sinners and the sanctification of believers, and calls for meetings came from every quarter.

I was glad to meet at this convention Rev. M. B. Fuller, who is at the head of the *Christian Missionary Alliance* work in India. He is a man of devout soul and strong mind, standing unflinchingly for the whole Bible and a full salvation.

It was like meeting with one's own kin to meet with Bro. Gregory and wife, Sister Codding, and other members of the Pentecostal Mission, from Nashville.

From this convention we went to Igatpuri, a railroad town up in the mountains. We were entertained in the home of Rev. J. C. Fisher, who preaches over a wide circuit to the natives. He came out some years ago from Kansas and is doing faithful and successful work among the natives. The meetings were held in the M. E. Church, Bro. Butterfield, pastor. The blessing of the Lord was upon us from the first and the altar was full of seekers at all of the six meetings. We could remain with them only three days. Several were pardoned, and others professed sanctification. Bro. Codding and some of his workers came up from their station and labored with us. Sisters Wood and Miller, of the medical work, were with us, and Sisters Hetchens, Nelson and Simmons, of the Nazarene Church, who are stationed there, were with us. It was three days of precious grace to our souls.

Early Saturday morning we left for Bombay in company with Bro. Codding and stopped off with him for a pleasant day at his mission station and orphanage. We had a horseback ride through the village near their mission, rested a few minutes, had a good dinner with much cheerful conversation about the work, made a little talk to the boys of the orphanage and had a prayer together.   Bro. Codding is a man of beautiful humility and earnest spirit, with a small force of intelligent and devoted workers.

The work of the Pentecostal Mission in India was started six years ago by Mr. and Mrs. Roy G. Codding, Miss Lizzie Leonard, and Miss Eva Carpenter, who were sent out by the Pentecostal Mission, a band of holiness people who have their headquarters at Nashville, Tenn.   Landing in Bombay, they consulted with missionaries who had been working for some years in India and felt led to choose their field in the foothills of the Western Ghats, having in view especially work among the Varli people, a hill tribe of the aborigines. This choice was in line with the policy of the society sending them out which is to endeavor to reach those who have not been reached by others.   The language needed was Marathi, so they located in Igatpuri during the first year to study this language.   While there they worked in fellowship with the M. E. Church.

When they began to look over their territory, they found there was just one building in it available for their occupancy.   A few years before a company had started a teak wood industry at Vasind and built a bungalow for their manager.   Later the company failed and the bungalow was vacated.   If it had belonged to a Hindu, no amount of money would have rented it, but it belonged to a Parsee living in Bombay and the superintendent secured it.   So it seemed in advance of their coming to India God had prepared one foothold for them in their territory.   The bungalow was unfin-

ished, resembling a barn more than a dwelling, and located near a river in a very malarious place, but was
thankfully accepted as God's provision. Every other
station in this field, as the work grows, will have to be
built. Vasind is on the G. I. P. Railway, about fifty
miles from Bombay.

In the autumn of 1905 Miss Long and Miss Williams from Louisiana who had been in India about three
years, felt the need of being associated with other Christian people and joined the mission.

In February, 1906, Mr. A. H. Gregory, from Hop-
kinsville, Ky., and Miss Pearl Thompson from Nashville, Tenn., reached the field. Something over a year
later they were married. Miss Bertha Davis and Miss
Bessie Seay, from Nashville, Tenn., reached the field
in February, 1909, and are at present studying the
language in Vasind. Miss Carpenter who now has
charge of the station at Vasind, devotes all her time to
evangelistic work and with her tonga and ponies is able
to reach many villages round about Vasind and is faithfully sowing the gospel seed in this virgin soil.

Mr. and Mrs. Codding are stationed at Khardi,
sixty-seven miles from Bombay on the same line of
railway as Vasind. Here is the Boys' Orphanage under the charge of Mrs. Codding. Possibly all but one
boy, who has recently come in, have been saved, some
sanctified and others seeking this blessing. Mr. Codding goes on a saddle horse by turns with the four native preachers to the neighboring villages. On several
occasions, in some of these villages, there has been some
expression of not wanting the gospel which might not be
regarded as encouraging, but on the other hand, it is
encouraging that the people who know absolutely noth-

ing about what Christianity means are beginning to at least get some little conception of it.

From Khardi a metalled wagon road is being built across the country northward into a section of country from which much timber is gotten out and where there are Varli's and other hill tribes living. Sixteen miles from Khardi, at Parali, which will be the terminus of this new road, a site has been secured for a station for Miss Leonard, who is now in America raising money for that purpose, and it is to be hoped that before long a house can be put up there for her work.

At Dhulia, something over 200 miles further from Bombay, on a spur of the same railway, is the station of Miss Long and Miss Williams. Miss Long is at present in America on furlough. Here is the Girls' Orphanage in which there are over forty orphan girls, the most of whom have been saved and some sanctified. With a tonga and oxen Miss Williams and her Bible woman go out in Dhulia and neighboring villages and preach the gospel. There are also two Indian men at this station who give their time to this line of work.

Mr. and Mrs. Gregory are at present living at Khardi. Mr. Gregory takes charge of the contracting, building and all kindred work of the mission and expects soon to begin putting up the buildings at Parali. With these four stations as a nucleus, it is their plan, as God sends in the men and money, to establish stations at intervals of twenty miles throughout their territory, and from these centers evangelize the surrounding territory. Even if these hopes are realized, the number of souls to be reached from one station is appalling, as each station will have from fifty to one hundred villages, ranging from a hundred to 10,000 inhabitants, depending on it for their knowledge of Christ and his salvation.

Another appalling fact is the amount of teaching they will need. At home the gospel has been preached until practically everybody understands that we are all sinners and whether or not they admit it, they know that Jesus Christ is the only Savior, and it is only necessary for the preacher to stir the consciences to act on the truth already known. But to say that the Hindu and Mohammedan people of India do not know that Jesus is the Savior does not tell half of it. They do not know that they are sinners in any true sense of the word; they scarcely know what sin is. They have words in their language for sin, but it is only those who do the most outrageous things that they look upon as sinners. Mr. Codding was trying to talk to a group of charcoal burners the other morning. They were more ignorant than the average Hindu, but their case will illustrate the point. He asked them if they knew what sin was. They did not appear to understand the word; it did not seem to belong to their vocabulary. To get at the thing more effectively he called on a converted Indian with him, who asked one of the men if it were wrong to steal, and putting it very personally before him, asked, "If somebody steals something of *yours,*" etc., and he admitted that that would be wrong. Well, said the preacher, that is what we mean by sin. And in this way they had to open up the truth to him and declare to him that we are all sinners and need a Savior, one who can give us new hearts and deliver us from sin.

Well, if day after day this same point could be brought more and more effectively before the minds of these same men and illustrated in a dozen different ways, by the enlightenment of the Holy Spirit, no doubt they would begin to get some understanding of what sin is. Then on this could be built some realization of our need of a Savior from sin. And thus one must work from the very bottom up, line upon line, precept upon precept.

We had to hurry away to catch the train for Bombay, and after a few hours' ride we pulled into the Victoria terminal and were met by Rev. G. B. Hill, who is district superintendent and pastor of Taylor Memorial M. E. Church. The church is a beautiful and substantial structure, the parsonage built into the front, and over the auditorium. The prophet's chamber is at the very top, and here Bro. Piercy and myself were soon comfortably quartered and praying for grace and guidance for the Bombay campaign.

Rev. H. C. Morrison, taken in India.

CHAPTER XV.

EVANGELIZING IN BOMBAY.

The city of Bombay claims a million inhabitants. It is situated on the west coast of the peninsula and is one of the great seaport cities of India. One of its principal industries is the manufacture of cotton goods. Much of the cotton crop of the country is woven into cloth in this city. From the flat roof of Taylor Memorial Church we could count eighty-six smokestacks, most of them respresenting great cotton mills in which thousands of natives work at wages far too small to sustain an American family.

Bombay has well constructed streets and sidewalks, a fine street car system, many beautiful drives with public gardens and parks, made especially beautiful by the luxuriant tropical flowers, plants and trees. There is an English population in the city aggregating about twenty thousand. These are largely officials, manufacturers, merchants and architects, and others engaged in the various professions.

The Parsees are a people who fled from Persia into India many decades ago to escape the persecutions of the Mohammedans. They were held down by the Hindu people until India came under British rule, and then they came to the front as merchants. The Parsees are called the "Jews of the East." They have immense wealth and are full of business enterprise and thrift. Many of them are highly educated and show much public spirit in reform movements for the uplift of the Indian people.   They have built hospitals and other charitable institutions in Bombay.   Many of them live in beautiful palaces with droves of servants about them.   They are fire worshipers and it is very rare that one of them is converted to Christianity.

When a Parsee dies he is taken to the top of a stone tower called the "Tower of Silence," where the naked body is laid in the open to be devoured by the vultures which are perched about the place in great numbers ready to pounce upon the corpse and rend it in pieces. One could hardly think of a more revolting method of getting rid of the dead than to feed them to these disgusting, ravenous birds which perch about the place like the black-winged imps of hades, eagerly awaiting the coming of the dead.

There are many wealthy and highly educated Hindus and Mohammedans in Bombay, some of them in high position in the government.   They are men of wide travel, are well versed in our English literature, and know much of what is going on in the world. Among these men of culture there are many reformers and various societies which have for their purpose the moral unplift of India.   They will accomplish some good no doubt, but the burden is too heavy for man to lift; it will take the omnipotent arm of Christ to lift India.

While at our meetings in Lanowli I met and had some conversation with a highly cultured Parsee gentleman.   He is secretary of a temperance society in Bombay and when I came into the city he and some other gentlemen asked me to speak in one of their public halls on temperance, giving them some account of the prohibition movement in America.   I spoke to them at six o'clock one evening. I looked forward to the occasion with no little concern. One of the Judges of the high court who is one of the great men of India was to preside, and many of their leading men would be present. The district superintendent accompanied me, with Bro. Piercy, and quite a group of missionaries were present. Every seat in the hall was occupied and many stood on the floor and in the gallery. Parsees, Mohammedans, Hindus and Christians were present. It was the most interesting audience I ever faced, with all sorts of brilliant colored robes and flashing turbans, with their clear-cut, classic faces and proud moustaches turned up almost like small horns. There was no singing or prayer, but the dignified Judge introduced me in a few sentences of as beautiful English as one could wish to hear.

I gave them some account of the widespread ravages of the whiskey traffic in America, its power in politics, and its grip upon the people. I told them something of the "Good Templars," the "Murphy Movement," and the W. C. T. U. The people cheered and I was as free as if in a holiness camp meeting in Texas. I told them of the awakening of the public conscience, of the long years of toil and prayer, and the victories won at the polls. I read them statistics to prove that prohibition would prohibit and informed them that the business of manufacturing and selling intoxicants in America was disreputable, that men engaged in the business had impoverished and murdered our people, and that we intended to drive them out of the Southland or out of the traffic. I made a plea for the South and told them that notwithstanding our past entanglement with slavery we were a great people who loved principle better than we loved money, and they rose to their feet and clapped their hands and called out, "Hear! Hear!"   I closed by saying, "And now gentlemen, I feel sure that it will give no offense to anyone in this audience of culture and thoughtful people for me to say to you that we are being saved from the power of this most subtle foe of the human race by the power of the Man who died on a cross just outside the gates of Jerusalem, nineteen hundred years ago.   It is the strong arm of Jesus Christ that is lifting us out of the darkness of drunkenness into the light of sobriety."   Before sitting down I offered a short prayer for the salvation of India.

At the close of the address it seemed to me that scores, if not hundreds of them, were on their feet. There was a vote of thanks, the Judge made some closing remarks, and a great number came forward to shake hands.   Two young Hindus followed us to the church and came to the altar for prayer that night. The next day a finely educated young man, a Brahmin, the highest caste of India, came to my room for instruction how he could get to America and what he could do, once there, to earn a livelihood.   Letters came to the pastor and myself requesting that I make a number of prohibition addresses, which I had to refuse, for my mission here is to preach holiness.

One of their leading lawyers called at my room to talk over the situation and begged that we would send out a temperance orator to help push the work for the suppression of the liquor traffic.   I promised to supply him with literature and statistics showing what the prohibition movement has done for our country.   It seems that certain Englishmen who are fond of their grog and who would blight this country with strong drink, have been singing the old song over here that "prohibition will not prohibit."

This lawyer tells me there is a movement on foot among the educated class, looking to the suppression of child marriage and many evils growing out of the miserable caste system which prevails in India. One of the greatest barriers to the progress of the people of India is the *caste*. It would be difficult to tell how many *castes* exist among the people and how wide and deep the social chasm is between these various castes. For instance, there is the *sweeper caste*. These people sweep the yards, public buildings, and streets; they clean the city. They are the very lowest and most despised caste. Once a sweeper always a sweeper, and so it goes from father to son, and there is no thought or effort of trying to rise above their caste. The sweepers live in certain sections of the city apart to themselves. I went into a number of their settlements yesterday to visit M. E. mission schools for their children. They live in miserable huts made of mud and sticks with bamboo poles supporting a roof made of old tin "Standard Oil" cans. The sweepers are so low down in the social scale and have so little pride that they are much more easily won to Christ than the higher castes and many of them are being saved by the gospel.

The charcoal burners are a very low *caste*. A few days ago while visiting Bro. Codding we rode on horseback through a village near his mission and in the outskirts of the village saw a huddle of mirerable shacks where the charcoal burners life, who are especially outcasts and despised because they will eat carrion. The dead body of a cow or goat found on the plains is readily appropriated by them.   Many of our Western Indians in America will do the same disgusting thing.

While on this same horseback ride we passed a group of Hindus burning the body of a dead woman. A large heap of dry wood was placed upon the corpse and set on fire in a field near the roadside.   When it came to a full blast the mourners turned and walked slowly away, the women of the group lingering to glance back at the roaring heap of logs.   The men of this funeral group were entirely naked except a small dirty breech-clout of cotton cloth, not much larger than a pocket handkerchief.   As I looked upon their poor naked bodies and their dead, ignorant faces, I could but think of a class of people we have in America, who say, "Let these people alone; they are contented with their religion.   Why should you bother them?"

The Brahmins are of the highest caste in India and they are so particular and fanatical on the subject that they would not think of eating food prepared by some one of a lower caste, or drinking water drawn from a well by some one of a caste below them.   If a missionary should draw a bucket of water from one of their wells it would be a polluted well, and they would not use the water again until they had gone through certain heathen incantations for the purifying of the well.   If you should go into one of these high caste person's house and touch him with the tip of your finger he would be polluted and would go off, perhaps a mile, to some stream to wash away his defilement.   Some of them dare not come within five, ten, or even twenty feet of anyone of a lower caste than themselves without becoming defiled, and they must bathe and pray to their idols before they can regard themselves pure, meanwhile they may be committing the grossest sins with apparently no conscience on the subject. This miserable caste foolishness is one of the greatest barriers in the way of the salvation of the people. To become a Christian is to break one's caste and become an outcast from one's home and family, and every old tie and friendship.

While I was preaching in Lucknow a fine young man of high caste was converted and baptized and immediately disappeared. He did not come to another service and could not be found. When inquiry was made at his home his people said he had gone to a city about six hundred miles away. The missionaries reported the matter to the police with the hope that he might be found. It was not supposed that he had been killed, but that he had been sent far away in order to get him out from under Christian influence and drag him back to idol worship.

Sad to say the devil of Unitarianism is busy in India. There is at least one influential body of missionaries there who are unsound in teaching, namely: the *American Board.* It is an organization of the Congregational Church, a church which is becoming pitifully unsound in doctrine at home and abroad. The educated Hindus are wide awake and know full well that unbelief in the *Deity of Christ* is widespread in America. They know that the incumbent of the *White House* denies the Deity of Christ, and that the chaplain of the United States Senate also denies His Deity. They have read Mr. Roosevelt's scolding and ridicule of those Christians in our land who dared to open their mouths in protest against this recrucifixion of the Son of God in our national capital. They know that our

church papers are practically quiet on the subject.
They talk of this among themselves and strengthen their
hearts in unbelief and wickedness.   All of this helps
to build the mighty walls of prejudice against which
the missionary must exhaust his arguments and energies.

The ignorance, stupidity and selfishness which are
now masquerading as statesmanship and patriotism under our dear old flag makes the heart of the true Christian turn sick with sorrow.

Since commencing to write this letter we were attracted to the window by music in the street, and looked
out and saw a brass band followed by two handsome
carriages richly decorated with silken colors, a little boy
and girl in each carriage seven or eight years of age,
followed by a large procession of people on foot.   It
was a child wedding.   Two couples of little children
were being united in matrimony.   After the procession
and feast these children will return to their respective
homes and will not live together as husband and wife
until they are somewhere in their teens.   If the boy
should die in the meantime the girl must remain a wid-
ow for life.   It is in this way that India has come to
have thousands of little widows who must spend their
lives in seclusion and sorrow.

We are having a gracious meeting at Taylor Memorial Church.   There have been from ten to twenty
young men at the altar of prayer almost every evening,
besides women and girls.   I believe the Lord will get
some preachers out of these young men.   At the close
of these meetings I am, D. V., to hold pentecostal
meetings at four annual conferences. I trust THE HER-
ALD family will continue to pray for us.   My health
is fairly good, though I have lost considerable flesh and

British Soldiers, most of whom were converted or sanctified in Bombay Meetings.

have aged rapidly, but I praise God for the opportunity he is giving me to witness for Christ in this land of darkness.

There is an open door here in India for a large number of Spirit-filled young Americans. In some portions of the country large numbers of natives are turning to Christ; in other parts the resistance is strong. Many people believe the truth of the gospel but fear to pay the price of caste and friends. The average intelligent Hindu would be willing to incorporate Christ into his religion, but he is not willing to give up his idolatries and his sins and trust in Christ alone for salvation. But there is victory all along the line, and the gospel is penetrating into every part of India. Heathen superstition and darkness are giving away before the onward march of the army of the great Captain of our redemption.

"Pray ye therefore the Lord of the harvest, that he would send forth laborers into his harvest."

CHAPTER XVI.

A GRACIOUS REVIVAL.

Taylor Memorial M. E. Church in which we spent our first week of revivals in the city of Bombay is out in the edge of the city, some four miles from the central business portion.   We put in seven days there stopping in the parsonage with the very pleasant family of Bro. Hill, who is district superintendent; also the pastor of Taylor Memorial.   I have never known a body of men more constantly occupied with their work than these M. E. missionaries.   They not only have their own English speaking congregations to look after, but native preachers and their congregations as well.   An immense correspondence must be carried on with the homeland raising money to support this pastor, that Bible woman, and the other student.   Some one must be found to pay the rent of a school building, to help pay a church debt, or pay the rent of a hall.   In fact, it seems that the missionaries are too much burdened with these more secular and material affairs of the church, and no doubt it would be far better if they could be relieved of much of this work and give more time to prayer and the great work of soul winning.

The Lord gave us a gracious meeting at Taylor Memorial.   Of course, seven days was not long enough, but the committee was eager that I should preach at as many points as possible, and gave me only a few days at each place.   The altar of prayer was filled most every evening, some coming for reclamation, some for pardon, and others for entire sanctification.   Many were blest. From time to time there was a number of Indians in the meetings and several of them came to the altar of prayer. A number of British soldiers came from the fort, some four miles away. Several of them were converted and others were seeking perfect love.

On Saturday we took our baggage down to the Y. M. C. A., which is in the heart of the English part of the city, within three blocks of Bowen M. E. Church, where we were to preach the coming week. This placed us much nearer the fort, and in close touch with the business part of the city. After being comfortably quartered in our room in the Y. M. C. A., where we are to be entertained during our work at Bowen Church, we went back to Taylor Memorial and held our last service of the series, Saturday evening, November 27. The Lord gave victory and a number were forward for prayer, among them an English sailor whose ship had recently come into port. He professed salvation, as did also a young infidel who has shown no interest in his soul's salvation until this meeting. We closed out after ten o'clock at night, and with a squad of soldiers who had come out to be at the last meeting, we boarded an uptown street car for the Y. M. C. A. There were enough of us to about fill up the rear end of the car, and we went sweeping up through the city, with its teeming tens of thousands of idolaters about us like a confused swarm of bees, singing aloud the sweet songs of Zion.

One night while at Taylor Memorial Church (this church is named in memory of the greatly beloved Bishop Taylor) I called for all the young men who were willing to lay themselves on the altar to preach the gospel in India to give me their hand, and seven

fine young men came forward. ' I have no doubt some
of them will preach. We are earnestly praying the
Lord of the harvest to send laborers into the harvest.
The pastor, Bro. Hill, informs us that on the Sabbath after the close of the meetings, he received on trial
ten new converts and that there will be more to follow;
we have heard since of other additions.

Saturday night we had a battle with the mosquitoes
and got very little sleep, but were up early for a busy
day. The order in India is a cup of tea, two slices of
buttered bread and a banana, sent to your room at 7
a. m. Preaching at half past eight o'clock; this early
hour is selected to avoid the intense heat of the later
hours.

When we came into the beautiful Bowen Church a
good congregation was present. There was a great
heap of soldiers' helmets piled on the floor in the rear
of the church, a stack of glittering army rifles stacked
against the wall and a fine body of soldiers in uniforms
white as snow, with belts and ammunition girded on
them. Since the great mutiny when the people were
slaughtered in church, the soldiers in India have gone
to church armed and ready for any emergency. The
Lord was graciously present in the morning service.
I offered Christ as a Savior able to save to the uttermost
and the Spirit was present to warm our hearts with
divine love. The pastor, Rev. Wood, is a man of
real devotion, and our hearts were united in prayer
and faith for the blessing of the Lord. We came back
to the Y. M. C. A., for breakfast a little past ten a. m.;
and had tiffin (a light lunch) at two p. m. The secretary
asked us to meet a number of English gentlemen at four
o'clock for a cup of tea in his room, and a quiet con-

versation on Christ's attitude toward social life.
"These men," he said, "would never come into a Bible
class, but they will come together for a cup of tea and
bit of cake, and conversation on some phase of Christ's
life or teaching."

It is marvelous how dead the sinner can become in
a heathen land where there is so much to draw him
away from God and so little to remind him of his soul
and his future. So we met in the parlor and an old
Indian, dignified as a prince and silent as the grave,
passed the refreshments and then the lesson was taken
up—"Christ's attitude toward social life," which led
to a discussion of the Christian's attitude toward world-
ly pleasures. The secretary maneuvered an opening
for me and after considerable conversation about the
theater and this and that, one young man suggested,
"Take the medical profession. You can scarcely find
a more degraded lot of men than medical students and
perhaps no class of men are more generally sinful than
doctors." It was his purpose, it seemed, to excuse
stage people. "Quite true," said the writer, "but the
study of medicine is not necessarily degrading and the
practice of medicine may and should be very elevating.
Many of our noblest and most unselfish benefactors are
physicians. The stage has always been degrading to
those who perform upon it; never more so than in the
days of Shakespeare himself. It is no doubt
entertaining to those fond of that sort of thing,
but not refining. The predominant suggestion
of the stage is downward." "Yes," said the young
man, "that is true of the theaters of the highest order
in London. I have often attended plays in them full
of low suggestions."

"It is the business of the Christian," said the writer, "to win other men to Christ. He will be successful in this great work in proportion to his influence as a Christian among his fellow men, and no Christian can afford to neutralize that influence by visiting questionable places or doing questionable things, and fortunately the Christian does not find his delight in such things but in the service of his Master. In deciding about the propriety of an action we should give Christ the benefit of the doubt and we will be kept on the safe side of every proposition." The big fellow with shoulder straps from a warship in the harbor, approved heartily, and almost every one assented to the soundness of the position, and the meeting dismissed itself and the men drifted out, in a serious thoughtful mood.

Preaching on Sabbath evening is at six thirty, and when we went in the church was packed with people. Some stood and some went away, but the Lord was with us, the word was with power, and the audience was very attentive and thoughtful. Europeans, Anglo-Indians, and Indians were present. After church we went to eight o'clock dinner with a doctor who is very zealous for the salvation of the soldiers. With some others he has opened up a hall where the soldiers meet for refreshments, song, and prayer, and where a number of them have found salvation. I am to speak to them at half past nine. Supper over, we drive to the hall and find a large company. A number of soldiers' wives are present and a civilian here and there. A Christian officer comes in and brings with him a private quite under the influence of drink, and seats him in the front row of seats and sits by him.

They pass tea and cake, then have songs, then solos,

then introduce the writer, and he tells them he is not much for tea, unless it is very weak; in fact, has always liked water in his tea, since we got so much water in our tea at Boston harbor. They laughed heartily and we got a good start, led them on to serious thoughts on sin, and offered a Christ who could save to the uttermost. The Christians were stirred up and two sinner soldier boys asked for prayer. We closed about eleven o'clock and a friend brought us home, dripping wet with perspiration, in an automobile. It was about 85 in the shade and blazing hot in the sunshine. A cold bath refreshed me, and I wrapped up in my Scotch blanket for rest on my little bunk; but the rest is broken by the mosquitoes, and before we could realize that the night was gone a crow was cawing on our window sill in a few feet of my pillow; and friendly crow he was, for we had to leap out of bed, eat our bread and banana and hurry through our preparations to get off to the eight o'clock morning meeting. During the week we preached at eight in the morning and nine at night. This catches the business people before going to their offices and gives them time for dinner at eight o'clock, before coming to the evening meetings.

Conference met on Wednesday and continued through the week. It was a great privilege to see the preachers and to preach full salvation to them twice each day.

There are many large missions in Bombay. The Episcopalians have large English speaking work here; several churches also work among the natives. Just below the Y. M. C. A., across the street is a great Catholic plant, church and school. Down the bay on Queen's Road is a large Presbyterian school.

There are Wesleyans, Baptists, and others. The M.
E. Church has two English speaking churches, one
large native church, and thirteen small schools for young
children, right down among the people. It is not the
purpose of the M. E. Church to do much institutional
work, but to give special attention to evangelizing
the city. This is, we think, a most wise decision. The
time has come when the gospel should be taken to all
men. Every heathen land ought to be swept over with
a fire-baptized evangelism proclaiming man a lost and
ruined sinner, and Jesus Christ a Savior able to save
to the uttermost.

The immediate need of India is a great revival in the
English speaking churches. This would spread to the
native churches, these would touch the heathen masses
and multitudes would be brought to Christ. There are
large numbers of young men out here in business and in
the army who would be saved in a great revival and
enter the mission field as pastors and evangelists. It
will not suffice to get the people converted, and leave
them at that. The means of grace are too few and
the pressure of unbelief and worldliness is too heavy.
The sanctifying power of the blood and the filling with
the Holy Ghost is the divine plan and anything short
of that must fail in a heathen land or anywhere else, as
to that matter. But there is not a large number of
English people there ready for the sanctifying grace.
They are in the church without regeneration; they have
backslidden or they are lukewarm and at ease in Zion.
Hence it will take time, patience, and much zealous
labor to bring about the great revival needed there.

One of the greatest needs of the M. E. Church in
India is several Spirit-filled evangelists devoting much

of their time to revival work in the English speaking churches. The fire, as just stated, would spread to the native churches and many young men who are already acclimated and speak the native tongues and are acquainted with the peculiarities of the people would enter the ministry and mightily promote the work of the Lord. The Englishman is conservative and the Indian is shy. These facts stand in the way of revivals. The Englishman is full of reverence. He will go to church, bow his head in prayer as soon as he gets into the sanctuary, sing, listen and stand with bowed head in deep silence for some time after the benediction is pronounced. He is a stickler for *decency and order.*

There is much to be learned from the sturdy, bulldog grit of the Englishman, but the influence of the *established church* is more or less over him, and is felt by the church generally in India. We Methodists should guard carefully here. We do not need any more forms than we have. We need power. We want to put life and spirit into our services. We want the heat and action produced by the Holy Ghost. The masses of the people care but little for the mere human forms of religion; they would like to see the unmistakable evidences of the supernatural power of salvation among men. Let Methodism separate herself from all worldliness, be filled with the Spirit, sing and shout and preach a free and full salvation from all sin. Then she will have to enlarge the seating capacity of her places of worship the world over. The world is ready for the proclamation of an unlimited atonement. Men are eager to hear of a Christ who is able to save all men from all sin.

CHAPTER XVII.

PENTECOSTAL MEETINGS AT THE ANNUAL CON-
FERENCE.

The Bombay Annual Conference convened in Bow-
en Memorial Church, Bombay, December 1, 1909,
Bishop F. W. Warne in the chair.   A more brotherly
and democratic bishop never presided over an annual
conference.   The revival meetings were under full
headway when the conference opened, and the coming
in of the preachers and their wives gave momentum to
the good work.   The writer preached each morning
at eight o'clock and in the evening at nine o'clock.
There was not a more earnest altar worker in the
meetings than Bishop Warne.   Every night the altar
was full of earnest seekers, some for pardon and some
for entire sanctification.

The doctrine of full salvation as a second work of
grace is nothing new in India.   The sainted Bishop
William Taylor, laid the foundations of Methodism at
many places in this country, and at every place thoroughly instilled into the people the doctrine of entire
cleansing from sin.   There is need of a revival of the
experience here, as elsewhere, but there is great advantage in the fact that that master workman, William
Taylor, wrought on the foundations.

All the great fundamental doctrines of salvation must
be preached to every generation and preached repeated-
ly.   The doctrine of the fall, the sacrificial death of
Christ, the turpitude of sin, and the final results of it,
repentance, faith, forgiveness, regeneration, the carnal

nature, and entire sanctification, the baptism and abiding of the Holy Spirit, are to the spiritual life of congregation what soil, sunshine, dew and shower are to a growing crop of corn in the field.

Many people were at the altar; misunderstandings were cleared up, differences were settled, and the entire church came into sweet fellowship. Preachers, both white and Indian, were at the altar; members of other churches and a number of soldiers from the Royal Artillery were among those calling upon the Lord. A number claimed pardon and a number professed sanctification.

The conference is made up of a sturdy body of men. Many of them have been in this field for five, ten and twenty years; some for a longer period. The reports of the district superintendents reveal a marvelous amount of heroic work; that many thousands of India's millions are hearing the gospel; that there is real salvation among the people, and that those who are being saved are becoming earnest witnesses and some of them devout ministers of the gospel to their people. The reports reveal the fact that the missionaries are fearfully handicapped for want of means. The possibilities of the field are unlimited. Multiplied thousands of Indians could soon be gathered into the fold if only the money was forthcoming to support a force of consecrated men and women to properly man the situation and cultivate the wide field so big with possibilities. I wish that this Bombay Conference could have been held in some one of the great wealthy Methodist churches in America. It would undoubtedly mean less tobacco, less feathers and jewelry, less of laid up treasures, and more money for missions.

The startling revelation to me was the fact that the missionaries do not only have to suffer cuts in their salaries, but they must by private correspondence raise from friends at home money for the support of the native preachers and workers. If the correspondence of one of these missionary superintendents for one year could be seen, you would think he was a secretary devoting his entire time to money raising. But if you knew the number of miles he travels on the train, in bullock cart, on horseback, any way to get there, you would think he did nothing but travel.

I learned with interest that most of the appointments for the native workers are made at the district conference by the district superintendent. It would be impossible for all these native pastors, evangelists, and Bible women to come up to the annual conference; so they gather at their district conference, make their reports there, receive their appointments and go on their way to spread the good news of salvation. This method means great economy, both of time and money. In fact, it would be impossible for the native workers of a district to come up to an annual conference. The distance and expense are too great, and the numbers could not get into any church or be entertained by any community.

On the closing Sabbath the brethren set aside their conference sermon, and Bishop Warne refused to preach at the regular morning hour that the evangelistic meetings might go forward without interruption. At the evening service the Bishop went away to Taylor Memorial, so that the writer might have full swing with the revival meetings. The Lord was with us in great power; many souls were seeking and many blessed.

This closing Sabbath evening service was held at six o'clock and lasted about two hours and a quarter. I went home to dinner, and at nine o'clock made an address to a fine audience, of men only, at the Y. M. C. A. At four o'clock in the afternoon I had spoken in a little hall packed with Hindu gentlemen who came for me with a handsome carriage and footmen. My theme at their request, was *Total Abstinence,* but I took pains to bear witness for Christ. Their attention and courtesy was delightful. Four services a day for the heat and enervating climate of India are too much for any man. I was suffering from dysentery, and the doctor had me on boiled milk and arrowroot, and I went through this Sabbath with no solid food until after eight o'clock at night. Dysentery is one of the scourges of India, and once it gets hold of you it is hard to shake off; it pulls you down and cuts your nerves in a remarkable manner. Thousands of white men who go out there die from this dreaded disease.

The conference and meetings closed at Bowen Church on Monday. We rested at our headquarters in the Y. M. C. A. Tuesday, and had a big Englishman, who had been convicted during the meeting, powerfully converted in our room. Wednesday we took it easy and left at nine thirty at night for the Jubblepur Conference. A number of friends, and a big squad of British soldiers who had been blessed in the meetings, came to see us off, one good sister bringing along a box of crackers, potted ham, a jar of three grain capsules of quinine and a bottle of medicine for emergencies. It cheered our hearts in this far off land to have these friends love us for Jesus' sake. We received many evidences of an awakening in various parts of the city and believe that with a six months' siege we could have seen a thousand converts. We heard of much conviction in one of the large medical colleges and of a general awakening in the Royal Artillery stationed in the city.

We were a night and a day going to Jubblepur; got off after dark and met the pastor, who hurried me to the church, where the congregation was assembled, with Bishop Warne conducting the introductory service. The pastor sent me off with a servant while he and Bro. Piercy looked after the baggage. The servant missed the way, but we found the church after a long walk, and I went panting into the pulpit and was soon preaching to one of the most appreciative and receptive congregations I have met in India. The congregation was largely made up of the members of the conference. We left the church at the close of the service for a large dining tent in Dr. Felt's yard where the preachers and their wives ate their meals during the conference. Dr. Felt is one of the district superintendents and has under his charge about one hundred and eighty native workers, pastors, evangelists, Bible women and teachers.

The second evening of our meetings, which were held at six o'clock, one of the pastors, a fine young Englishman, was sanctified at the altar and gave a clear testimony. Later on one of the most experienced missionaries in the conference who once enjoyed full salvation, but had let it leak out, received it back again. It was my pleasure to meet here with three missionaries from Hamlin University, near Minneapolis, who were sanctified under my ministry at Red Rock camp meeting several years ago. It was a happy meeting. One of them had lost the holy glow out of his heart; he came to the altar and was soon graciously restored. Among those who were blessed was the sister at the head of the large orphanage and girls' school, located at Jubblepur. The altar was filled every night and a number were saved or sanctified, among them some of the "The King's Rifles," a crack regiment of British infantry stationed in the city.

I preached morning and evening throughout the conference, and Bishop Warne gave his hearty support, and labored faithfully with the seekers for pardon, or purity. A little after eight o'clock we retired to the big dining tent in which six tables were set and we all sat down to supper (dinner in India). It was a great time, one that I shall never forget. These brave souls have been scattered over a wide range of country for a year; they have seen, some of them, but few white faces. Now they have come together to recount their conflicts and victories. The beloved Bishop is among them as a big brother. Now this group is at his table, and at the next meal some other company, so that there is mixing and mingling freely and close touch and pleasant acquaintance, while beautiful brotherly love prevails. It was good to be there.

There is big Bro. McMurry, and his wife, a strong fearless woman, and their three fine children. They have an orphanage and when provisions get scarce he takes his rifle and goes out into the jungle and kills deer for the children. He has brought in as many as four at once. Now and then they have bear meat for a change. His wife has nursed hundreds of people down with cholera and seen them die by the score. Three times she has been smitten down with the dread plague and three times the Lord has raised her up.

. . . .

There is young Ward, the son of the sainted missionary Ward, who recently took leave for rest at the Master's feet in glory. His work is far out in the jungle, five days' travel from the railroad. He looks like a boy, but for years has done a man's work. A few years ago he was going to annual conference with two Indian boys in a cart, when just as the sun was going down, a huge tiger leaped into the road behind them; the driver stopped the cart and in an instant Ward had his Winchester leveled on the beast. His fingers tarried for a second at the trigger while he prayed God to guide the bullet. At the crack of the gun the tiger leaped halfway to the cart and then wheeled for the jungle. Ward pumped another bullet into him as he fled. To follow a wounded tiger into a jungle is almost certain death. Many hundreds have perished this way. They camped for the night a short distance from the place. Next morning early, a wealthy Indian came by on his elephant with his servants. Ward mounted up behind him; the men spread out and made their way into the jungle. Ward soon saw the wounded animal crouched in a clump of bushes and gave it a death shot. His men skinned it and they took the hide with them to conference. This young man could fill a book with the interesting stories of thrilling experiences with wild beasts and wild men. The people among whom he labors live largely from hunting. They kill their game with bow and arrow and spears. Ward's Winchester comes in handy among them and they have a great love for him, frequently meeting him in the road and asking him to get down from his horse and pray for them. And just to think the collection box was passed to you, taking up money for the meagre

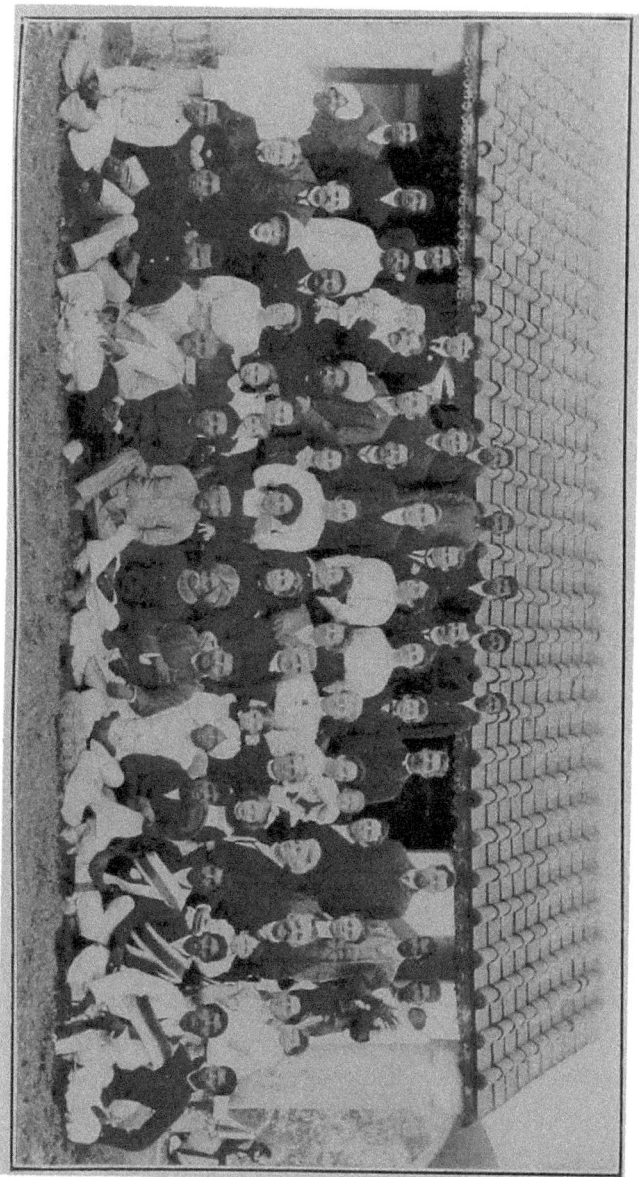

Methodist Conference of Jubbalpure, India.

support of this man and those like him, and you looked
straight into your hymn book with head covered with
flowers and plumage and did not cast in one cent, and
the man at your side with a pocketful of fine cigars cast
in a dime. It would not be so bad on you if it were
not for the judgment day. But we must come to the
judgment day and stand there before Jesus with these
missionaries and those naked, neglected heathen.

On Sabbath morning I preached to one of the native
churches to a large congregation of Indians. I wish
THE HERALD readers could have seen them. Almost
every seat was occupied and some dozens sat on floor
about the pulpit. The contrast between these Christian Indians making the rafters ring with their songs of
praise, and those poor, naked idolaters in the street, is
as beautiful day to the darkest night. It would seem
that the devil would feel ashamed of his crowd, but he
has no shame. He has lost the power of faith, or
love, or shame. At the close of the sermon the altar
was packed with native seekers after full salvation,
most of them pastors or theological students. There
was a time of strong crying unto God and many glad
testimonies followed and a time of joy and praise. At
this service it was my privilege to baptize four Indians,
three of them adults and one of them a babe in its
mother's arms.

During the conference Bro. Piercy and myself had
a comfortable room in the home of the president of a
school of the Christian Church. A fine group of people out from the United States, some of them from In-
diana. The day after our arrival in Jubblepur, Bro.
Piercy and myself drove in a cart through the city with
its ninety thousand people and scores of idol temples

and shrines. The whole place was a swarm of humanity, but the Black Plague had broken out and some of the shops were closed and people were beginning to leave the city. The day after the conference closed we drove through the city again. Most of the shops and bazars were closed, the general market was shut up and the people were fleeing to the country. The streets, full of people five days ago, were now almost empty. Dead rats were found all about, and the fleas from these rats scatter the plague. A little dead squirrel lay near the church door, where the conference was held, and some one called out, "Better not go near that dead squirrel, Bro. Morrison, it might have plague fleas on it." "Yes, thank you, I will keep away," and I changed localities with alacrity.

After the conference closed I went out to see the great Methodist orphanage, riding the two miles in a bullock cart which is the missionary method of travel about the country. It is a fine large place with something near two hundred girls, ranging all the way from grown young ladies to a babe in arms. I poked a little creature, about two years of age, in the side to make her laugh, and she liked it so well that she followed me up for more fun. Finally she reached up her little brown hand and took me by the finger and walked about, singing to herself in sweet baby voice. She never let go until we reached the compound gate and looked sad at parting, but I feel those baby fingers yet. India had at no time touched my heart so deeply as through the grip and prattle of this little orphan child.

CHAPTER XVIII.

GOING INTO SOUTHERN INDIA.

Returning from my visit to the orphanage Bro. Piercy had everything in shape for our start to Southern India. As we drove to the station every jar of the cart wheel sent pain through me for my malady contracted at Bombay was still clinging to me, and I was becoming very weak and sore from the effects of it. It was about dark when we got on the train and Piercy put my quilt, blanket, and little pillow on a seat and I lay down at once. Passengers were in and out of our carriage through the night and there was not much sleep, but the reclining position was helpful.

The next day we arrived at Monmad about ten o'clock where we changed cars, got breakfast, and Piercy bedded me down on a bench in the station for a six hours wait for our train going south. Leaving at four in afternoon we ran through a great Indian country, scarcely seeing a white man, but thousands of the native people. We arrived at Dhoud (pronounced Doan) at nine o'clock; Piercy bedded me down on a bench and went to supper. When I awoke from a short sleep he told me he had quail for supper, the very thing I had been wishing for during the day. I got up and made my way to the dining room to find the dishes cleared away and no chance for anything to eat, so I went back to my bench. Piercy spread his quilt near me, and we made a shade of our coats and hats on the back of a chair to save our eyes from the glare of the

lamp.   Two other men were stretched out in the waiting room for their rest, but one of them snored merci-
lessly.   Piercy slammed his shoes on the stone floor a
number of times hoping that he would be aroused
enough to change his position and perhaps make less
noise.   We felt sure he could become no worse.   Our
ruse failed, but tired nature overcame the situation and,
with door open and hundreds of cat-footed Indians
moving about in the moonlight and cuddled in the corner and stretched on the stone floor of the station shed,
we slept with no thought of danger.

About one o'clock I awoke and walked out into the
wonderful India night.   There was not a cloud in the
sky; the moon rode through the heavens, flooding the
earth with beautiful golden light, while the great stars
shone out with a brilliancy I have not seen in the
West.   When there is no moon to dim the starlight the
heavens bending over this fair land are wonderful to
behold.   I tried to count the Indians sleeping on the
stone pavement, wrapped up head and heels in their
blankets, but they were so mixed up, interlaced and
crisscrossed that I could not walk about among their
prostrate forms, so I gave it up and went back to my
bench.   I am confident there was more than a hundred
of them.

At four o'clock we were up and off.   During the
day we ran through broad valleys bordered on the one
hand with mountains of great boulders piled in mighty
heaps upon each other.   Some of them were as large
as small temples or good-sized houses, and thousands
of them from the size of large tobacco hogsheads down
to that of a man's head.   There seemed to be neither
soil nor verdure on these great stone mountains, but at

the top there were towers and peaks shooting up into the air. They looked like silent sentinels of nature watching the tired feet of the centuries as they went slowly marching by.

We passed through great plains that spread away to the drooping horizon, with vast fields of cotton and a variety of grain from which the Indians make their coarse bread. The predominating growth is much like Kaffir corn that grows in the western part of our country with a head on it quite like our sorghum cane. There were great herds of cattle with long lines of water buffalo, one of the most useful animals of India, an ugly creature, but giving far more milk and much richer, yielding more butter than the ordinary cow. There were scrubby little short wooled sheep and numberless flocks of goats, valuable for skins, many of which are shipped to the United States. You will see large goats with teats almost as large as those of a cow. If she is followed by a kid her udder is pocketed in a little cloth sack tied with a string over her back, to keep the kid from getting more than his share of the milk. All of these animals are followed by shepherds who attend them closely that they may be kept out of the unfenced harvest fields.

As you run down into the southern end of India you would expect the heat to become intense, but fortunately the land rises to a high altitude above sea level, making the district about Bangalore one of the cool and healthful regions. We do not mean to say it is cool, but it is not nearly so hot as some other parts of India.

I wish our HERALD readers might have seen the little railway carriage in which we traveled the last day of this journey. It was quite an old worn-out affair, the floor and walls covered with dust, cinders, grime, boxes, trunks, bundles of luggage, racks with umbrellas and walking canes and big Toquets (Indian hats) which we must wear on every occasion of going out, to prevent sunstroke. There were five of us in the carriage and tobacco smoke in profusion. We stopped, started and clattered along, stopped again and waited so long at one station that a barber came in and shaved three of us and then had time to spare. Indian merchants stood at the car windows and offered rugs for sale to the passengers, and boys called attention to candies and fruits. Scores of people chased about and lounged around and no one seemed to know why we waited or when we would start. After awhile some one would ring a station bell furiously. The engine whistle would answer and the people would begin to run about like a hill of disturbed ants. A few minutes later the *guard* (conductor) would blow a whistle like a police whistle and, after a minute of scurrying about, we would slowly pull out from the station and dash away for a few miles and stop, visit, trade, glance up at the sun, yawn, ring bells, blow whistles and move on to the next village where the throng languidly awaited the coming of the train; and so we went toward Bangalore.

The last night we traveled on a narrow gauge and Bro. Piercy and myself were thankful to have a little carriage all to ourselves. We made our pallets down on the seats, the sun went down like a ball of fire, the stars came out, the cool wind sprung up, we hoisted the windows of our jerking, jolting little coach and my feet, which seemed to be burning to blister through the day, were soon bare and hanging out of the window.

Our panting little engine puffed and wheezed along drawing us something more than one hundred and twenty-five miles during the night. Friday morning we were passing through a beautiful country of little rice fields, orchards and gardens, and a little after seven a. m., pulled into Bangalore. Rev. C. F. Lipp, pastor of the M. E. Church, gave us a hearty welcome, and drove us to the parsonage where his wife had some refreshments ready for us, and I was in the pulpit preaching by nine o'clock. After preaching I came to the parsonage and went at once to bed, the first real bed I had touched since Monday night. We had two services each day, at eight in the morning and six in the evening. On Sabbath after the evening service in the church we drove out two miles to the camp of a Scotch regiment just over from China held in quarantine outside of the city, and I preached to them in a tabernacle made of bamboo poles and matting. The place was packed with soldiers and in the dim light of a few swinging lanterns I looked into a mass of thoughtful Scotch faces while I preached from the text, "Ye must be born again." I felt the Spirit's presence and believe for fruit in the time to come.

Methodism has a strong place at Bangalore—a large school for girls, a large school for boys, a large church building, and parsonage. The real estate and buildings are worth from seventy-five to a hundred thousand dollars. The schools were out for vacation; the students were off for home, the excitement of preparation for Christmas was on, and it was a bad time for revival meetings. During the ten days of the meetings a goodly number were at the altar; some were converted, a number professed full deliverance from sin through the

sanctifying power of Christ's blood, and others were
greatly refreshed in their souls.

On the afternoon of Christmas eve, Bro. Piercy and
I went up into the city to a little park where the
people had built a kind of village of bamboo, matting
and green boughs, and in neat little booths had all sorts
of Christmas toys for sale.   The Christians were
making arrangements for the glad tomorrow, and the
Mahommedans were having a feast in memory of Abraham's offering up of Isaac, which consists of killing a
fat goat, one-third of which they keep for themselves,
one-third they send to neighbors, and one-third they
give to beggars.

It was a lively scene.   Antomobiles were honking
about, and carriages with gay parties were hastening
from place to place.   The bullocks were going at a
lope with their carts full of laughing people, gay colored clothing was on every hand, an Indian band was
playing, two big government camels were striding about
with Indians on top of them and laughing little English
girls riding perched behind.   The broad-shouldered
Scotchman, in kilt and bonnet, strode about as if he
owned the whole thing, and the neat "Tomey" in flashing uniform was in and out of the throng.   The jewel
merchant had a rich display of diamonds and pearl
necklace and golden belts and bracelets for arms and
ankles.   The silk merchant had his marvelous patterns
of silks and gold.   The side shows were all about in
tents, none of which we saw inside of, the grab bag at
so much a chance was well represented, and gambling
tables with various coins over which men and women
and boys tried to throw little rings were scattered along
the line, the monkey man squatted on the ground with

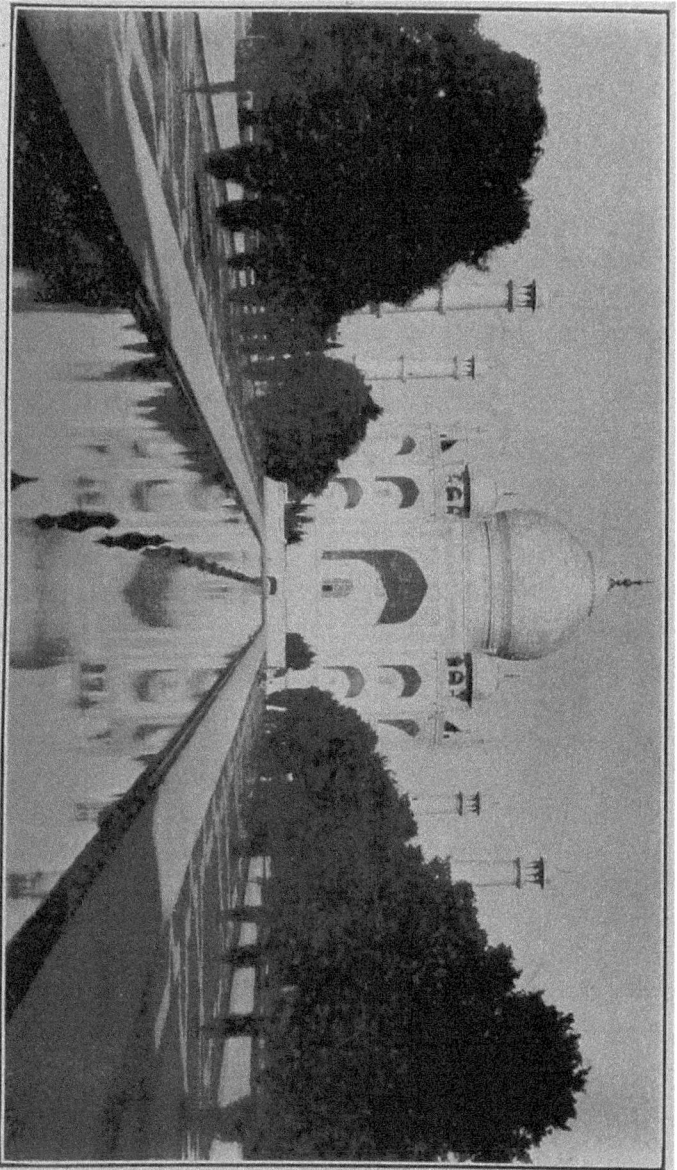

The Taj Mahl of India. The Magnificent Tomb of a beautiful queen.

his big monkeys, and the snake charmer with several baskets of vicious serpents, beat his tom-tom.   And so the strange peoples mixed and mingled with each other in their preparation for the coming Christmas day, the heathen improving the opportunity to make a penny. We had our Christmas dinner at the boys' school with Rev. P. J. Roberts and wife.   Bro. Roberts is at the head of the school.   Rev. A. B. Coats and wife from Iowa who teach in the school, and Bro. Lipp and wife were with us, and we had a pleasant hour.

Bangalore is a city of two hundred thousand people, the capital of the Mysore presidency, which is under the rule of an Indian rajah, or king, with a British resident for his adviser, and from four to six thousand British troops stationed there to keep order with a fort large enough to hold all the Europeans in case of trouble with the natives.   One of the most interesting places to visit in this city is a massive fortification of the olden time which has stood for some hundreds of years and about which the native factions fought before the days of British domination.   A marble tablet marks the spot where British cannon breached the walls and British regiments charged in to vanquish their opposers.   The place is deserted now and the massive stone walls overgrown with weeds and shrubs, a desolate memory of the bygone days of barbaric splendor.

Standing on the walls we looked down into one of the strongholds and saw an almost naked Indian with a big knife in his hand chopping up plague rats.   They had been caught in traps and killed, some hundreds of them, but to make doubly sure that they might not be brought back to the official for additional

reward, for there is a premium on rats in a plague strick-
en region and bubonic is in Bangalore, the Indian was
hacking each rat into three pieces.   A flea from a dead
rat is more dreaded than a tiger in the jungle, and the
tiger is bad enough.   I hear tiger stories that I would
not dare repeat, but for the reliability of those who tell
them, and the general familiarity of the people with
the startling facts.

A man-eating tiger is not a special species, but simply
the big striped tiger.   As he grows old and cannot
chase and bring down cattle as in his younger days, he
picks up some man from a pathway in the jungle.   Once
he has eaten human flesh he will eat nothing else.
Sometime ago one of these ferocious beasts made his
den near a native village and in time killed one hundred
of the population, often running into the village and
seizing woman or child and loping off with his victim
as a large cat would with a young rabbit.   Finally the
villagers got together with drums, horns and pieces of
board and anything that would make a noise, surrounded this murderer on three sides and drove him into a
nearby river.   He swam the stream and, making his
haunts near another village, during the succeeding
month carried away eighty people.   The news of his
ravages spread abroad and one of our Christian Indian
boys in one of the Methodist schools took a gun and
went after the brute.   He came to a frightened village
from which a girl had been recently taken, and refusing
all company, took the trail alone.   When far out in
the jungle, moving cautiously and looking carefully
ahead, he saw near the side of a large log the uneaten
palms of the victim's hands.   He had scarcely time to
bring his gun to his shoulder when he saw not far from

him the blazing eyes of the tiger fixed upon him. He took good aim and fired, killing the savage creature the first shot.

Securing assistance, he skinned the beast and brought away the hide and feet as a trophy. When he came modestly walking back to his school, it had taken him nine days to make the trip. His friends were surprised, as well as amused, to find that on this long and dangerous hunt he had carried only two cartridges in his pocket. When asked why he had not taken more he quietly said, "I had no need of more; I could not possibly have had time for more than two shots. If I had failed to kill him with these, he would have killed me." And that was the Indian way of looking at it.

Our meetings closed on Sabbath evening with twenty-two people at the altar, some of them claiming salvation in Christ. Monday afternoon we started on our long journey for our next meetings, the pentecostal services at the North India Conference which meets at Bareilly, in northern India. It is about eight hundred and fifty miles to Bombay and something near one thousand miles from there on to Bareilly. We stopped off and preached a few days at Baroda, and spent a day in the ancient and famous city of Delhi.

CHAPTER XIX.

THE GREAT WORK OF RAMABAI.

Going up from Bangalore to Bombay, we stopped off a day at Kedgaon, to visit the famous orphanage and industrial school of Pandita Ramabai.   Many of THE HERALD readers have heard something of this remarkable Indian woman.   I have heard nothing but good of her and her work since coming to India, and was glad of an opportunity to meet her and see her orphanage and school.   Her school is situated only a short distance from the station and as one approaches the institution it seems to be a very simple and plain affair.

I was expecting spacious grounds and splendid buildings, but found only a narrow strip of ground between the country road and the building, neatly laid off, planted in shrubs and flowers.   There were buildings on both sides of the road, I believe the boys and men of the institution residing on one side, and the women and girls on the other.   We got off at the station before day and walked up to the school soon after sunup.

As we approached, and while we were yet a hundred yards from the place, we heard the noise of many voices lifted up in prayer.   As we turned into the yard Ramabai came out to meet us.   She was so simple in her dress and so humble in her appearance and manner, that I could hardly believe we were standing in the presence of one of the most remarkable and widely known women of all the world.   She gave us a cordial but quiet welcome, and some one conducted us to a little guest chamber furnished in simplest fashion.   Tea and bread were sent to the room and, with other guests, we were soon seated in a small sitting room waiting for an interview with Ramabai. We found her quite deaf and had to converse with her through an interpreter. The little interview was not very successful. I said to her that it had been reported in America that her institution had been about broken up with the tongues movement. She laughed very heartily at this and said, "Well, we will have you shown through the place directly and you may judge for yourself if it has been broken up."

I forgot to say that before our conference with Ramabai, we went into the church in the large court back of the building where some hundreds of young women and girls were engaged in morning prayer. Most of them were praying aloud with great earnestness; it was an affecting scene and we bowed down with them in gratitude to God for what he hath wrought in this place.

During our interview Ramabai and her interpreter insisted that I should remain over and preach for them on Sabbath, which I could not possibly do, so they asked that I preach at twelve o'clock. This I agreed to do, as our train did not leave until three. We were then shown through the industrial portion of the institution. There were at least a hundred looms going, weaving cloth for the clothing of the orphans and household, of some fourteen hundred people. There was a large department of needlework and some very exquisite work being done. There was a department of embroidery where a number of girls were doing work on handkerchiefs. The very small girls were making buttons of cloth and thread. There was industry, order, and peace everywhere.

There is a large printing establishment and a great force of people engaged in bringing out a revised version of the Bible in the Marathi language. Ramabai is a profound scholar and is devoting much of her time to the work of putting the word of God into the tongue of her people.

Having been sick, and on a limited diet for weeks, I was very weak and stumbled about, cane in hand, over about two-thirds of the institution, when I gave out and had to lie down. They took me to a room in the yard which seemed quite apart from the residence of the people, told me not to come down to the dining room, but sent food up for Piercy and myself. After an hour's rest I preached to a great audience in a church with a capacity for two thousand people. The people of the institution sat on the floor. Ramabai's daughter, a very sprightly looking young woman, interpreted for me. After the sermon I went back to the room to which I had been taken when I gave out on the inspection tour, and remained there until about time to leave. They seemed a little shy and said nothing more of my remaining over. As I was from a city infected with bubonic plague I have an idea that they were just a bit uneasy. I could fully sympathize with the sisters if they felt a little fear.

I have no doubt this is a great work, both from a spiritual and industrial standpoint. This woman was once a devoted idol worshipper of the highest caste of India, but was powerfully converted to Christ and afterward sanctified at the Methodist meeting at Lanowli, and is without doubt one of the chosen instruments of the Lord in India.

We left Kedgaon at three o'clock and got into Bombay something after twelve o'clock at night and stopped at the Watson Hotel. The next day we spent in Bombay and I kept close to the bed, but found the food quite like home cooking and a big American flag hanging up in the dining room, which gave me a home feeling, so I broke over and ate two square meals. We left on the night train for Baroda, got there a little before day and were met at the station by Rev. A. A. Parker, president of the theological school at that place. When I got off the train at Baroda the two meals eaten at Bombay had doubled me up like a jackknife. Bro. Parker and wife took me in hand at once. I had met them some years ago at Wichita, Kan., holiness camp meeting, and had been longing to get to their home, so that if I had to make a fight of it I would be among those I knew. They cancelled all my engagements for preaching and had me go to bed. Parker had suffered from India dysentery. It is one of the worst enemies a white man has in this country; he told me my entire alimentary canal was out of fix and sore, and that any sort of solid food was bound to irritate the situation and was liable to produce a condition that could not be successfully dealt with. I told Piercy we had experienced no little trouble with the Panama Canal, but it was a mere pleasant diversion when compared with a disturbed alimentary canal in India. Dr. Eldridge gave me some helpful medicines and a few days of rest, soup, eggs and boiled milk did wonders for me.

Methodism has a great plant at Baroda. Here is one of the largest Methodist churches I have seen in India—a fine boys' school, the large girls school and orphanage, a handsome building for the missionaries and a large row of little brick cottages for the forty or fifty theological students and their families. The building for the theological school, the gift of a man in Kansas, is a handsome structure. The district superintendent, Rev. L. E. Linzell, resides here. His wife is a daughter of the much beloved Pastor-Evangelist, Rev. S. A. Keen, D. D., who fell asleep a few years ago in great peace. There isn't anything more delightful than to find preachers' children following up the paths their fathers trod.

Mr. E. J. Leocraft, presideent of the *Laymen's Missionary Movement* in the M. E. Church, is traveling with his wife in India. He has a son-in-law and daughter in missionary work in India and is out looking over the situation and picking up information. He spent the Sabbath with us at Bro. Parker's.

I improved rapidly and was able to get out New Year's day and watch an Indian regiment of the British army drill on the broad field just in front of the Methodist buildings. You could hardly conceive of a finer looking body of soldiers than these tall, graceful Indians in their beautiful red uniforms and moving like clock work. We also drove through the grounds of the king of the presidency. He has a palace many times larger than the White House, or Buckingham Palace in London, with vast grounds surrounding the place. He has quite an army under the command of English officers whom he hires to train his soldiers. The British government keeps a representative residing near the palace as adviser to the king and one regiment of Indian troops to look after the situation if events should make it necessary. We saw the king walking on his grounds near the palace dressed in plain clothing like an English country gentleman with a big Panama hat pulled down over his face.

Great monkeys were leaping about in the trees and scampering about in every direction. If any one came too near an old mother monkey she would catch up her baby and fling it between her front arms. It would entwine its arms about her neck and its hind feet around her waist, and she would dart up a tree, the whole maneuver being accomplished in a few moments.

Methodism has a great field for work in and around Baroda. There are populous villages in every direction and the young preachers from the theological school go out all over the country Sabbaths preaching the word to the multitudes. This sowing of the seed is already producing good results and in the not distant future will bring multitudes of souls into the kingdom of heaven.

By Sabbath evening I was able to preach to the people. The Lord gave us a gracious meeting and a large number of young preachers were at the altar of prayer seeking full salvation. I forgot to mention the fact that a judge of the high court, a Mohammedan, and his family, called at Bro. Parker's Saturday evening to see the visitors, and we had a pleasant conversation with him. He is a man of education and travel, and seemed fairly well posted on affairs in the United States. On Monday I spoke to the tehological students, about fifty of them, and found them a fine looking body of young men. One of the interesting and excellent features of this school is the fact that the preachers' wives (most if not all of them are married), attend the school and study with their husbands in order that they may be prepared to enter fully into the work.

The contrast between these Christian women, studying the word of God and seeking to lift up their fallen sisters, who worship cows and monkeys, is most remarkable and all in favor of the Christian's Bible and the Christian's Christ. The man who claims that the inspired Scriptures are a human fabrication concocted and written by designing men in order to deceive and enslave their fellow-beings to a false system of religion, ought to come out to India and see what the Bible is doing for the land of idolatry. The Baroda missionary plant, with its church, homes, orphanages, schools and hospital, the consecration and energy of its missionaries, the intelligence and devotion of the Indian professors and pastor made a most favorable impression upon me.

Bro. Parker, the president of the school of theology, was a few years ago the secretary of the holiness camp meeting at Wichita, Kan. He is a man of strong intelligence and deep conviction, the personal friend of the king and high officials, with large influence among the people and is standing foursquare for full salvation. His wife is marching at his side in the great work God has given them to do. If some sanctified brother or sister has some of the Lord's money they would like to invest to good advantage, let them write to Rev. A. A. Parker, Baroda Camp, India, putting a five cent stamp on the letter.

We rested Monday and arose sometime before day Tuesday morning to start on our long journey for the conference at Bareilly. Bro. Parker was up to see us off and conducted us to the yard gate and pointed out to us just above the tree tops that constellation of stars, called the *Southern Cross.* How beautifully the form of the cross hung there in the great blue depths of the Indian night, in the deep, deathlike stillness of the hour before dawn.   Sweet peace rested on my soul as I gazed at those stars which seemed to flash back from heavn a signal of divine love and gracions promise.   I could not feel that it was a mere accident that these stars are thus arranged, but the God who gave his Son to redeem the race has placed them thus as a constant reminder of the price He paid and the full redemption we may have in the precious blood of Jesus.

CHAPTER XX.

A DAY IN DELHI.

From my boyhood I have been interested in the famous and ancient city of Delhi (pronounced *Dellie* in India.) We did not come to India for sight-seeing and have not departed from our line of travel at any time in order to see any of the marvels of this land of wonders, but I was greatly pleased to find that our line of travel from Baroda to Bareilly, the seat of the North India Conference, led through the city of Delhi. Leaving Baroda a little before daylight, we traveled all day and night over the vast plains of India with cities and villages on every hand, coming into Delhi about eight o'clock the following morning. After a very poor breakfast at the station restaurant, we went forth to look at the city. In the olden time this city was surrounded by a massive stone wall, much of which remains to the present time, apparently as perfect as if erected only a decade ago. The wall is built high with a deep moat at its base on the outside, with embrasures for cannon and port holes through which the soldiers fired their muskets at an approaching enemy with little or no exposure to themselves.

Within the city stands the palace of the kings of long ago, surrounded by the buildings of his court, barracks for his body-guard, the temple in which he worshiped, with ample grounds, and all of this protected by a great wall of red sandstone which, from the bottom of the moat surrounding outside the walls, is from forty to fifty feet high. This wall from base to battlement is made of great red stones, hewn and laid with most graceful curves, arches and parapets, towers and embrasures, with a number of gates every one of which is in itself a strong fortification, the whole a triumph of the stone mason's art at once massive and beautiful.

The palace itself is made, floor, wall and ceiling, of white marble, with much intricate and beautiful carving and inlaid work which required great skill and much time. The baths are of white marble, large rooms with beautifully decorated arrangement of fountains for hot and cold water. The kings who once dwelt here in the midst of polished marble, glittering gold and flashing diamonds, surrounded by beautiful women and armoured men, feasting on the most delicate and delicious food that could be secured, sleeping on beds of down, almost worshiped by millions of devoted subjects whose lives they held in their hands and snuffed out for the gratifying of their foolish ambitions, have passed away in their vanities and left these marble palaces and great strongholds as silent and empty monuments of their pride and tyranny.

Had the vast millions of money which they squandered upon their selfish lusts been devoted to the building of canals for irrigation, railway for transportation, schools for education, and drainage for sanitation, India would not today be so frequently swept with famine and cursed with plague. The old Indian kings, so full of self love that they were unfit to rule the people, were unable to lift them out of the darkness, misery and sin that have engulfed India through the centuries.

Delhi was one of the strongholds of the rebellion during the mutiny of 1857. The English had great stores of arms and ammunition in this city without anything like an adequate white force to protect them.

In fact, there were no English troops in the city, except a few soldiers in charge of the military magazine. The English officers with their wives and children stationed about the palace, were slashed to death with the swords of a body of mutinous cavalrymen who galloped into the city and killed on sight every European found in the place. The city was garrisoned by several Sepoy regiments. A Sepoy is an Indian soldier in the British army   Many of the officers of these regiments and their wives were shot or bayoneted by their soldiers; some of them leaped off the wall, crawled out of the moat, hid in the jungle, and finally made their escape.

One of the bravest deeds done in Delhi on that awful day of slaughter was the blowing up of the magazine. It contained arms and ammunition sufficient to have equipped a large army and was held by only nine Englishmen, Lieutenant George Willoughby in command. When the Lieutenant found that the mutineers had come into the city and that the Indian regiments had joined them and slain their officers, he prepared himself for the best possible defense, rolling out ten cannon, planting them so as to rake the streets approaching the magazine, loaded them almost to the muzzle, broke open several barrels of powder in the magaine, lay one end of a fuse in it and the other out in the yard, with one of his nine men ready with a torch to fire it. The Sepoys rushed upon the place like a maddened human flood, broke down the gates and poured into the place, while other hundreds scaled the walls by means of ladders and poured a hail of musket balls upon the little band, who fired their shotted cannon into the on-moving mass until almost every man of the little group was dead or wounded; then Willoughby waved his hat for a signal, the torch was applied and the next moment the city shook as with an earthquake, red flames lit up the heavens, with a thunder crash, walls were rent asunder and hundreds of human beings were hurled into eternity. Five of the brave defenders, along with the rest, four of them blackened and singed, picked themselves up out of the ruins and, at least for the present, had escaped death. A white marble slab nearby marks the spot and records the names of the brave men who died at their post of duty.

It would take a volume to tell the story of sufferings endured by those who leaped off the walls and escaped into the jungle. Little babies died and were buried in unmarked graves in the dense thickets, never to be seen again. Fair women, worn out with fatigue, sorrow and hunger, fainted away in their husbands' arms to awake in another world. Brave officers lay down and died of their wounds, whose shallow graves marked the trail of the retreat of the wasting group of sufferers. Twenty-seven Europeans, eleven of them children and eight women, took shelter in a house near the great mosque, where they successfully fought off the enemy for three days, and then suffering untold agonies for water, were induced to surrender and were set down in rows and shot to death without mercy.

Fifty Europeans and Eurasians barricaded themselves in a strong house and made a brave resistance, but were captured and huddled together in a cellar in the king's palace, where they were kept in the suffering heat for five days, and then all tied together with one huge rope, were taken to a large tree in the palace garden where their tormentors gathered about them and

tormented them to death and stood gloating over the
heap of mangled, lifeless forms. A small army of
British and loyal Sepoys was hastened to the relief of
Delhi, but when they arrived the city was completely
in the hands of the rebels who numbered ten to one of
those sent against them. The British camped on a
long ridge overlooking the city and fortified themselves
as best they could, waiting for reinforcements and fighting almost daily with the powerful forces sent out
against them.

If you want a man on your trail who will never leave
it until he overtakes you, just mix in his veins Scotch,
Irish, and English blood, and then mistreat his women
and children, and it matters not how much the start you
have of him, how fast you travel or how far you go, he
will doggedly hold on your trail until he comes up with
you and then resistance is useless. Through heat and
scalding rain, wasting plague and repeated battles of
odds of ten to one, the little army held the ridge.

The Jumna river rolled back of the city, while a massive stone wall, nearly six miles long, bowed gracefully
around in front of it. This wall is twenty-four feet
high with a deep ditch at its foot, twenty-five feet wide.
On these walls were mounted 114 heavy guns, besides
sixty field guns, with 40,000 trained Sepoys in mad
revolt, and hundreds ready to lend a helping hand,
wherever possible, while perched on the ridge overlooking the city were 3,000 British soldiers, with twenty-two light cannon and a few battalions of loyal
native troops. Thus the unequal forces confronted
each other, the Sepoys marching out and charging up
the ridge again and again to be beaten back with heavy
loss.

The first reinforcement to reach the fort, says the historian Fitchett, was a baby boy. The wife of an officer who had been unable to be sent out of the camp, found a rough shelter in a wagon bed and there gave birth to a baby boy, who was gladly welcomed by the rough soldiers. One old powder-begrimed veteran said, "Now, we will get our reinforcements. This camp was formed to avenge the blood of innocents and the first reinforcements sent out is a newborn infant."

Gradually small detachments of reinforcements came up and, after long weeks of desperate fighting, the British determined to attack the city. I will not detain the reader with the story of the fearful conflict. The three thousand British had been recruited to five thousand, they divided themselves into four storming parties and charged upon the defenders of the city now 50,000 strong. At the Cashmere Gate there was a heroic conflict. Ten men ran forward, each with a bag of powder in his arms, five of them fell before they reached the gate, the others ran single file on a log over the mote and threw their bags of powder against the gate and leaped into the ditch below. A number of men were shot down while running forward to ignite the powder, but finally a brave fellow succeeded and the gate was blown open, and the column swept forward through the entrance and drove all resistance before them. The walls about the gate have never been repaired, but stand as silent witnesses of the fearful carnage of that tragic morning of fifty-three years ago.

Bro. Piercy and myself climbed up the walls and stood over the gate and looked down on the stage where the awful tragedy had been enacted. The parapets had been shot away, the stone walls bore many a deep scar made by cannon balls, and everywhere were evidences of the fearful struggle of men striving to take away each other's lives. Little vines and shrubs have sprung up on the walls and in the rents and with their tender leaves and modest flowers, seem to be trying to hide the ugly scars of war and blot from the minds of men the memory of the days of cruelty and hate.

An English Church stood within the walls not far from the Cashmere Gate; on its tower there was a metal globe and cross, which was taken down when the church was repaired, after the mutiny, and is now standing on a platform near the church door, as a souvenir of the dark days. We counted more than seventy-five bullet holes in this globe and cross.

We wandered slowly over the ridge where the British camped and fought, and stood long at the foot of the great monument erected to the memory of the gallant dead. The ancient city spread out at our feet with its temples, palaces and bazaars. Shining up through the great groves of wide-spreading trees, the river swept away in its course and the wide plain stretched out to the distant horizon. What an amphitheatre lay before us! What startling tragedies have been enacted upon this vast stage! For thousands of years men have lived and fought, laughed, wept, sinned and died, and gone away to the judgment bar of God. Nothing short of infinite wisdom understanding the intricate workings of the human mind, and the hidden motives of the heart will be capable of judging them, and of assigning to each his place and portion in the coming years of eternity.

Much is said of the "open door" and the progress of civilization, commerce, and the opportunities for the propagation of the gospel in the East, but comparatively few people of my native land realize how much of British blood and treasure have been poured out that the door of the East might be opened, that courts of justice might be set up, that the trader might travel in safety and that the missionary might carry his message of salvation unmolested.

We got away from Delhi late in the evening for Bareilly, the seat of the conference. There was no one in our railway carriage, save Piercy, a railway employe, a Catholic priest and myself. The priest lived out a short distance from the city and had come in to lay in supplies for himself and a brother missionary who were working among the natives. I said, "It seems to me that the priest who has given up all the world and all his life for others, who is saved from all sin through the blood of Christ, and has no care but the one great desire and purpose to carry the gospel to the lost about him, should be a very happy man." His face lit up and he answered, "Such a man must indeed be happy." I wondered if he knew the joy of such an experience. The train stopped and we assisted him off with his parcels and exchanged kind farewells.

We spread our quilts and stretched out on the seats to be awakened frequently by passengers who came and went. At one o'clock we alighted at the station at Bareilly and, knowing that all were asleep at the parsonage, we rolled up in our blankets and lay on the benches in the station, where I was aroused from my slumber by some one pushing open the door of the station waiting room, long before the stars had quit the sky. I could see a man standing in the dim light of the door, who called out, "Well." Though far away in

India and in the night, half asleep, I could feel the soul
of a Methodist preacher near me, so I called out from
my dark corner, "This is H. C.;" and in he hastened
with outstretched hand and cordial welcome.   It was
Dr. Mansell, the president of the theological school
and pastor of the Methodist Church in Bareilly.   His
father, one of the saintliest men I ever met, has been in
India for almost a half century, and this, his worthy
son, cultured and devout, a strong and gentle man, is
beloved by all who know him.   We found comfortable
quarters in his house and were soon introduced to the
conference, composed perhaps, of some fifty of our missionaries, and not less than one hundred and fifty Indian
pastors, evangelists and Bible men and women.

I was still on diet and Bishop Warne who had just
been sick, took me to eat with him, in a quiet room,
where a faithful old Christian Indian who has cooked
about this mission for seventeen years, prepared our
food for us, consisting almost entirely of milk and eggs,
with toasted bread.   The missionaries attending the
conference, with those resident, ate their meals in a
large hall at the school.   This is a great conference.
Three of the district superintendents were Indians,
many of the strong pastors are the same.   They represent 65,000 native Christians.

Dr. Mansell interpreted for me, and I preached to
them twice each day, besides addressing in English
the missionaries.   The native preachers flocked to the
altar and many of the missionaries mingled with them,
seeking the sanctifying power of Christ's blood.   I
think it safe to say scores were blessed, and something
like a dozen missionaries claiming full salvation and
many of the Indian brethren claiming the same, while

Indian Conference at Bareilly, India.

there seemed to be a general uplift and blessing on the conference. While here I went one night to the "Soldiers' Home" and preached once, afterward hearing of good fruit among the soldiers.

In almost every large military station in India there is a large building with halls, reading rooms, dining rooms, rooms for exercise, verandas and attractive yards for a general meeting place for the soldiers. These institutions are in the care of motherly women who look after the moral and religious training of the soldier boys. It is encouraging to know that at least one-third of the British soldiers in India belong to a teetotalers organization and never touch strong dronk. When Mr. Roosevelt was president, Mr. Taft was secretary of war, and Mr. Root secretary of state, and the three of them were doing their best to open up drinking saloons in all our army posts, Lord Roberts and other great military men of the British army were using their influence to enlist the British soldiers in a great temperance organization. The time will come in the progress of scientific and moral civilization when those who contend for the saloon in the American army will feel ashamed of their unpatriotic and impractical position.

There was a stalwart intelligence and depth of faith and zeal in this conference which stirred one's soul with hope for the regeneration of India. It is now some fifty-three years since Dr. Butler and his colleagues planted Methodism here. In that time God has wrought wonders of grace. There is now a large school, a hospital and large orphanage, two Methodist churches and several good resident buildings for those engaged in the work, altogether making this one of the strong centers of Christian influence in India.

CHAPTER XXI.

BAPTIZING CONVERTS.

From Bareilly we went to Muttra, the seat of the Northwest India Conference. We traveled by daylight to Agra through a beautiful country and saw many wild deer feeding quietly in the fields. With the Hindu people all life is sacred. They live on grain, vegetables and fruit. Even eggs are excluded from their bill of fare, because they have the life germ in them. As a result, birds and animals are far more gentle in India than in our own country. Should India ever become civilized, fashionable women will have a great harvest of plumage for their head decorations. A poor, benighted Hindu woman would not think of slaughtering an innocent songster of the forest in order to decorate herself with its plumage. Would that our American women might learn a lesson from their heathen sisters in this particular. On this day's travel we saw many scores of large birds, some of them with beautiful plumage, many of them as white as snow, feeding in the fields and marshes along the way. None of them seemed to have the least fear of harm, as our train dashed by them.

At one station where we had to wait for some time we were interested in watching the monkeys, which were thick in the trees and up in the iron structural work of the large station shed. Their agility as climbers is most remarkable, and the care of the mother monkeys for their young was at once touching and amusing.

The monkey is a sacred animal in India, and is not slow to take advantage of the large liberties and many advantages which are granted him. He robs fruit trees, helps himself to grain in field or bin, pulls the tiling off the roof in search of food, and often comes into the dining room and snatches bread from the table, darting into the yard and up a tree in a few seconds. He will sit on a roof and catch a peanut tossed to him with as much skill as a boy would catch a ball. One day as we walked up a street of Muttra, a large monkey leaped from the roof of a nearby porch upon a heap of peanuts on a blanket on a sidewalk, grabbed a handful of nuts, scampered up the porch, up the wall and over the roof, out of sight so quickly that the peanut vender scarcely knew what had happened.

We spent the night in Agra at the home of the Methodist minister, and the next day went to see the famous Taj Mahl. It is the tomb of the favorite wife of one of the rajahs of India. It was erected some three hundred years ago, built of snow-white marble, with much beautiful carving and inlaid work. The cost of this magnificent tomb ran high into the millions of dollars. In it sleep the remains of the beautiful queen and the rajah who loved her so devotedly. In view of the Taj Mahl stands the great sandstone fort which has stood for some three centuries and, with the exception of a sealed rock here and there, looks perfect as the day the master masons gave the last hammer stroke which completed it. Within this fort stands the marble palace of the rajah, who built the Taj Mahl. One of his ambitious sons killed his brothers, seized the old king and held him in captivity for many years in the splendid palace where he was once supreme master.

The guide pointed out to us the spot on the white marble veranda where the old king died looking out upon the beautiful tomb of his wife, by whose side his dust is now sleeping.

On the afternoon of the day we visited these historic spots we ran down to Muttra, an hour's ride, the seat of the Northwest India Conference. On our way down we counted twenty-six deer in one herd, within easy rifle range of the train. The conference meeting at Muttra had hardly so many missionaries or native pastors as the North India Conference, but they represented 95,000 Indian Christians.

Here again I preached through an interpreter twice each day on full salvation and saw the altar crowded again and again with seekers after sanctification. A number of the missionaries were among those seeking, and a host of the native preachers, many being blest. At both of these conferences Bishop Warne gave me the largest opportunity and the fullest endorsement in preaching entire sanctification from sin. Bro. Buck, an old veteran missionary, interpreted for me twice; Miss Green, who was sanctified at our Lucknow convention, interpreted once, and then Dr. Mansell who came down from Bareilly, became my medium of communication. He is an excellent interpreter, and the word loses nothing passing through his mouth, but rather gains in warmth and unction. It was a season of great grace and blessing, especially the evening meetings.

In these evening meetings I spoke to the native ministers alone and made the doctrine of the remains of sin in the regenerated and its cleansing away by an act of God's grace as clear as

I could possibly put the truth; then I appealed to their personal experience in the matter: "You well remember the time when your sins were forgiven; you know you love God and would not turn back from his service, but you often feel something within your breasts, a war within your members, the flesh lusting against the Spirit. Your intelligence and conscience condemn all these unholy uprisings; you deeply lament their presence and oft have longed for freedom from them. This deliverance may be had in the cleansing blood of Christ; it is received by faith." Almost the entire body of ministers would come to the altar and mightily cry out to God for freedom from all sin, and a number of them claimed the witness that the blessed work was done.

We left Muttra a day before the conference closed in order to keep our engagement with Bro. Grey at Arrah. A few years ago Bro. Grey located in this place and commenced gospel work in the villages around him, and has been blest of the Lord in a most signal manner. He now, with his assistant workers, has under his care nearly a thousand new converts, and the number is being constantly increased. Spending the night with Brother and Sister Grey in their new parsonage just completed, we ran some thirty miles next morning on the train to a station where we were met by Bro. Sampson, one of Bro. Grey's workers, and one of the most devoted of the Indian pastors. Here we also met a young preacher, being supported by my cousin, Will Godbey, son of the famous Dr. Godbey, of Perryville, Ky. We got a most cordial welcome into Bro. Sampson's home. His devoted wife and cultured son did all in their power to make us comfortable. A Hindu gentleman who heard of our coming had sent over a rug, chair, and a beautiful vase of flowers, as a token of good will. May the Holy Spirit draw his heart to Christ.

After a noon breakfast I baptized three converts who had come from an outlying village for the purpose. All idolaters here in India wear a long lock of straight hair in the top of their heads; this is always cut away before baptism. With my own pocket scissors I cut the long lock from a young fellow's head before baptizing him and later sent it home to my children in a letter.

In the afternoon we mounted little two-wheeled carts with our backs together and our feet hanging over the wheels, and started for a village some distance away, where some new converts had just been made and were awaiting baptism. Grey, Piercy, and myself, with four Indian brethren, made up the party. There were two rifles along, in case we should see deer near the road. Leaving the main thoroughfare, we had to jump off the carts occasionally, because of the bad roads, and as we neared the village, left them entirely, to walk through the fields, where we were surprised to find barley, mustard, flax, and a little vine of some sort of peas all growing together on the same land, the natives wading about in the growing grain and pulling up each harvest as it ripened.

On reaching the village we found the home of the first convert had been burned because of his throwing away his idols and coming to Christ. Many who were to have been baptized were frightened away from the place by their persecutors. A family came out in front of their hut and sat down on the ground, and a great company of angry people gathered about us while we cut their long locks of hair, thus destroying their caste and then baptized them in name of the Trinity. With Bro. Sampson as interpreter, I exhorted the surly crowd to seek salvation from their sins in Jesus Christ. We then went to another part of the village to baptize converts, but they had all been frightened away. As we left, the head man of the village, with a number of his followers, with their big sticks, came out of the tall grain growing by our path and we had quite a parley. It was very plain that these men were quite mad because of our visit and would like to have broken our necks if they had dared. Bro. Sampson answered them in the most straightforward and fearless manner. The two rifles in our party had a salutary effect on the motley, scowling crowd that gathered about us. The head man said: "These are our people and you have no right to come here making Christians of them. They are in our houses and we will put them out," etc., etc. Bro. Sampson gave them to understand that we had a perfect right to preach Christ to them and that they must not be molested.

Just then a runner came after us saying that some of the people who had been frightened away had come back and desired baptism, and back we went with the head man yelling in anger after us. We sang, prayed, cut the long locks off another group crouched by the wall of their hut, outside, with the fierce heathen neighbors glowering at us. Seeing that we were not to be frightened away, the head man sent out one of his henchmen to speak kindly to us and assure us that no harm should be done our converts and that they wanted friendly relations with us, all of which we knew was untrue.

᾽ believe I baptized seventeen in all, and was deeply impressed with the calm, determined manner with which these new converts looked upon their angry neighbors gathered about them. No words could express the solicitude and sorrow I felt for this little group of Christians, as we left them at the mercy of thousands of idolatrous heathen living about them in the deepest depths of sin and bestiality. How little they knew of the word of God, the love of Christ, the witness of the Spirit, or the wiles of the devil and the corruption of their own natures. But God knows how to enlighten and lead them on. May he keep them by his gracious power, is my prayer. The missionaries will visit and teach them from time to time, and as the years go by others will be converted and sometime, no doubt, a chapel will stand in this village, and from here immortal souls will go up to sing praises at the feet of Jesus.

When we got home after dark, a number of Christians had come in to see us, and when we had eaten our late dinner, we had songs and prayers together. Three cots were fixed in the best room for Piercy, Grey and myself, and we were soon sound asleep, while Bro. Sampson and his wife were up until after midnight feeding, comforting, and finding places for the people to sleep. A blanket or mat on the floor makes the average Indian a good bed. The next morning we were up early and I baptized the head man of one of the villages who had been a great debater against the Christians, but had been convinced and converted to Christ, had cut away his long lock and come in for baptism.

As our train did not pass until afternoon, we took the guns and went into the jungle near by. Piercy and myself each got a running shot at a blue buck, but the deer was none the worse off for our shooting.

When we came in to noon breakfast a number of Christians, most of them women, who had heard of our coming had walked nine miles across the country to see us. We sang and prayed and gave them some words of exhortation and comfort, and commended them to God. They all declared their firm faith in Christ and their purpose to be faithful to Him. What a harvest field for souls is this, and how white for the gathering into the kingdom, if only the reapers would come out in the name and spirit of the Lord.

After a day's rest in Arrah we came on to Calcutta, and were welcomed at the station as the sun was rising by Dr. Gross, pastor of the English speaking Methodist Church of the city, and other friends who had come out to greet us. Thoburn Memorial Church is a large structure with seating capacity for about fifteen hundred people. The present membership, I believe, is about six hundred. The ceiling of the church curves overhead like the half of a barrel turned downward. This always makes a hard auditorium to speak in. In building a church, large or small, never put in a curved ceiling. Avoid curves of all sorts if you desire the best acoustics. I preached eight days in this church at eight in the morning, and nine at night. It is hard for me to have faith for victory at such hours. But it was claimed, and no doubt true, that these were the hours when we could hope to get the most people.

The heathen here in India are very devout and give much time to pilgrimages and the worship of their multitude of gods, but the European is over here after rupees, and they have but little time for the sanctuary. Their dinner comes at about eight o'clock in the evening; nothing must interefere with that, and it is no easy task to preach to people on a full stomach at nine o'clock after a hard day's work in an India climate. All we could do was do the best we could, and so we did, and the Lord blest the word.   Almost every night there were a number of people at the altar, some for sanctification, some for reclamation, and others for pardon.   The sinfulness of sin and the fulness of salvation was the burden of my message.   I evidently made sin look too sinful and salvation too great for some of the people, though a number claimed to be blest, a few witnessed to the cleansing from all sin, others to reclaiming love, and still others to pardoning mercy.   The head of the boys' school said a number of his boys were blest and the matron of the orphanage, herself greatly blest, reported a gracious blessing on her children.

Calcutta was the only place in India where the Methodists seemed at all shy of the term *sanctification*.   It is claimed that reproach is attached to the term here, because sometime ago it was much used and abused by those who were unworthy.   It is a religious honeycomb to me, and I will not give it up anywhere for fear or favor.   If we surrender Scriptural terms because of fanatics or hypocrites, the devil could soon run us out of the Bible for words with which to proclaim the message of the Lord.   One week is too short a time for a meeting in a great city with but few Christians and more than a million idolaters in and immediately around the city.   We should have had six weeks with a number of gospel singers, a band of trained workers, the most constant and thorough advertising, much house to house visiting, powerful gospel preaching and nights of fasting and prayer, with the presence and leadership of the Holy Ghost to awaken the sleeping conscience and arouse the drowsy soul of Calcutta.

Dr. Gross has only been pastor a few months. His congregations are increasing and spiritual interests are deepening. The people spoke in high terms of his strong, earnest sermons. I was informed by an outsider that this church has more people in it on Sabbath evenings than all the other Christian churches of the city put together. With a mighty outpouring of the Holy Ghost upon the membership, this church could become a great factor in the problem of the evangelization of this part of India. This church was built and for some time under the pastoral care of Dr. Thoburn, afterwards elected Bishop. He gave fifty years of most earnest and consecrated service to India, and his name is like ointment poured forth throughout the length and breadth of the land.

CHAPTER XXII.

A BEAUTIFUL MONUMENT.

While stopping in Calcutta we were entertained at the Lee Memorial Mission.   It is a home and school for girls, and one of the very best institutions of its kind in India.   Connected with this beautiful building and this peaceful, Christian home and school here in the midst of paganism, there is a most pathetic and tragic story.

Rev. D. H. Lee and his wife, Mrs. Ada Lee, have been devoted and successful missionaries in India for many years.   Calcutta has been their special field of labor.   In and around this city God has greatly used them in winning souls to Christ.   In Calcutta they now have a training school for boys and girls, preparing them for regular government examinations and for preachers, teachers, colporteurs, and Bible women.

In the year 1899 Brother and Sister Lee had placed their six children in school at Darjiling, a healthful place in the mountains some twelve hours ride on the train from Calcutta.   The six bright children under the care of a devoted sister, who was blessedly sanctified at Mountain Lake Park while on a visit to America, not long before the incident of which I write occurred, was keeping house with her little brothers and sisters in a cottage on the mountain side.

Calcutta, it must be remembered, is a place of intense heat almost the entire year, and many people go up to Darjiling for health and to escape the intense

Indian School Children.

heat of the hottest part of the season. Here a school had sprung up for the education of English speaking children. The Lee children were attending this school and saving expenses by renting a little cottage, which their fond parents had made as comfortable as possible, and where from time to time they visited and looked after them.

The monsoon, or rainy season, came on, and floods poured out upon the mountain. One night the storm was something fearful and in the midst of the darkness and tempest, that part of the mountain where the Lee cottage stood gave way in a great landslide and the cottage and six children were soon buried beneath the stones, mud, and uprooted trees. A great company of people sought for days, removing earth and stones, but the mass of earth which had fallen away from the mountain was so vast that only one of the children, a little boy, was ever found. He had life remaining in him and, after careful nursing, told the story of the tragedy and how they had met it on their knees, committing themselves to God. He told his mother of the brave words of the elder sister and said that at the last awful moment her face looked like an angel. After telling his parents of how the calamity came, and with what faith and resignation the children met it, this little fellow, all bruised and crushed by the fearful fall, fell on sleep down here and awoke up there with the happy group who had gone before. I forgot to mention the fact that there was a Christian Indian girl with the children who was also translated with them.

The news of the sweeping away of the children spread far and wide, and friends commenced sending in money with which to erect a monument to their memory, and this splendid building, in which we found such delightful entertainment, this home for orphans and little widows, and a training school for girls and Christian workers, is the Lee Memorial. It is one of the very best school homes we saw in India, costing about $35,000. I should think the same building in the States would cost $45,000 or $50,000. Labor is much cheaper in India than with us in the States.

A girl can be kept in this excellent home, well fed, comfortably clothed, and receive good school advantages for $25.00 per year.

I noticed a shy little Indian girl, a meek-faced little creature, sitting quietly by the door. I asked about her. "Yes, they gave her to us over at the jail. Her mother was a prisoner and she was born in prison. They gave her to us, and afterward her mother died." Poor little creature, what a sad advent into the world, but how fortunate that she fell into such good hands.

No man I met in India impressed me more profoundly than did Rev. Henry Mansell, D. D. He came to India when a young man, and is now well up in the seventies. He speaks Hindustani with great fluency and is much beloved among the Indian Christians. Many years ago he experienced the sanctifying power of God's grace, and is in life and character a beautiful example of Christ's power to save and keep and fill with His own Spirit. He is a strong, gentle, happy Christian, praising the Lord for full salvation and praying for a great outpouring of the Holy Spirit upon India. Though not in the active work, his presence

---

Any one desiring a part in this great work write Rev. D. H. Lee, Calcutta, India.

in India is a blessing and he plans to remain yet some
years on the field, holding up the hands of those who
labor in the more active service and blessing all with
whom he comes in contact.

REV. A. L. GREY

Came out some years ago from near Baltimore as an
independent missionary, and has known much of hardship and something of real suffering. He could write
an interesting pamphlet on the unwisdom of a man coming out into a heathen land and undertaking to do successful mission work independent of church organization, without the sympathy, counsel, and fellowship one
so much needs everywhere, but especially in
a heathen land surrounded by heathen darkness and bitter opposition. After years of
single-handed effort, not without success, he
realized his great need of church relationship
and Christian fellowship, of regular support for his
family, and of the assurance that if he should fall his
labor would not be wasted, but have some one else to
step into his place, preserve and carry forward his work,
so he joined the Methodist Church and conference and
is one of the much beloved and most successful missionaries. Hundreds of people have been converted
under his ministry and all about him people are casting
away their idols and coming to Christ for salvation.
The following from Bro. Grey's own pen will be interesting:

"Until two years ago our work in Shahabad District was of a general character. We worked in the
bazaars, villages and melas, and, of course, among all
classes. With our small force of workers we attempted

to drive back the entire anti-Christian forces, and compel the whole army of Hindus and Mohammedans to surrender to Jesus Christ, instead of concentrating our efforts upon one position until the line should waver, fall back, and surrender to the Captain of our Salvation.

"We heard and read with interest all that other workers had to say and write about mass movements. We visited and studied at short range the work across the Ganges from us, and returned to our own work with the conviction that what God was doing over there he was willing and able to do in our midst. After much prayer we determined to pass none by, but make a very special effort to win the low castes first, as one of our native workers put it, 'to wash India's feet.'

"As soon as arrangements could be made a preacher was stationed in a large town in which are two mahallas of Chamars, with instructions to preach the Gospel to all as opportunity was given, but make a special effort among the Chamars. At first the people were suspicious and ill at ease because of his frequent visits to their mahallas, but gradually doubts gave place to confidence, friendship followed, and in less than six months I had the great joy of baptizing sixty-three in that town in one day. Others followed until now the people of both mahallas are Christians.

"This break occurred in March of last year and since then the work has spread from village to village until now we have a Christian community of over 800, and at this time about 300 inquirers are waiting for me to visit their villages and give them a chance to confess Jesus in baptism. Not only so but hundreds more have come under the influence of the Gospel and might be said to be in the valley of decision, and in their distress are calling us to send some one to teach them about the true God and the way to Him.

"In the civil district of Shadabad where this movement is, there are 121,000 Chamars, and I believe if we could get the workers and the support for them that all this vast multitude could be turned from their idols to Christ in an incredibly short time. Moreover, I believe the work would spread to the surrounding districts and continue to widen its circle, and increase in power and momentum until mass movement would touch mass movement, and we could no longer speak of the mass movement of the Punjab, North India, among the Telugus, or in Behar, but of India. God help us to do our part to hasten that time."

There are hundreds of thousands of people, especially of the low caste, who are ripe and ready for the gospel. Men filled with the Spirit of Christ can gather a great harvest in this land. Who will go, and who will support those who are willing to go?

REV. E. STANLEY JONES.

was for some years a student at Asbury College, a leader in things religious, and an enthusiast on the subject of missions. No young man who ever attended that school had a wider or better influence over the student body; even the unconverted students said, "Stanley Jones lives all he professes," and he professed a full salvation. He has taken high rank as a missionary in India. He is a hard student, an earnest preacher, a devoted pastor, with the evangelistic fire burning in him. In a short time he will give up the pastorate of one of the best English-speaking churches in India and devote his entire time to evangelistic work, giving half his time to the English-speaking churches and half to the Indian churches.   If the Lord preserves his life and he gives himself up fully to the Holy Spirit in this work for five years, he ought to be able to visit all the English-speaking congregations of Methodism in India, at least twice, and a large number of the Indian congregations, stirring up the people with revivals, seeing a host of sinners converted and a great company of people enter the Canaan experience.

BISHOP WARNE.

I saw him at the Lucknow convention and was with him in four annual conferences.   During the Bareilly Conference we ate our meals alone, except the Indian cook who served us.   We conversed most freely on many of the vital subjects that appeal to the hearts of Christian men, both at home and in the foreign lands, and I had the best of opportunity to see the man as he is.   Bishop Warne was born in Canada; he was a pastor in America when called to India.   For thirteen years he served the church in Calcutta and then was elected Bishop.   Since then India has been his field of labor.

In the homeland a bishop comes once in eight or ten years, holds the conference and leaves on the first train.   Bishop Warne comes year after year, gets in a few days ahead to plan, holds conference and remains over to meet the board and plan how to patch out the salary and make ends meet.   The burden of the churches is upon him. He knows the heart secrets of the people. Letters pour in to him by the hundreds from missionaries and native pastors.   He spends many nights in a second-class coach traveling through India from place to place where his presence and counsel are needed. I doubt if there is as hard-worked bishop in any church in all the world, nevertheless he is always patient, always hopeful, always helpful. When a session of the conference is dismissed the children of the missionaries gather about him and hold to his hands and count it a privilege to walk from the church door at his side. He is a big, broad-shouldered man, with a constitution which has stood up against this trying climate for twenty years, and promises strength and vigor for many years to come. When India is saved and the history of the long, hard battle that conquered her for Christ is written, the name of Bishop Warne must figure largely in its pages.

But the time came for me to say good-bye to India and sail away to other fields of labor. I left much of my heart behind me. Bishop Warne treated me as a brother. Most all of the missionaries treated me with as much courtesy and kindness as if I had been a bishop; the Indian people melted my heart with their evidences of Christian love; the Lord kept and blessed my soul, and I believe all will bear me witness that by His grace I have preached a full deliverance from all sin in the blood of Christ. Though to some my message may have at times seemed severe, I think they will agree that it was spoken in love. My heart ached at the thought of leaving, and in the years to come I will ever love and pray for India.

CHAPTER XXIII.

METHODISM IN INDIA.

It will be impossible for me to write of Methodism in India for these pages only in a very general way, but I hope to be able to put down some facts, and make some observations which may be interesting to those who followed me in the evangelistic tour.

Rev. William Butler, of the New England Conference, was the first Methodist missionary appointed to India. He landed in Calcutta, September 25, 1856. He was sent out with instructions to select a field and begin the work of planting Methodism in India. He located at Bareilly, and commenced the work by having preaching each Sabbath at the morning hour for natives, and at four o'clock in the afternoon to English-speaking people. The Presbyterians kindly loaned Dr. Butler a native preacher to begin with, but a few weeks after the mission was opened, the mutiny broke out, the mission was burnt to the ground, and the missionaries were in flight for their lives.

The Methodist seed was next planted at Naini Tal, where Dr. Butler with his family were refugees during the dark days of the mutiny. Shortly after the mutiny, the work was opened up at Lucknow, then Maradabad, and then the missionaries got back to Bareilly, from which place they had been run out by the outbreak, one of the native Methodists at that time being killed, so that directly after the coming of the missionaries, India's soil was wet with Methodist blood, and this first Methodist martyr headed the procession of a mighty host who have since been marching home to heaven, not of martyrs, but of believers who have died in the faith.

Within six years of the date of Dr. Butler's landing in India, or at the close of the year of 1863, nineteen men and nineteen women, having given themselves to do mission work in India, landed from America. In those days it took four months to make the voyage from home, and most of the missionaries received their appointments for life, never expecting to see their native land again. The woman missionary has been a great factor in the Methodism of India. She has built hospitals and ministered to hundreds of thousands of the sick and suffering, finding the way to a sad, sinful heart through ministrations to an afflicted body. She erected orphanages and gathered suffering children from the huts and alleys of villages who were homeless, starving little waifs of desolation and misery, nursed them to health, taught them their letters, how to cook their food, make their clothing, led them to Christ, educated them and brought them up to intelligent womanhood; many of them becoming the helpful wives of the young native preachers, and many of them going out as Bible women, to lead their heathen sisters to Jesus. She has established many schools, deaconess homes, and at least one fine young ladies' college, but aside from all this the women missionaries go out into the villages and preach the gospel to thousands of deeply interested natives who gather about them and hear the story of Jesus.

I doubt if the Woman's Foreign Missionary work is better organized, carried forward with more intelligence and success anywhere in the world than in the

M. E. Church in India. The western women of the United States cannot be surpassed for strong, healthful physiques, clear minds, deep spiritual devotion, and high resolution that wills and finds a way to execute. India is sprinkled over with such a womanhood from Iowa, Kansas, Illinois and the other states, who trusting God and loving the lost millions of India, face Bubonic plague, cholera, and the wasting fevers of this disease-smitten land without fear or complaint. For their sisters at home to forget them, standing at their post in this far away land, and waste the money that should be given for their support on jewelry, feathers, fashions and selfishness, would mean that they must hang their heads with shame in their presence in that great day when we shall stand before the King.

The Deaconess Training Schools of the M. E. Church are sending out a body of women well equipped for the work of the mission field. At the Mutra Conference, I was asked to sit at the dinner table with thirteen women who labor in the Northwest India Conference, from the Chicago Deaconess Training School. It was a happy group full of reminiscences and good hope for victory in India. These women rank with the heroines of the times, faithful soldiers of the cross, fighting nobly for the salvation of the race.

Methodism has been wise in planting herself in the great intellectual and commercial centers of India. In Calcutta, Lucknow and Madras, she has large printing establishments, not only for the printing of her own paper, *The Indian Witness*, books and tracts, but for all sorts of contract and job work for the business world about her; so that the printing press, one of the most powerful agencies for the spread of the gospel, is firmly footed and helping to sow the gospel down in India.

Methodism has a Theological School in Baroda, also one in Bareilly, where scores of young men are being prepared for the ministry, who are getting their practice with their theory by going out to the villages about them and preaching the gospel to the multitudes. The school, one of the truest handmaidens of the Church, is keeping step with the onward gospel movement. Methodism has forty-two thousand young people now in school in India. What a power these young people will be in India, five, ten, fifteen and twenty years from now. How important that these young people should be thoroughly evangelized, soundly converted, sanctified and Spirit-filled; that they may go forth to be a real spiritual force among the people.

There are some two hundred and fifty thousand native members in the Methodist Church in India, while from five to seven thousand Methodists go up from that country every year to join the mighty throngs gathered at the Master's feet. What a great colony is gathering with Dr. Butler, Bishop Taylor, Dr. Parker, and a goodly number of missionaries who wrought in India, at the feet of Jesus over there. There are now something like one hundred and fifty missionaries in the field, and more than a thousand native workers. Among the Indian preachers there are several district superintendents and many strong preachers. In the schools there are a number of Indian professors, men of character and culture, who are most hopeful specimens of the possibilities of men saved by grace and developed in a Christian school.

It is encouraging to know that there are some self-supporting native churches, and many that contribute something to the support of their pastors. The Indian mission field is peculiar in that a western civilization has thrust itself into this great eastern mass of humanity. The British have ruled India for more than a half-century. In every city of consequence there is an English settlement—a well-laid off and well-built European residence portion, in which live the civil officers, the European merchants, retired military and other men who have accumulated as the decades have passed. The Eurasians, or mixed-bloods, Anglo-Indians generally with Indian mothers and British fathers, form a large class of cultured people, who speak the English language, hold many official positions in civil government, railway and business life. Many of this class stand high in the professions, such as physicians and college professors. These people all attend the English-speaking churches, and as a result Methodism has a number of English-speaking churches in which missionaries just arriving on the field may preach while they study the language and become acclimated that they may go to the jungle seeking the lost sheep of the native population. One Englishman in one of these English-speaking churches, a man of large wealth, has made some munificent gifts to Indian Methodism, aggregating in all something near a quarter of a million.

There are several churches in the great cities of India, whose pulpits should be supplied with the very best talent in Methodism. Such men as Dr. Mitchell, of St. James, in Chicago, and Dr. Wilbur Sheridan, of Kansas City, would find ample scope here for all their gifts and graces, and a white harvest field for the gospel sickle. These words are not written in any sort of depreciation of the stalwart men on the field but they should be reinforced, and that with the largest brains and warmest hearts in Methodism. There is at this moment the direst need of men and money at the front in this great field. The lines have stretched so far that the ranks are thinned, and the call is to move forward. The church at home must hasten men to the field, those at the front are struggling against powerful odds, the multitudes call for help, will the church at home, loaded with luxuries and with millions of idle money in the bank, fail to rise to the emergency, seize the opportunity, and furnish the forces to sweep forward to one of the greatest victories of the cross since its precious victim on Calvary made it the emblem of our holy religion.

Yes, India needs a great revival of religion; a mighty out-pouring of the Holy Ghost upon the missionaries, and the English-speaking churches would spread rapidly among the Indian preachers and native churches and would touch and salt that part of the population that stands near the border line of the kingdom of heaven; mass movements would be set in motion, human landslides would take place, multitudes already convinced would be emboldened to profess Christ, and tidal waves of revival power would sweep over India, bringing millions of souls to Christ. It is a well-known fact that the ironclad caste systems is one of the most powerful barriers to the evangelization of India. To break one's caste is to become an outcast from home and people forever; it means much to come to the point where one literally gives up all for Christ. The Episcopalian caste is a barrier to spiritual progress in India. The British race is a great people. That is, I mean to say that the people of the British Isles, the English, Scotch, and Irish combined, make by far the most powerful people of Europe and the East, but the *established*, or Episcopal Church is becoming the blight of this great people. That there are many great and good people in this church, no one will deny; some of the most devoted, saintly and successful missionaries in India are Low Church Episcopalians, but the great *established* Church of England is a fallen church and will prove a spiritual blight wherever her shadow falls. The rank and file of this church seem to have almost no conception of what New Testament Christianity is. In the recent elections of England, the State Church and the liquor traffic combined their forces to crush the rights of the people, and force the iron yoke upon their sore necks. The position of the State Chuch is driving many of the great masses of the people to hate the very name of religion. The whiskey-loving, autocratic clergy are fast helping to dig the foundations from under British society. In India the official classes, both in the military and civil service, belong to the *established* church. The great mass of them drink whiskey, attend the theatres, dance, go to horse races, and plunge greedily into all sorts of worldliness. Not long since a Mohammedan gentleman stood in a street in Bombay and looked through a window into a hall where a big ball was in progress. He knew the whole company belonged to the Episcopal Church, and were called *Christians*. He turned away and said to a friend of mine, "And is that what you want me to do? If I become a Christian must I bring my wife to a place like this, naked half-way to her waist, and have other men encircle her with their arms, and caper about in this fashion?" "No, that is no part of Christianity," said the friend. "But," said the Mohammedan, "These are Christians; they claim to be such. You recognize them as Christians. Here are their great churches and bishops. They are the most highly cultured people, and the ruling class come over to govern us heathen." If the manhood of England would rise up and overthrow the *established* Church and crush the liquor traffic, and inaugurate a reign of freedom from the brewer and the clergymen, a new era would come to England, with a revival of spiritual, moral, and commercial life. I must and do love England for what she has been and done in the great work of the world's civilization and evangelization, but I fear for her if she does not set on foot some radical, deep and far-reaching reforms. It is well understood that in the marshalling of her powerful military hosts and the building of her great fleets of battleships, Germany has her military eye upon the British Isles. If Germany should hurl her three millions of soldiers against those islands, then dear old England would have to give an account of her stewardship and if she stood the shock and came out of the smoke of the conflict victorious, she would nevertheless come a chastened nation, bleeding at every pore.

But this has been a diversion. Whatever comes, Methodism must win in India. She is well-distributed and strategically fortified and moving forward on all lines. It has been one of the highest privileges of a lifetime to spend three months with the Methodism of India. I traveled about seven thousand miles, and preached some one hundred and fifty times, besides a number of addresses, in one hundred days. I met most of the missionaries and saw not less than two hundred native pastors kneeling at the altar of prayer seeking full salvation. Many of them claim full salvation. I trust and believe many of them got a larger view of Christ and will be able to preach him with more power to the millions of Indians one mighty to save to the uttermost; whose blood cleanseth from all sin.

CHAPTER XXIV.

THE UNREST IN INDIA.

Most of my readers understand that India is a part of the British Empire. The story of how India came under British rule is too long to undertake to tell in these pages. First came the traveler, then the merchant, then the East India Trading Company was formed, great commercial houses were erected, homes were built, factories arose, and English settlements sprung up about them. In due time the East India Company employed police to guard their property. This force grew into a small army. Complications arose, conflicts followed; British soldiers were employed by this or that Indian king against a neighboring king. Their superiority over the native soldiers was so marked that the fear of the white man fell upon the people, and the white man took advantage of it. The camel's head was in the tent, and he steadily advanced until the tent was his.

The French had established trading stations in India, and England and France were at war, and the war reached India, soldiers came, in the end the French flag went down, England acquired small strips of territory, and out of the complications and the conflicts, her territory grew, concessions were granted, and a governor was sent over, constables and British judges appointed. Natives were enlisted into the British army, the empire grew, and in the end, the Sepoy Rebellion came with its blood and tragedy, and at the close the British Lion had his paw firmly planted in India.

Since the year 1857 British word has been law in India. Large portions of India are entirely under British rule, while many small principalities are under the government of Indian rajahs, or kings, who pay tribute to the British government, and are really under the supervision of an English resident, with plenty of "Redcoats" handy who virtually dictate the policy of the little king, or at least see to it that nothing is done that would be injurious to the interest and prestige of the British government.

The unrest in India arises out of the fact that many of the people seriously object to foreign rule. They complain that India is taxed to keep up the army, consisting of some eighty thousand British troops and one hundred thousand Indian soldiers, in the British service. The British viceroy at Calcutta, the chief civil officer of India, and various governors, besides most all of the most remunerative offices, civil and military, are occupied by Englishmen supported by taxes collected from the people. The Indians complain that these officials remain in India for only a short time; that they are not fully identified with the people or the interests of the country, and that they gather millions of money and take it away to England for investment, and that by these methods India is being drained of her wealth. The Indians claim that they once governed India, and that they are able to do so now.

The educated class, especially those persons who have been educated in the government schools in modern science and by up-to-date methods are, as might be expected, eager for freedom and power. Hence the *unrest in India*. I have talked with people who would like to make light of the situation, and they say, "Oh, it is of no consequence—a few turbulent fellows making a noise. The people know that they have a better and more stable government now than ever before; they desire no change; they are content." That they are talking with their eyes closed is easily seen. In the first place the people do not so reason. Comparatively few of them know but little of the former times. They see the remains of the magnificent palaces and the great forts and walled cities, and hear the stories of the great battles and victories, the pageantry and pomp of the old kings and rulers. They listen to the stories of the wealth and wisdom of the great men of the India that was. Looking backward through the dim years, distance lends enchantment to the view, and, as is common among all men, they have the notion that former times were better than the present, and they would like a reinstatement of reign of the rajahs, with their long trains of elephants and armies, conquest and loot. It goes without saying that no people with any sort of intelligence or ambition are willing to be governed by foreigners. No nation of men are willing to be heavily taxed in order that immense salaries may be paid to men of some other nation, language and color, who may come in and govern them. However low down in the scale of civilization a nation or race of men may be, they are only governed by another nation and race of men when they cannot help themselves.

British rule in India is simply a question of bullets and bayonets; hence the powerful army of one hundred and eighty thousand men and, "We must be taxed to support this army, while it holds us in subjection at the muzzle of the gun," is the complaint of the intelligent and ambitious Indian. The unrest in

India is manifesting itself just now in the assassination of British officials.   Not long since a young Indian went to England and killed in cold blood a high civil officer, who had held a responsible position in India. Two efforts have been made to assassinate the viceroy since I came to India.   Just a few weeks ago a collector of taxes was shot dead by an Indian youth. Within a few blocks of the room where I am writing this article, a high police officer, an Indian, in the service of the British government, who had been active in an attempt to secure the punishment of political prisoners was shot down and killed three days ago. These assassins are young men, scarcely out of their boyhood.   It is well understood that there are old heads and a regular propaganda back of them that has for its ultimate end the overthrow of British rule in India.

So far as my personal opinion is concerned, I believe that India is incapable of self-government for the present, and that she has received inestimable benefit from British rule and the progress that has come with it that could not have come without the strong hand of a civilized people at the helm.   The Indian rajahs of former times put the people's money into palaces, fortifications and tombs.   The English have put it into great railroad systems, irrigation canals, government schools, and thousands of miles of the fine country roads.   These country roads are broad and smooth as the streets of a city, with a row of great spreading trees on either hand, protecting the traveler from the burning sun as he pursues his journey.

Yes, large salaries are paid the viceroys and the various governors of India, but it is as nothing to what would be paid for the maintenance of half a hundred rajahs if India ruled herself. No doubt the tax for the maintenance of one hundred and eighty thousand soldiers is considerable, but it is a trifling sum compared with what it would take to maintain fifty or more armies of separate states or small kingdoms if the English should withdraw from India. Now there is peace and great industry throughout the entire realm, then there would be perpetual war and the waste of property and life because of conflicts between the multitudes of small nations. The outsider in judging the situation in India must remember that the three hundred millions of people in this country are so equally divided between Hindu and Mohammedan, that neither one could safely control the other, and that the bitterest of hatred exists betwen these powerful peoples. Take away the British Lion and they would leap upon each other immediately.

There is no union among the multitudes of India. There are many races, tribes and languages, and the high, thick walls of the most bitter and fanatical religious and race prejudices exist between them. The Mohammedans would never submit to be governed by the Hindus, who worship bulls, monkeys and luxuriate in idolatry and image worship in its most gross and revolting form. The Hindus would never submit to the Mohammedans, who would feel duty bound to burn their temples and break up their idols, kill and eat their sacred bulls and shoot their monkeys.

India's sins make her helpless. If she had flung away her idolatry and rallied around the cross of Christ fifty or even twenty-five years ago, she would easily be a free people today. A united India, elevated by the gospel and Christian education, could easily hold her own with any nation on the earth. But she is so far from this that the heart sickens to contemplate her condition. Fortunately for her, the British keep peace within her borders, and protect her from any outside interference. How much better the British Lion than the Russian Bear. How gladly Russia would move down from the north and plant her flag in the great seaports of India, but it is evident that for some time to come in the providence of God the English jack, which stands for equity in the courts, the open Bible in the land, and freedom and conscience in worship, will float over India.

Whatever of mistakes England may have made in her Indian policies and their practical application in the administration of the complicated affairs of this great country, it was impossible for any other European power to have improved upon or to have approximated what she has done for the uplift and progress of the people. No one can tell how widespread the present disaffection is or whereunto it may grow. Next door to the building in which I am now being entertained, there stands the mansion of one of the wealthy men of this city. Recently his house was found to be a hotbed and center of opposition to the government. He was secretly printing and circulating literature calculated to foment unrest and rebellion. He was arrested and his printing press confiscated. I noticed a few days since that ten Indian soldiers were arrested in one regiment and cast into prison under suspicion of disloyalty, and their regiment transferred to another station. I conversed not long since with a Mohammedan gentleman high up in culture and social position, and it was quite easy to see that he had no tears to shed for those who had been assassinated. As certainly as physical conditions may exist in a city, which invite and breed disease, so moral conditions may exist in a country which breed crime and lead to riot, bloodshed and death; those conditions now exist in India. The simple fact is that the western world had educated without evangelizing the eastern mind. Government schools have taught heathen men how to manufacture and use the most dangerous explosive, without permeating the heart with the gracious influences of the gospel of Jesus Christ.

In all of the heathen or idolatrous countries, where Christian evangelization fails to keep abreast with scientific education, we will have on our hands conditions that will put in jeopardy our civilization. Japan has made remarkable progress in all branches of modern science; she stands easily equal to the foremost in the arts of war; her brain is wide-awake, but her conscience sleeps; she does not know God; at heart she worships idols.

The victory of Japan over the Russians stirred the whole heart of the East with a new ambition; it had much to do with the present unrest in India. A new era is dawning. The more than seven hundred millions of colored men in the East believe they have an unbalanced account with the white man of the West; they believe that in carrying the world's burden, the white man has given them the short end of the handspike; they are eager to balance the books, settle up old scores, and have a full share of the handspike. The time has come when the white man of the West must evangelize his eastern brother or pay a fearful penalty for his neglect, at some time, perhaps in the not distant future.

For the present England holds India with a firm hand. Any sort of an attempt at an armed uprising would meet with a fearful retribution. The native population are not permitted to have firearms. The Indian regiments are officered by white men and the soldiers are not permitted to have access to or to keep upon them any ammunition. Ball cartridges would only be issued to them in case of demand for immediate use in firing upon an enemy. The general opinion is that the Indian regiments are quite loyal to the government; what they would do in case of a general uprising, no one can tell. If England has no military complications with a European power, it will be easy for her to hold her Indian possessions, but if she should become engaged in war with Germany, India would be quick to take advantage of the situation; and if under such circumstances, she should rid herself of British rule, strife and war would break out among her contending factions, her wheels of progress would be checked, and the great missionary movements now going forward with so much promise would be greatly hindered, if not swept away.

It is not lack of natural ability, education or culture, that unfits India for self-government. It is the lack of conscience and character that can only be produced as the result of acquaintance with, and faith in, the teachings of the word of God. It is a lack of that sympathy, fellowship and union, which will never come to India until India comes to Christ. Much has been given to our Christian civilization of the West. God has honored her with light and power above her fellows, not

Entrance to the Old Fort, Agra, India.

out of partiality, but that she might lead the eastern peoples out of darkness into light. If the West hold the truth committed to her in unrighteousness, if she refuses to enter the open door of the East with the saving truth of the gospel, if she is indifferent to the pitiful hands which are held out to her for help, then in the end God will avenge himself upon her with those same neglected hands.

When the Hebrew people failed to fulfill their mission, the peoples they should have saved became the instrument of their destruction. Shall history repeat itself?

CHAPTER XXV.

DOWN THE STRAITS TO SINGAPORE.

On the morning of February 1, we went on board our ship, the "Fultala," which lay in the river near the wharf at Calcutta, soon to sail for Rangoon, Burma. The river was full of all sorts of water craft, from the great steamships from over the seas to the clumsy barges, with sixteen to twenty natives, their naked bodies, except a small loin cloth, glistening in the morning sun, while, with a little chant to keep time, they bent their long oars, shoving the noses of their stout vessels up against the muddy current. Little boats, with one man at the single oar, shot in and out from shore to ship, and stout tugs with hoarse whistles hurried about in all directions, while men called, clamored, commanded and gesticulated at each other in the most frantic manner.

The shore, like the stream, was crowded with a moving, blustering mass of humanity. There was a little group of American tourists and a troupe of English theatrical people, perhaps thirty strong, and a few others, with about seven hundred and fifty natives, a flock of sheep and a herd of goats all to be gotten on board. The English officers of the ship stood in their white duck like marble statutes on top of the ship, looking quietly down upon us, and let us fight it out among ourselves with the coolies, who chased each other up the gang plank, with perspiring women screaming after them, and scattering the baggage about the ship generally. For a time, it was hard to tell what would become of us, but the hands moved slowly over the face of a compassionate looking clock, and in time we were all stored away somewhere and came upon the deck smiling, happy that the big ship had pulled in her cables and was swinging around in the river to point her prow to the sea, almost a hundred miles away.

We were three days and a half making the trip over from Calcutta to Rangoon, sailing southeast over a comparatively calm sea, on a steady ship, a most welcome rest to me, for I had worked in India quite as I would at home, a thing no man could do long at a stretch without complete collapse. We were some two hours steaming up the Rangoon river, the tide being out, our ship cast anchor in the stream and a steam launch came off for us and took the white passengers ashore. The M. E. Church has a good work in Rangoon, but has not done much as yet in the interior of the country. In the city there is a large church and girls' boarding school and a girls' day school for English-speaking people. There is also a girls' school for the Burmese and a boys' school for the same people, with some five hundred young men and boys in attendance.

I preached twice a day for five days in the Methodist Church which has about one hundred and fifty English-speaking members. Many were at the altar during the meetings; some professed to find the pardon of their sins, and others were definitely seeking the sanctification of their hearts. At the close of the meetings the interest was deep and we doubt not some souls will press on into Canaan, while some, who had once enjoyed the experience and had lost ground because of failure of definite testimony, were stirred up to a renewal of faith and activity.

The British lion rests his paw gently on Burma and a few regiments of soldiers keep the peace, while the people follow undisturbed their industrial pursuits. The English residential part of the city is very beautiful in the midst of a luxuriant growth of tropical trees and flowers. It was a relief to note that the Burmese women seem to have more freedom and recognition than the women of India. They were better clad and walked about with their heads up, many of them with bright, intelligent looking faces.

In Rangoon is located the largest heathen temple we have yet seen, or rather a hilltop covered with scores of temples and hundreds of gods and a swarm of people coming and going all the while, engaging in a variety of ways in many forms of worship. Their faces were sad and dead and hopeless.

We had a gracious closing service on Thursday morning at the church. I had spoken to one of the schools and to a fine body of men at the Y. M. C. A., and have firm faith that the Lord will bless the seed sown here. We passed the medical inspector and at about half past two o'clock, clambered over a big ship onto our launch and steamed out amid stream to the ship "Dunera" on which we were to sail for Singapore.

The chief engineer on our ship was a big Scotchman with whom I had some interesting conversations. "It is a dark blot on the page of American history that the early colonies should have gone to war with the mother country when her hands were full of European troubles," said he, with much gesticulation and great emphasis. My answer was, "Why should you bring up the unpleasant past and tear open the old wounds? Let them heal and be forgotten. No doubt the hand of God was in it all. It was His will that we should become a free and independent people and build up a great democratic republic and give the race a new start in a new world, under new and better conditions for the development of men." To all of this he readily agreed and we became good friends and disputed in a good humor about the creed of Calvin. "Ye must judge a tree by its fruit," said he, "and look at what these great doctrines have done for Scotland." I answered, "The Scotch are great in spite of the creeds. Calvinism gave them a great supreme God—a God of absolute power and supreme rights among men. In a word, a *great* God. It makes men great to worship a *great* God. These redeeming features of the creed blessed the sturdy Scotch. But the ironclad features of Calvanism drove men from the church and into infidelity. Much of the popular unbelief of our times is the pendulum swinging back to the other extreme from ultra Calvinism." To this he partly agreed and admitted that because of the extreme teachings of foreordination, he had joined the Free Church of Scotland.

At Penang, a point down the straits, near halfway between Rangoon and Singapore, we took on some five or six hundred Madras Indians, who were on their way to the straits settlement to work in the rubber woods. They were a pitiful lot of almost naked, half-starved humanity. After carrying them a day and night down among the islands of the straits, we put them off on boats and sent them ashore at a place called "Sweatman." Some years ago but few ships came in here, and then at great peril, for these waters, islands and shores were swarming with pirates and if a sailing ship was becalmed in these waters these human fiends made short work of her.

While on board the natives were fed on rice with a cupful of minced meat and gravy, hot with red pepper, poured over it.   A piece of a large leaf from a banana stalk was placed on the deck answering for a plate and the rice and curry were poured upon it.   They had neither knife, fork nor spoon, but flung their food into their mouths with their fingers.   There was no trouble washing dishes when the meal was over; they threw the bit of leaf overboard, wiped their fingers on their loin cloth and settled down to sleep in the sun.   Just before they were sent ashore some of the passengers threw them down some oranges and bananas.   It was pitiful to see the outstretched lean hands and hundreds of eager faces longing for one mouthful of the fruit. In it I saw a picture of these perishing millions of our brown brothers stretching out their hands for the gospel of Jesus Christ. What a hopeful field these rubber camps would be for a devoted missionary to labor in, among these destitute multitudes who have so little to give up, and so much to find in true Christianity.

It was near the middle of the afternoon when we cast anchor far out in the harbor of Singapore and a number of steam tugs put off from shore to meet us, the first one being the medical inspector, who lined us up, one and all, passengers and crew, to see if we were free from contagious disease.   Ships come into Singapore from all quarters of the earth and the authorities are very careful to guard the place against plague.   We passed and were soon on a boat steering for the shore.

When we landed from our ship at Singapore on the afternoon of February 15, we found our meetings at the M. E. Church well advertised and made haste to the parsonage to get ready for the first service at 5:15 o'clock in the afternoon, to be followed by another meeting at 8:15. And so I preached twice each day for the four days we were in Singapore, at the hours above mentioned. It put the meetings close together, but the brethren felt it was the best they could do and it seemed to fit in very well. One afternoon preached at the Scotch Presbyterian Church. The M. E. Church has a beautiful plant in Singapore. The English speaking church is quite new, and a very attractive building in a choice location with an excellent parsonage conveniently situated.

Rev. Chas. R. Vickery, the new pastor out from New York State, a few years ago, who has seen service in India, has just been installed as pastor and appears to be in high favor with his people. For a hurried up meeting held between Sabbaths, the attendance was good and the fruits gracious. The schools were out, and a number of the missionaries were away at the time of our visit, but those who were at home were very constant in their attendance, and as bright, devout, zealous a company of missionaries as we have met with thus far on our tour of the world. Not one word did I hear from one of them against any other one of them, but a happy band like a large family; they appear to be living together in beautiful harmony and faithful labors.

There are two large Methodist schools here, one for boys and one for girls, with an attendance of something near fourteen hundred students. There is a neat chapel for the native congregation and a most hopeful work among them, their young pastor, Rev. Bro. Sullivan, who is a graciously sanctified man, pressing the work with earnestness and a great faith that promises large things for the future. Every night during the meetings there were from thirty to forty young men, Chinese, Japanese and Malays, in the meetings, who could understand the gospel in English, and from ten to fifteen of them were at the altar seeking pardon or purity at each evening service, conversing with an intelligence and praying with an earnestness that was truly encouraging. A number of them were blest and we heard of one fine young Japanese who said to his pastor that he had surrendered to a call to become a preacher of the gospel. We believe several Spirit-filled preachers will come out of these few days' labor at Singapore. God grant that it may be so.

We were especially impressed with the thoughtfulness and humble earnestness with which several cultured young Chinamen sought the experience of perfect love. When we left, the light of Canaan seemed breaking in upon them.

On Friday morning, our last day in the place, we arose early and from 7 to 8 o'clock I gave an address to the assembled missionaries at the home of the superintendent. At 9 o'clock we had breakfast at the parsonage. We then looked after our sailing to Hongkong on Saturday, and went with a brother to look at a large property recently purchased for a training school. At 1 o'clock we took tiffin with a group of missionaries at Oldham Hall; at 2 o'clock we drove out with the pastor and a friend four miles in the country to see a rubber grove, and a vast stretch of cocoanut palms, where we called at the cottage of the Mohammedan manager, who explained to us the process of producing rubber for the market. We drank cocoanut milk with him and walked a mile in the intense heat, got back to our vehicle and returned in time for a breath of rest, and the 5:15 meeting, dinner at 7:00 with the family of Bro. Cherry, and back to the church at 7:15 with a good long altar service. A Scotchman past middle life was converted, several missionaries sought full salvation, and other souls were under deep conviction. A good time and a great forward impulse in a number of hearts.

The next morning we were up early and while Bro. Piercy got our baggage on board the "Princess Alice," our German steamer for Hongkong, I held meetings from 7 to 8 a. m., in the native church, with a group of earnest souls that more than filled the long altar—some of them missionaries, others the young men of the various nationalities above mentioned. The Lord was graciously with us and it was a deep, tender hour. I had to close the service and hasten to the ship some two miles away at her dock, booked to sail at 9:00. I got on board in time, but the ship was delayed for some hours and we did not sail until 1 o'clock.

Singapore is a city of about two hundred and fifty thousand people, situated on an island at the extreme lower end of the Malay Peninsula. It is only about one degree and a half north of the equator. It is a very warm spot and but for the ocean breeze fanning it from three sides, would be intensely hot. Tropical trees, fruits, and flowers luxuriate here and the parks and drives are very beautiful, as is the best residence portion of the city. The city itself is well built, with many fine public buildings and large commercial structures. Almost one half the population is made up of Chinese. There is also a large population from India, an over-flow from that full country of merchants and coolies. Japs and Malays and men from all eastern climes may be seen here, while the English jack flutters peacefully over all, and "Tommy Atkins" in neat uniform and little walking cane under his arm, reminds you that the British lion is the king of beasts in this part of the world.

CHAPTER XXVI.

EVANGELIZING IN MANILA.

Directly after our arrival at Hongkong a letter and cablegram came from Bishop Oldham calling us to Manila for revival meetings during the conference week. Having spent all the month of February at sea, except nine days, we dreaded the trip just a little, especially as we had to make the voyage on a small steamer and everybody prophesied a stormy sea, which is generally the case between Hongkong and Manila.

Friday evening we went on board our ship but the night was so rough and foggy that the pilot refused to take us out to sea. Saturday morning the clouds of fog coming up from the ocean obscured from view the hotels on top of the peaks back of the city, and although we were soon under way the heavy fog stopped ours and two other ships at the mouth of the harbor. After considerable loss of time the fog rose and we put to sea, but the "log" at twelve o'clock showed that we had traveled less than fifty miles. The fog vanished, the clouds rolled away, the ocean smoothed out and contrary to the expectation of every one we had a beautiful voyage. Monday morning early we could plainly see the mountains of the northernmost island of the Philippine group and we steamed along close to the shore until about 11 a. m., when we passed the famous island of Corregidor, which stands at the entrance of Manila Bay. There is an entrance on either side of the island. It was here that Admiral Dewey slipped by the Spanish batteries in the night not receiving a single hit from the guns of the batteries which fired some belated shots after him when he was safe within the bay.

Our ship soon came to anchor in the harbor behind the immense wall or breakwater, built by our government since occupation; white launches were circling around us—some of our friends to welcome their loved ones and others with government officials.

Two Methodist preachers who had come out to greet us, sought us out, and, as quickly as we could have our hand baggage inspected, took us ashore in the steam launch of a friend who kindly gave us a free passage. We whisked around through the harbor and shot up the river for a short distance to the landing place. Both sides of the stream, which was narrow, were jammed with watercraft, and boats of many sorts and sizes were coming and going almost as thick as vehicles on a busy street. The shores, wharfs and docks were piled high with merchandise and Chinamen and Filipinos by the hundred were at work with truck, poles and noisy gabble while discharging cargoes and ladened ships.

We got into a carriage and hurried away to the native M. E. Church, where some thousands of people were gathered celebrating the tenth anniversary of Methodism in these islands. The church which held near two thousand people was packed and many people standing on the outside. Many missionaries of other churches, and prominent officials, among them the Consul-General of Japan, were present. Bishop Oldham gave me a seat on the platform where I had a good opportunity to look at the sea of faces rising in the huge gallery to the ceiling. I was deeply impressed with the many finely-shaped heads and strong, intelligent faces and the perfect attention given to the speakers, even by the children.

After the ceremonies at the church, there was a parade through the streets with mounted officials, hundreds of people carrying banners with religious designs and mottoes on them, and not less than a dozen brass bands, with some thousands of Methodists in line while streets, vacant lots, verandas, sidewalks, windows, and doors were crowded with a multitude of spectators. Everybody found out that the *Methodists* were in town.

That night I preached at the English-speaking Methodist Church and in the same church next morning spoke to a group of missionaries coming in to attend the annual conference. The conference opened the next day and through the session I preached each morning through an interpreter to the Filiponos and at night in the English-speaking Church. The hot weather with a swarm of mosquitoes had broken in upon the city and many of the people had gone to the mountains, but the soldiers came and a goodly number of citizens, young fellows from North Carolina, Texas, Georgia, Ohio, Kentucky, and all about, came smiling in as if they were surprised to see a "feller from way back in the States." The altar was filled every morning with people seeking the Lord for pardon, restoration or full salvation. Missionaries and natives flocked together to the mercy seat, and prayed and sobbed out their heart longings into the ear of our compassionate God, and he blessed them. I think four missionaries claimed to get through to the full cleansing; most all

of the others witnessed to a gracious refreshing in grace
and many of the Filipino brethren were blessed.

I was highly pleased and deeply interested in the
native preachers.   They have fine heads, clear-cut, intelligent faces, very genteel and neat in dress and manners, and deeply attentive and interested in the message
I brought them.   I have nowhere met with a body of
young men to whom my heart has gone out with truer
and tenderer sympathy.   They are yet babes in Christ,
and have a long steep climb ahead of them and will
need the help of strong hands asnd tender hearts, but
some of them are making most encouraging progress
and no doubt will become mighty men in the uplift of
their people.   A number of them witnessed to the belief
that they were cleansed from all sin and others manifested great desires for deliverance from the carnal nature by the baptism with the Holy Ghost.   I think
they will talk and tell about and preach it until all the
thirty-odd thousand Methodists of the island will hear
and think of the glorious fact that our Christ is able to
save and keep from sin.

I was delighted with what I saw and heard of our
soldiers.   I never saw a bigger, healthier, cleaner looking bunch of men in my life.   I think they enjoyed my
plain, straightforward preaching more than the citizens
did.   There is something fine about a soldier. He has
a contempt for hypocrisy and doesn't have much use
for a preacher up in the pulpit firing blank cartridges.
He loves a lick that makes the fire fly.   I would love
to have a life to give to the American and British soldiers.   To live in their barracks, camp in their camps,
go with them to the front and evangelize everywhere;
what a ripe harvest field, what a fine quality of grain

and what a life work for some young man, not a "sissy" sort of easy fellow, but a man with the heart of a soldier in him, a man who has power with God and power over men.

The American citizen in the Philippines went out as government officials or to hold down jobs in civil service, or to make money, or as lawyers, doctors, and scientific men in engineering and other pursuits. The old pious families of the East, South and middle states have not gone to Manila to reside. The Filipino sees many poor specimens of professing Christians.

The carnal nature flourishes in a tropical clime where the days are long, hot, and lazy, and the nights are cool and bright; the multitudes seek after pleasure, the moral standards are low, the conscience has never been awakened by the thunders of Sinai, and the heart lifted and purified by the story of the Cross.

The city of Manila is built on the lowland of the bay shore at the mouth of the Pasig River. The old city is situated on the right-hand of the river as you enter the stream from the bay. It was built in the fifteenth and sixteenth centuries and has passed through some stormy and tragic experiences. The original city was entirely surrounded by a wall of considerable height and thickness, pierced by a few small gates through which a wagon without a high load might be driven. These gates were strongly fortified, both in front and above, so that in the olden time a comparatively small force shut up within could bid defiance to a powerful enemy without. This was not only for protection from the wild tribesmen from the islands, but from the old piratical rovers of the sea. The walls still stand in perfect order, except where modern progress has charged them here and there and made a breach for the passage of electric cars.

In the year 1762 Great Britain and Spain being at war, an English fleet sailed into the harbor, and after a stubborn resistance from the comparatively small garrison, the city was captured and held by the British for some eighteen months, when on payment of a heavy indemnity the conquerors sailed away, and again the Spanish banner floated over the city.   During the weary years of cruel Spanish rule the natives arose again and again and flung their lives away in vain attempts for freedom, which never came, and never could have come, had Uncle Sam not appeared upon the scene.

When the crash of Dewey's first gun swept over the bay and echoed through the hills, it announced the dawn of a new era in these islands.

The greatest boon that the American flag brought to the Philippine Islands was the Protestant religion, —the Bible, and the gospel of pardon and peace with a pure heart and a righteous life.   The Catholic Church offers a salvation in *heaven* to a lost, burdened soul after a life of penance, suffering, and submission to all sorts of soul slavery to ignorant, money hungry, tyrannical men and a longer or shorter period in purgatorial fires, the time to be gauged by the amount of money left the priests to pay for the deliverance of the soul from said tortures.   The Protestant Church offers salvation through faith in Jesus Christ, here and now—a life of peace and joy, and an abundant entrance into the heaven of the holy.   It would take a set of large volumes to tell of the dark situation after all of these years of absolute Catholic control in the Philippines.   A church could not have had a better opportunity to show its power to Christianize, civilize, educate and lift a people into happy homes and prosperous life than the Romish church had.

For centuries the pope, and priest and friar had their own sweet will. Yet, what did Mr. Taft find when he went to Manila as governor of those islands? Poverty, ignorance and superstition, with a greedy priesthood stealing away the substance of the people. If he had eyes to see, (anything more than a splendid opportunity of a great political coup of the Catholic vote) he saw a fearful picture of human degradation.

In the Philippines the priest placed the marriage fees so high that it was impossible for the poor people to meet the expense of a legal church marriage, and so they lived together in the most indiscriminate manner. Of course, the well-to-do could pay the heavy *tariff*, but the great masses of the people could not pay for a church marriage and lived together without the sacred rite, separating when they choose to do so. In this way the church tore up the very foundation stones of society and Christian civilization.

A fawning politician, with his greedy head in the government trough down in Manila, said to one of our Methodist preachers, "I can't say that I approve of your method of proselyting," by which he meant to say that seeking the conversion of these poor, benighted creatures from their sins was proselyting Roman Catholics. Thank God, in the past ten years the Methodist Church has thus proselyted something more than thirty thousand of these remarkably bright people who only need the Bible, the religion of Christ, and the education, uplift and enlargement that it brings to take their proper place among the great brotherhood of civilized men.

Next to Bible salvation the greatest boon that the flag brought to these islands is *education.* The free public school is, and will be, of incalculable benefit to the people. The man who would find fault with the Filipino must remember the terrible disadvantages under which he has lived. He must remember something of the long period in which the Anglo-Saxon was climbing up to the position which he now occupies and the ignorance and selfishness which yet cling to him. Give the Filipino the public school, with all it means, and give him time and he will come rapidly and will make a strong, courteous man, ready to do his part in the world's work I don't think he will ever learn to be cuffed and ordered about like the African and the Soure Indian have been, a most serious delinquency in his make-up as viewed from the standpoint of some observers.

Perhaps next in the order of blessings is the scientific physician and what he means and brings with him. The American flag brought with it salvation for the soul, education for the mind, and health for the body. The improvement in health conditions is quite remarkable. The cities are being cleaned up, pure water supplied for the people, modern and up-to-date hospitals erected, and long strides are being made toward hygienic living.

Next we would say in the order of blessings come the courts of justice. The old Spanish courts were an abomination, slow, uncertain and hopeless. The United States has appointed a high class of men to the judicial bench in the Philippines who are bringing order out of chaos, clearing the innocent, punishing the guilty in a humanitarian way, and lifting the people up to a true appreciation of equity. Thus the church, the school, the hospital and the court have joined hands and are standing shoulder to shoulder for the uplift of the people. This means the quickening of industry, the increase of commerce, the awakening of the dormant mind, the multiplying of wants, the stimulating of effort and the forward march to a higher life all along the line.

The people are not yet ready for self-government as an independent nation. They have large liberty and much to say in the matter of local affairs at the present time. What they need is to be let alone in the peaceable pursuits of knowledge and comfortable homes and healthful surroundings. Give them time and every possible help in learning their lesson. They should raise up among themselves a great company of ministers of the gospel, teachers for the public schools, physicians for the healing of the sick, strong, patriotic men for the administration of local government, large merchants to manage the commercial affairs of the country and thus develop themselves, and their country until no true man can deny their capacity for the largest liberty, and self-government. Meanwhile the Christian Churches of America are under the highest obligation to do all in their power for the rapid evangelization of the Filipino people.

We closed our meetings at the English-speaking church in Manila Sabbath evening, and Bishop Oldham gave us the entire time Monday morning at the conference, from nine to twelve o'clock, for pentecostal meetings. The Spirit was present and we had a gracious time. Almost the entire body of the native ministry was at the altar seeking holiness of heart; quite a number of the missionaries, also several of the young Fili-

pino women.   There were tears, prayers, songs, heart
searching and crying out to God.   Quite a number of
persons, some missionaries, and some native people professed full salvation. and a number of the native ministers rejoiced in a new found grace. We put the doctrine
of regeneration, the remains of sin, and the sanctifying
power of Christ's blood before them as clearly as we
could, and believe it went into their heads and hearts.

The whole band of missionaries is a zealous, happy
company with their hearts set on the salvation of people.   Bishop Oldham is a strong man, with a culture
and intellectual power that appeal to the highest, and
a gentle tender heart that makes him easy of approach
and beloved of all.   I doubt if there is a man on the
islands who counts for so much for all that is good as
this devoted Bishop.

Tuesday morning we looked in on the conference to
say good-bye and Bishop Oldham suspended business
long enough to have Bro. Piercy and myself stand up
while a song was sung and the missionaries and native
brethren and sisters marched around, and we had an
old time Methodist handshake, and they gave us many
good words of appreciation and encouragement.   So
ended another chapter in our world tour of evangelism
and we hurried away to be ever thankful that we came
to Manila with some more beautiful pictures of altar
scenes to hang on the walls of memory.

Tuesday afternoon, March 8th, we sailed out of the
Bay of Manila on the *Eastern,* a good English ship.
We were hardly out of the bay until the wind was
singing through our rigging and as the curtains of
night fell about us the whitecaps were rolling up in
every direction.   The next day we hung on to the
ropes and watched the waves which rolled by in a

succession of watery hills with great yawning valleys between them.

Our ship was like a pony in a hurdle race, standing up on her beams with her prow high in air, leaping the big waves all the way to Hongkong. Late Thursday evening, through the mist and spray, driven by the shrieking winds, we caught a glimpse of the flash light from the tower standing on an island near the mouth of the Hongkong harbor. The captain had thought of casting anchor outside, but finding the fog was not heavy, he put on steam and in a few hours we were passing under the great searchlights into the quiet waters; our anchor dropped and we went to berths with grateful hearts for the privilege of a quiet night's rest. We were awakened early by the clamor of the people on the launches and sampans about our ship eager for passengers to be transferred to the shore.

Some weeks after we left Manila, I received a very encouraging letter from Bishop Oldham. I will quote a paragraph from this letter, which gladdened my heart, and will be interesting to our readers. "When I cabled you, I did not know how marked a step forward your coming would bring. I called the mission together yesterday to discuss especially the matter of revival and I found the men's hearts are all aglow, but they all feel that we must organize Revival bands in which Americans and Filipinos shall go together all over our territory to call the people to repentance and the Christians to a deeper life of holiness. Your coming has practically fixed the holiness idea as the birthright of every man in the Methodist Church, and I desire these revival bands to move through the country not only for the sake of sinners, but that we might have sincere saints."

CHAPTER XXVII.

OUR CAMPAIGN IN CHINA.

One does not like to go back to sea after so short a time on shore when it is out of one storm into another. But there was no way out of it, so after a day and night on shore after our voyage up from Manila we went back like a tired horse takes the bit. Saturday morning there was cold rain and mist and such a heavy wind that we had to refuse the eager entreaties of clamoring men and women who offered to take us out in their sampans, and go out on board a large steam launch. The harbor was very rough and the little boats were being tossed about in a fearful manner. We were surprised to see many women in charge of boats who seemed quite indifferent to the fury of the gale and managed their boats with a strength and dexterity truly remarkable. We noticed a little Chinaman; he could not have been more than three years of age, in a padded suit, with cap pulled over his ears, his little limbs spread wide and his tiny feet braced like an old sailor, he gripped a plank with his little hands and while his father in one end of the boat and his mother in the other with oar and hook pole made their way amidst a fleet of small watercraft, all tossed about by the tempest, he looked about him as fearless and brave as the "boy who stood on the burning deck."

The Chinese are remarkable sailors. Often we saw them far out at sea in their little fishing boats, mast bending to the wind and frail craft crawling up the sides of a great billow and pitching down into the trough of the sea looking as if every moment would be their last, but John seemed utterly fearless, steadily holding the helm and driving on into the storm.

We sailed from Hongkong on the afternoon of March 12th, on the *China*. She is a fine old ship, having weathered many a rough sea in crossing the Pacific ocean almost two hundred times. It was a delight to climb up her high iron side and leap upon her deck with a joyful thrill at being once more under our own dear flag. The *China* is an American ship, carrying the U. S. Mail with American officers and a fine look and feeling of United States all over her. The officers seemed glad to welcome us on board. There was a good list of passengers, a large number of missionaries, most all on board our own people, and we were delighted to see and mingle with them. On this voyage we experienced the strongest wind, and the greatest waves of our entire trip. When the mountain waves would strike us our ship would tremble in every timber, but would leap forward like a living monster flinging the spray high into the air with her great steel prow pushing steadily forward toward the desired haven. Standing at some sheltered spot on deck we watched with awed admiration the magnificent battle of the winds and waters.

Sabbath morning I braced my feet upon the tilting floor of the reading room and preached Christ mighty to save to the uttermost, to a good audience of thoughtful people.

Shanghai is a wonderful city. As you approach it coming up the river the huge buildings fronting the stream sitting back from the bank far enough for a narrow stretch of park, dotted with monuments, and then a broad street with wide sidewalk on each side, remind you of an European city. In fact, the great hotels, bank, business houses, clubs and shipping companies offices in architecture and appointment, are European. Traveling in one direction for many blocks, the city is so European in its architecture, but for the multitude of Chinamen in the the streets you would not know you were in China. The Britons and Germans are fighting their commercial war here with energy, and while they are thus engaged, you look about for the American enterprise, factory and business house but see little to congratulate yourself over. But when you come to investigate, you are rejoiced to find a host of Americans here, looking not after the Chinaman's gold, but laboring for his moral uplift and his spiritual enlightenment. The American missionary is here with church, school, and printing press, Y. M. C. A. and Y. W. C. A., helping in the introduction and nurturing of those forces that will redeem China.

After two days and nights in Shanghai we took the train for Soochow, a place some fifty miles up country, and one of the strong centers of the Southern Methodist Church. The country through which we ran was broad, flat land, closely cultivated, very fertile and green with growing grain and vegetables. We were surprised to see mounds everywhere in the fields, which we learned were graves. Some of these mounds were small, while others were from twenty to thirty feet square, and from seven to ten feet high; others were even larger. These graves are scattered indiscriminately all about the fields, the mounds themselves covered with a rank growth of

Chinese Bible Woman.

grass, while the vegetables and grain grew right up against the base of them. We could see hundreds of these graves in every direction from the car window, as far as the eye could reach. I should think many of these fertile fields are from one-sixth to one-tenth taken up with graves. This indiscriminate method of burying the dead deprives the farmer of much soil. There are vast cemeteries but in spite of that fact, you see hundreds and thousands of graves scattered about everywhere, some of them in most unexpected places. We also saw many coffins sitting about in the fields not yet deposited within the mounds, some of them without any sort of covering, while others were neatly thatched with straw. It is not uncommon for a coffin to sit thus in the fields for many months. The timbers of the coffins are sometimes several inches thick and one of the Chinese methods of expressing good wishes to a friend at parting is, "May you live long and the timbers of your coffin be thick."

Our train stopped at a station a few miles outside of Soochow and the first thing we knew W. B. Burke, was on the train hustling us off for a near cut to the Methodist mission. It was our first meeting since we separated in Wesley Hall at Vanderbilt, more than twenty years ago. Bro. Burke has been in China for something like two decades and for a number of years has been in charge of Soochow district. He had come up the canal for us on a boat and we were soon stowed away in the same, bag and baggage, and on our way to the city, the canal almost as full of boats of various sorts and sizes as a city street of carriages, carts and wagons. Our boat was propelled by two oars put out behind and worked like the tail of a fish, driving us through the water at a good rate of speed.

We were quite interested in two boats we met coming up the canal, each with eight or ten cormorants in it, a Chinaman standing in the center with a long pole in his hand having a hook on the end of it. The birds about the size of a small wild goose, but with long neck and very long, sharp bill, are great fishers; they dive through the water with remarkable rapidity, catching and swallowing a good sized fish. The Chinaman has a ring tied around the bird's neck down against its body to keep the fish from going down into the bird's stomach; another string is tied to the bird's leg. When it catches and swallows the fish the Chinaman thrusts out his pole and hooks the bird and drags him into the boat by the cord attached to his leg, shakes the fish out of his throat and tosses the bird back into the water. If the bird catches a fish too large for his wide mouth and capacious throat, John knows how to manage the situation. It was an interesting sight.

We passed through a great arch in the wall which surrounds the city and pulled to the shore, visited the snake temple which stood near our landing in which there were many images of snakes, carved in wood and cast in metal of many sorts and sizes. A doleful and disgusting place, dusty and dim, with some poorly clad, sad looking old priests. Coming out we climbed up to the top of the city wall and walked along some distance, perhaps a mile, when we came upon our Southern Methodist mission. At the foot of the wall on the inside runs the canal, and just across the canal is the mission compound wall. A street runs up through the Methodist territory, the woman's work on one side and the university on the other. Standing on the wall and looking down we could see well over the plant.

"Trueheart Home" stands in the corner next to the canal. It is a plain, neat, substantial, roomy house, built to stand the test of years. In it the women who conduct the work of the college for girls and young women live; just beyond it stands the beautiful new "Laura Haygood Memorial." It is a splendid structure, well adapted to the work for which it is intended. A large parlor and beautiful chapel, good recitation rooms and spacious study hall, a large dining room and well ventilated dormitories, with a long, wide hall for exercise when the weather is inclement. There is also a good front yard which offers room for exercise and recreation. On beyond this college is the woman's hospital with several buildings, fairly well equipped, and one of the cleanest, neatest places I ever saw. Still further on is the male hospital, a large place of many rooms and wards, and a procession of sick people coming and going from the two hospitals almost constantly. On beyond the male hospital is a large, substantial residence, recently erected, the home of one of the missionaries.

On the opposite side of the narrow street stands the Soochow University. This is a substantial, attractive, commodious building. In the rear is a large playground and back of the playground a long, well arranged dormitory building for the students. In front of the main building is a beautiful campus, not large, but with sufficient room for four or five good residence buildings for the families of the professors of the university. Just above the university block and on the same side of the street is the residence of Dr. Margaret Polk, who has charge of the woman's hospital, and just beyond her residence is that of Drs.

Snell and Mosea, two of the doctors in charge of the
male hospital. Altogether it is a splendid plant, well
located, well laid out, with attractive, substantial buildings that will remain through the decades. Situated between the Laura Haygood school building and the
hospital for women is the church, a poor little structure
with Chinese pastor in which the schools and others in
the neighborhood meet for worship. Each one of the
hospitals has a small chapel in which religious services
are conducted daily for the patients and their visiting
friends. By this means the gospel is constantly finding
its way into the minds of the people. A few steps over
the Methodist boundary and you are in the great
Chinese city. The presiding elder of the district, Bro.
Burke lives over the line in a rented house among the
people.

The great stone wall around Soochow is from twenty
to thirty feet high, and from ten to twelve miles in circumference. The outside of the wall is perpendicu-
lar, with a wide, deep canal at the foot. On the inside there is a vast bank of earth, like a railroad fill,
piled up against the wall within some six or eight feet
of the top. This bank of earth is wide enough for a
wagon to drive around upon it. There the soldiers,
who defended the city marched and fired their cannon
and muskets or arrows through the embrasures and port-
holes near the top of the wall. The rebels captured
this city in the great rebellion, and held it for many
months. All about the city are heaps of ruin and
rubbish, mute witnesses of the fierce struggle of those
days. Chinese Gordon came here at the head of the
imperial army, captured the city and restored it to the
king.

Soochow, within the walls and in the suburbs immediately around the place, claims five hundred thousand inhabitants. Many narrow canals, spanned by stone bridges, wind through the city. The streets are too narrow for wheeled vehicles, and one must walk, ride in a Sedan chair carried by Chinamen, or ride a donkey, the smallest variety of that homely, but patient and sure-footed quadruped.

On the day of our arrival in Soochow, I was asked to preach at a regular weekly union meeting of the missionaries of the city, which I did, and at which time we met quite a company of missionaries of various denominations. I made a short address to the students in the University chapel, at the invitation of Prof. Smart, a much beloved missionary, son of Dr. Smart, pastor of Broadway Methodist Church, of Louisville. I addressed his Bible Class on "Pentecost," which happened to be the lesson for the hour.

I preached Saturday evening in *Trueheart Home*, to a group of Methodist missionaries. Sabbath morning, early, I preached to the young ladies, in the beautiful chapel of the new *Laura Haygood School.* This school is fortunate in having Miss Martha E. Pyle for its principal. We had a good meeting, and I got away in time to walk two miles across the city and preach in the great chapel of Miss Atkinson's school at eleven a. m., while Brother Piercy preached at the same hour to the students and missionaries in the University chapel. At four in the afternoon I preached at a union meeting of the missionaries of all the churches, in the home of the Atkinson school. Folding doors were thrown open between dining room and sitting room for the purpose. There was a large gathering, among them several Presbyterian ministers, Baptist and Episcopal clergymen, a number of teachers, physicians and workers, with several Chinese who could understand English. It was a gracious service. The sermon on the "Baptism with the Holy Spirit" as a subsequent work to regeneration, cleansing, comforting and empowering for service, was well received by the audience.

Soochow is in need of a great revival, and I do not think we have found a place more ripe for it. Concerted action among the missionaries, importunate prayer and a plain putting of the word of God would bring it in gracious power. The fruit is ripe and the tree suffering for shaking.

The Methodist plant in Soochow is one of the great strongholds of Christian activity in China, having grounds, buildings, institutions, equipment and consecrated intelligence.

The agents and representatives of the Methodist Church, the Lambuths, C. F. Reid, Dr. Park, and many others, who have planned and worked here, have not wasted or misused the money the church has committed to them. No doubt the Lord has guided and blessed. Burke is one of the best of them all. A devout, pure man, beloved of missionaries and Chinese people. All had a good word for him. One prominent missionary said, "I tell you it made a big difference in Bro. Burke when he got *the blessing.* We all know that he lives a holy life."

From Soochow we went up to Nanking for a short visit. The city of Nanking was founded some two hundred and fifty-five years before Christ. It grew rapidly, and in due time became the capital city of the

Chinese Empire. It was noted for its great wealth, and as a seat of learning. In time the capital was moved to Peking, but Nanking continued to be a city of great importance and influence. During the Taiping rebellion, the city was captured and pillaged by the rebel forces, and great damage was done, but through the centuries it has remained a populous and influential center. It is situated on the Yangtze River, the most famous river in China, and one of the greatest in the world. A number of beautiful mountains surround the place, and there are one or two smaller rivers and several beautiful lakes nearby, making it naturally a most attractive situation.

At the present time there is a great revival of education in the city. The Chinese people themselves are taking hold of a far more advanced educational system, and doing a work for the young Chinese boys and girls, which will be much more in keeping with the progress of the times than formerly. At the time of our visit they were very busy preparing for an industrial exposition. Many handsome modern buildings were nearing completion, the grounds were systematically laid off and being beautified and the people were anticipating a great gathering.

It is plain to every one that the thrills of new life are going through China. The spirit of progress and patriotism is animating her teeming millions of young men, and the China of today is an entirely different China from the one the Japanese fought and conquered. She is a different China from that of the Boxer war. What she will be in twenty-five years, would be hard to prognosticate. It will be safe to say, however, that she will be far up the highway of modern progress from where she is now. The Boxer war had no little to do with her awakening. China learned that there was a powerful outside world and that in the matter of military science, she was far behind the procession. She saw that she must give up some of her old notions, or be at the mercy of any nation that desired to take advantage of her. She also had an opportunity to see that Christianity was a powerful force; that the Bible was a most marvelous book. Her people who had professed faith in Christ went cheerfully to death by the thousand, rather than surrender their loyalty to Christ. This made them think. When men, women and children die this way for the cause they love, there must be something in it. She also got a good look at the missionaries. They really love us. They suffered patiently and died calling on Christ in great peace. Those who escaped came back immediately after the persecution with reinforcements to take up their old story of the love of Christ for China. All of this is having a deep and far-reaching effect.

Another thing worthy of note; China has recently made a great discovery. She has found a new weapon with which she can defend herself against all nations. It is a wonderful device, and can be used effectively on any foe, without the loss of a single man to China. The new invention of China surpasses dreadnaughts, and airship are nothing compared with it. It can be put into effectual working order and bring America, England, France, and Germany to their knees, one at a time or all at once. This new contrivance is much cheaper than building a navy or organizing an army— it is the "*Boycott.*" When China turned up her nose

Scene in Woman's Hospital at Soochow, China.

at American goods and refused to buy, Uncle Sam
pulled off his hat and commenced bowing and smiling.
"John," said Uncle Sam, "you remember that war indemnity we levied against you? Say, that was all a
joke; we don't intend to collect it. Ha! Ha! We are
going to make you a present of that. What is a matter
of a few millions between old friends like you and
me. Oh, don't mention it! Here, have a cigar, and
let's take a walk." John bowed and smiled, and then
shook hands with himself in the most cordial manner.
He thoroughly enjoyed the joke, and fully understood
the situation. While the American newspapers were
bragging on the generosity of the United States, John
slipped his hands up his big sleeves and hugged himself.
He realized that the *"Boycott"* had reminded Uncle
Sam that he never did intend to collect that indemnity.

This new apparatus of Chinese defense is so delicate-
ly adjusted and so powerful an instrument that if a
mean American boy should pull the queue of a Chinese
boy, or kick him off the street in San Francisco, Seattle
or Denver, the "Boycott" is liable to go off in China
and cost American commerce ten millions of dollars.
It would pay Uncle Sam to hunt up all the mean boys
at home, who intend to kick and cuff Chinamen and put
them in prison for life now, before the kicking and cuff-
ing is done, on the principle that an ounce of preventive
is worth a pound of cure. *China is too big to be kicked.*

While in Nanking we were entertained in the home
of Dr. Russel, who was in charge of the large Methodist hospital in that city. We visited and made an address to the students of the large Christian School in
that city. It is a union of the Methodist, Presbyterian,
and Disciples schools, the three having united into one

large college, with a Methodist president, and a number of professors from the various Churches represented. Returning to Shanghai we went out fifty miles to Sungkong where the Southern Methodist Church has a fine Christian plant. We were entertained in the home of Prof. Reed, head of the boys' school, and preached three times each day, while we remained there in his school, in the Church, and in the large female school.

We here found a most devout group of missionaries, and a company of intelligent and consecrated native Christians. The Lord was with us graciously and the altar was filled at the close of each service by those who were eagerly seeking forgiveness or sanctifying grace. Since leaving China, we have heard most encouraging reports of the results of our few days' meetings in that place. Going back to Shanghai we spent a few days, during which time I spoke twice to groups of missionaries, and delivered an address to the students of the large Methodist School located in that city. Deeply regretting that it was out of our power to remain longer in this ripe, rich field for full salvation evangelism, we sailed away on a Japanese ship to Nagasaki, Japan.

CHAPTER XXVIII.

KOREA'S TURNING TO THE LORD.

We sailed from Moji, a seacoast city of Japan, for Fusan, a Korean port. We had some trouble getting tickets fo th voyage, but finally found a Japanese who could speak a little English, who helped us out of our dilemma.

We went out at nine o'clock at night in a launch and scrambled up the ship's side,—a Japanese steamer with Japanese officers, sailors, cooks, waiters, and most of the passengers. Being second class, we were taken to a room in the aft part of the ship about twenty-two by twenty feet, with sixteen bunks in it, eight below and eight above. Piercy and myself were given upper bunks which were almost as hard as a plank, but we had plenty of blankets, which I prized very highly having been cold all day. We pulled the blinds over our bunks and wriggled out of our clothes some way, piling them up in a rack overhead. In due time every bunk was filled, and from twelve to twenty people lay down on the floor, and a number of them lighted their pipes and filled the place with the fumes of tobacco smoke. It would have been a rough night on us, for the room had no ventilation save at the door, had we not fled to the land of nod, and so passed through our tortures in blissful unconsciousness.

The next morning on awakening, we got up at once and got out of the stifling atmosphere into the pure ocean air as soon as possible. Away to our left in the dim haze we could see a small, rocky island, lifting itself high up out of the sea. It was behind this island that the Japanese fleet hid itself while the Russian Black Sea fleet came into these waters and at the strategic moment, steamed out pouring a stream of crashing shells and death upon their enemies. Someone who knew the range of battle, said that in all probability we passed over some of the sunken wreckage of the conflict.

Fusan is one of the principal ports of Korea. The town itself is not large, crouched on the narrow strip of land between the mountains and the sea. There is now in course of construction a fine long dock, running out into the sea, which, when completed, will be of great use to travel and traffic. An immense passenger depot is just being completed, with vast train sheds and many side tracks. We heard people asking why should the Japanese build so largly here? The Japanese know full well what they are doing. They not only intend to annex Korea, but they have their eyes on Manchuria also. When Korea becomes a part of Japan, it will be easy for the little brown men to make encroachments of the vast, rich regions of Manchuria.

Our train pulled out for Seoul a little aften ten a. m. The line lay through a country quite like the most barren and mountainous parts of New Mexico. The sun shone brightly, and the atmosphere was fine and bracing, quite like our far West. We passed many villages, an occasional town, and one considerable city. The small bits of level ground at the foot of the rugged, barren mountains were in cultivation, and the hillsides were terraced up and green with growing grain. We frequently crossed streams of water, and here the level land was carefully laid off into rice paddles or small

Korean Methodist Preachers at Seoul, many of them sanctified during the revival.

fields, with banks of earth thrown up around them to hold water on them, for rice must be planted in mud and grow in water. The human habitations along the way were poor structures, small, dark, little huts, built of stones or sun-baked mud, and covered with rice straw. These thatched roofs are laid on with great skill and neatness, and sometimes more than a foot thick.

We arrived in Seoul a little after dark and were met by Dr. Hardie, Rev. J. L. Gerdine and Bro. Rockwell. They gave us a very hearty greeting which we appreciated, for at no time have we seemed farther from home than up here in Korea. Southern Methodism has a fine work in Seoul; there are three good homes for the missionaries high up on the hillside near the city wall, overlooking the great harvest field of souls, they are there to gather into the kingdom. They have four native congregations in the city, a large new church edifice going up almost completed, besides a large girls' boarding school and four day schools. I suppose there is no mission field in all our Methodism, where the church has made so small money investment as in Korea, and holds so much valuable property. I doubt if there can be found in any mission field of the church a more consecrated and devout body of missionaries than our church has here. We have found a beautiful spirit of union, devotion, and zeal among them. Bro. Cram, who is an old Kentucky boy and was for some years a successful young minister in the Kentucky Annual Conference, is at home with his family on leave for a year of recuperation and agitation of the church on missions, and especially the needs of this field. He is much beloved out here, by the whole missionary body and the native people. It is said that there is perhaps no mis-

sionary in the field that speaks the Korean language
more fluently than he. The old Asbury boys and
girls will remember Cram as one of the best students and sunniest souls of his time at college. They
tell me that he is still in a good humor, that there is life
and joy in him, and that he can find the hopeful side of
a situation and press the battle to victory with a Christian cheerfulness that helps to roll the clouds away from
other souls.

The M. E. Church has a strong foothold in Seoul.
They have four native congregations in the city, with a
number of large brick churches, a fine boarding school
for girls, also a boys' boarding school, besides a number of day schools.

There is a most beautiful spirit of union and harmony
between the two Methodisms here. They are now arranging to build a union theological school in which to
educate the ministers for the two churches. This is as
it should be. Throughout the mission field where I have
met the two Methodisms, I have found them working
together as one, and my impression is that all of the missionaries of both churches would rejoice in the union of
the churches. Such a union would give Methodism a
powerful influence in the East, and would result in great
economy in men, money and time, and would doubtless
make possible the saving of many souls, who otherwise
would die without hearing the gospel. The native
Christians know nothing of our church prejudices, and
it is to be hoped they never will know of or partake of
them.

The Presbyterian Church is very strong in Korea.
They were among the first on the field, and the home
church has poured money into the field and has kept a

Korean Country Woman.

great force of workers in Korea. They have about seven congregations in the city of Seoul. They have a large school for boys, also a school for girls; they also have the largest hospital in Seoul and some strong, devout men. The Church of England also has work in the city, and there are some Japanese churches for the emigrants who are coming up from Japan. The two Methodisms and the Presbyterians have in Seoul about four thousand members, and large numbers of people are being converted as the weeks go by. Seoul is rapidly becoming a city of churches.

We arrived in Seoul at an opportune time. The Korean Methodist preachers of the two Methodisms, about ninety in number, had come in from all the country round for a few weeks' study and training. They were just closing out their work, and were in their examinations when we arrived, and it was at once arranged that they should remain over a week and that I should preach to them each morning. The program ran like this. I should preach each morning in the Methodist Church to these young ministers. In the afternoon I preached to the more advanced Christians in the large Y. M. C. A. Hall, and in the evening I preached to the missionaries in the chapel of the girls' school, and so the meetings went forward. The altars always full at the two Korean services, many claiming either pardon or cleansing.

Our home at Dr. Hardie's was far away from all of these points, involving much travel, making it one of the most strenuous weeks of my life, but a most blessed time. Both in the church and at the Y. M. C. A., all the altar space was full at the close of every service. Dr. Hardie was my interpreter, and a good one. Piercy,

who has been so faithful in altar work, suffered in his
soul that he could not speak the language of the people,
but he *amened* me up the hill, and helped to find a place
to pack the people into the altar, motioned the Christians on to the work and wept for joy.   Thus the work
went on, three services a day, until Friday, there being
only two meetings that day and Saturday off for rest.
Every evangelist should rest Saturday if possible.   On
this trip, the nature of our meetings has been such that
we could not do so, and I have fully realized the importance of one day in seven.   On Friday evening,
while I preached to the missionaries, Dr. Hardie held a
praise and testimony meeting for the young preachers,
and says they have all been greatly blessed and not less
than thirty of them sanctified.   For this I praise the
Lord, and want our Holiness Association to give him
glory, and beg them to pray that these thirty men, with
many others who believe in a Christ able to save to the
uttermost, may spread the news of full salvation all over
this peninsula until every Korean shall know that Jesus
Christ is able to save all men from all sin.

One of the most delightful incidents of this meeting
was the coming down of Dr. Reid to see me.   Almost
twenty years ago when Rev. C. F. Reid, missionary
from Kentucky Conference to China, was at home on
rest leave, he was with his family at Winchester, Ky.
During their stay there, I assisted Rev. W. F. Taylor
in a meeting in the Methodist Church.   Sister Reid,
who was a niece of Bishop Wightman, was graciously
sanctified, and her two children, then quite small, were
converted.   Sister Reid, though a quiet woman, was of
strong mind and radiant soul.   She remained a faithful
witness until the Lord took her to himself.   Once a year

South Gate in Songdo, Korea.

for many years, she wrote me from far-off China renewing her subscription to The Herald, and every time witness of the saving, sanctifying and keeping power of Christ. This Dr. Reid, a fine big fellow, the son of this sainted mother, is the outcome of the little boy converted that night at the altar of the Methodist Church at Winchester. What could be more delightful than after these nineteen years, to meet him here, one of the most consecrated missionaries I have met in all my travels. He remained with us for several days, and we walked and talked together. If I were Dr. Clarence Reid, I would rather be the father of this son, living here among these poor people, ministering to their diseased bodies, and telling them of the Christ who can save their lost souls, than to have all the wealth of the Rockefellers.

Seoul is a city of three hundred thousand population. The city is built upon a plain surrounded by mountains. It has been the capital of Korea for five hundred years. A vast stone wall encircles the city, erected upon the range of the hills, and climbing up the great mountain to the topmost rocky crags. The plan was that no enemy should be able to stand on an eminence above the wall, and look over into the city, or be able to throw any missel or shoot an arrow down upon the defenders of the place. The guards on the inside of the wall looked down upon every approach and stood high above any advancing enemy. There is a legend that when the capital was moved to this place and the king's palace was built here, sixty thousand were put to work upon this great wall, many miles in circumference, and that they completed the great structure in three months. We spent an hour looking over the old palace, the extensive grounds and buildings. There are gateways

leading back from the street through the vast stone wall
that surrounds the place, which cost sums of money
sufficient to have built large houses.   There is the king's
audience room or court, his winter palace, summer
palace, the beautiful artificial lakes, two of them, in
which the Lotus flower bloomed.   There are buildings
for servants, soldiers, and councilors, and it is said three
thousand wives,—entirely too many wives.   There is
the spot where the late queen's palace stood.   The
queen was foully murdered a few years ago by the
Japanese, her body burned and her palace torn down
and carried away.   The former glory of the palace has
departed, the grounds are neglected, and the palaces
are falling into decay.

An incident that touched my heart in the meetings at
Seoul, was the coming of Bro. Moose and his two little
daughters, on pack horses two days' journey across the
plains to attend the meetings.   He is pastor of a church
and presiding elder of a district back in the interior.   He
is one of the most devout men in Korea, and is full of a
joyful faith for the coming of a great wave of salvation
over the people for whom he labors.   He stopped at Dr.
Hardie's.   The Hardies seem to keep a hotel; I would
not undertake to tell how many people were at their
table while we were there, and there was a glad glow of
welcome for them all.

Bro. Moose had the pleasure of seeing his eldest
daughter, a very bright girl of twelve,, graciously blessed in the meetings.   He had business in the city, which
he looked after during the day, attending the meetings
at night.   One afternoon a telegram came that his wife
was quite sick.   Their little baby boy, *Morrison*, is only
three months old.   At once Bro. Moose was away,

leaving his little girls behind, and taking his faithful Korean servant with him.   The sun was soon down, and we followed him in our thoughts as he hastened forward under the stars, with prayer and hope.   If there should be dining rooms in heaven, and the serving of meals, it would be a joy to me some sweet day over there to gird myself, and walk behind the chairs and serve these missionaries.

Early Monday morning, April 25th, Bro. Piercy and myself were off for Songdo.   It is only about fifty or sixty miles from Seoul, traveling north toward the Manchuria border.   We found the valleys between the mountains broader than down in the region through which we came up to Seoul, and the carefully cultivated fields have the appearance of fertility.

When we arrived at Songdo, Dr. Reid and Rev. F. K. Gamble met and gave us a most cordial welcome. Songdo, like Seoul, lies in a valley surrounded by a circling chain of mountains.   Many centuries ago it was the capital city of Korea, and is now the second city in number of population.   The grim old walls, gray and crumbling with age, encircle the city, running along on top of the ridge and up the mountain crest, not only taking in the habitations of the people but the low, surrounding hills and many hundreds of acres of land, growing gardens, rice, wheat and barley fields.   The beautiful hills within the gates are covered with spreading chestnut trees, and at this time underneath the trees masses of wild flowers are blooming.

The Southern Methodists have set themselves to the splendid task of capturing this city for Christ.   A band of missionaries never gathered about a richer harvest field or one more ready for the sickle.   The Missionary

Board of the church has been very fortunate in securing seventy-two acres of land beautifully located for their purpose. The Woman's Board has fifteen or twenty acres on which has been erected a handsome stone structure costing some $15,000; such a building would have cost far more at home; this is *Holston Institute*, a school for girls. They also have a large, brick building, a home for the women who have charge of the girls' school.

There is the *Anglo-Korean School* for boys. They have a handsome, stone dormitory costing $6,000. Stone is on the ground for the main building of the Anglo-Korean School. It will cost $50,000, Mr. T. H. Yun, of the school, is now in the United States raising money to erect the building. There are four excellent residences for missionaries, and a fifth now being erected.

The Ivey Hospital, of which Dr. Reid has charge, is a beautiful, stone structure costing $6,500. Another large ward or wing is to be added to the hospital plant soon.

The church was fortunate in securing a fine stone quarry on the mountain side near the building site of the mission plant, and cheap labor has made it possible to put up the above buildings at much less cost than could be done at home. I doubt if there is a handsomer, or more substantial church property on the globe for a smaller outlay of money, for beautiful situation, attractive architecture, substantial material, workmanship and general convenience. We have seen nothing quite up to it in our tour around the world.

We have four congregations here, with three houses of worship, a baptized membership of about eight hun-

East Gate in Songdo.

dred adherents, with some sixty or sixty-five thousand people ready for the gospel. The churches are very poor houses and entirely inadequate to accommodate the people.

The band of missionaries now in Songdo, are a most devout, zealous people. We have not met a company of missionaries with larger vision and greater heart burden for souls than these people. The first baptism here took place December 4, 1898, about twelve years ago. As stated above, some eight hundred have followed, but now the harvest time has come, the trained workers are on the spot; there is a great company of Koreans ready to help press the battle for souls. Stand by this band of missionaries, supply them with churches and a proper force of workers, and within the next few years a very large number will be brought to Christ.

There are many reasons why the church should at once possess this land. First, the Holy Spirit is mightily moving the people to accept Christ; while he is so manifestly at work, the church should follow his leadership with zeal. Second, the scenes are shifting rapidly on the Eastern stage; no one can tell what a day may bring forth. A conflict in Manchuria, between Japan and China, or Japan and Russia, would mean that Korea would be overrun with marching armies and the whole social and moral life of the nation would be demoralized. Third, a generation will be in their graves directly; the church owes it to those who will soon pass into eternity, to let them hear of Christ's salvation before they go and stand before the throne of God in their sins, to accuse us of our neglect of their salvation. Fourth, the sister churches have entrusted this rich field to Southern Methodism and she owes it to those who have confided in her to met their expectation, and bring forward her wing of the army of conquest, abreast with the advancing hosts. If the church will send forward the munitions, our faithful little band at the front will not only hold their position, but will sweep the enemy before them, and capture Songdo for Jesus.

I would to God I could put the cry of my heart for this people on paper, so that it would awake in the hearts of all who read these lines, a cry to God for the salvation of Songdo.

During our three days' stay in this city it was my privilege to preach in three of the mission homes, once in the girls' school, twice in the boys' school, once in one of the churches, and twice in another one of them. In neither instance, when preaching in the churches, could the congregations be seated, but they packed the houses, and gathered in great numbers about the doors and windows, filling the altar with seekers always at the close of the sermon.

Since our visit the missionaries have inaugurated an aggressive evanglistic campaign in Songdo, and as many as two thousand have given names for instruction in the things of salvation.

While in this city I had a room in the new hospital with Dr. Reid. He has not been able to move his patients into the new building, as he has not yet secured a nurse for the place, but the old hospital is very near the new and he has his office and bedroom up at the new hospital, and hopes to get into it soon. He gave me a quiet room, and I had three nights of gracious rest and sweet sleep in the place. A Korean brother prepared our meals for us at the breakfast hour, and most of the other meals we ate with some of the missionaries.

I wish the readers of these pages could have looked upon what our eyes saw these three nights in Songdo. Far more people can be seated on mats on the floor, than can be seated on pews in a church. The Koreans can fold up their lower limbs gracefully and sit in the most compact manner imaginable. Everyone sings during the song service; everyone prays in the most humble a.... de, and almost everyone has his Testament and turns to the text. Many of them have pencil and note book, and make copious notes.

When we left for Pyeng Yang, the students of the boys' school, marched in a body out to the station, almost a mile, to tell us good-bye, and were drawn up at the gate in beautiful order in two long lines, some two hundred and fifty of them in all. The officer in command doubled up the lines, and I made them a short address. They gave us a tune from their drums and trumpets, and we waved them a farewell with our hats as the train pulled out. As far as we could see, their caps were all in the air. So we went on our journey, leaving much of our heart at Songdo.

I would to God the church at home could understand the devotion and zeal of this little band of missionaries and the heart hunger and need of the people; then with joy she would pray and give for the salvation of this city.

From Songdo, we traveled almost due north one hundred miles to Pyeng Yang. This is, I understand, the third city in point of population in Korea. It is situated in a broad valley through which flows a beautiful, clear river, emptying into the ocean fifty miles away. The mission stations are on the hills overlooking the city, which lay between the hills and the river. Beyond the river is a broad plain, with the mountains towering up in the blue, hazy distance.

The Presbyterian and the M. E. Church, both have strong centers here, working out from this place into their separate territories. Pyeng Yang has a native population of thirty-five or forty thousand, and there are some eight thousand Japanese in the city.

The city of Pyeng Yang has seen some stormy days in her history. In and around this city, a considerable battle was fought between the Chinese and the Japanese during the war between those nations. Many Chinamen fell here, and for months after the conflict there were some places not far from the city fairly white with their bones. The Chinese army on that occasion was armed with spears and swords; some of the troops were equipped with old antiquated firearms, and some of the officers carrying umbrellas and fans. They waved banners and beat gongs while the Japanese soldiers, with their modern rifles and well-trained regiments, mowed them down with little or no danger to themselves. The Chinese military machine will not compare with the Japanese in its efficiency to-day, but it has made marked progress in the past few years, and will in the time to come, be easily able to take care of the interests of China. Even now, China is no longer the plaything of the nations.

Near this city occurred the first land skirmish between the Russians and the Japanese in the recent war between those nations. Only a few shots were fired, and the Russians fell back to a point, from which they later fell back to a place, from which they withdrew to a position, from which they retreated to rendezvous, from which they fled in confusion. Thousand of troops

Street Scene in Songdo, Korea.

passed through this city to Manchuria, the border of
that great land of promise being only a few hours by
train from here. The troops were under good disci-
pline, and gave little or no trouble marching to the war.
It was thought if they should be defeated, and driven
back throuh the place, the situation would be quite serious. Other white people fled from the place, but the
missionaries held their ground, kept in the best possible
touch with the situation, having all their arrangements
made to get away if there should be a reverse at the
front.

There was no railway here then, and the weather was
bitter cold. Oxen were engaged with pack saddles to
convey the luggage and the women and children, and
on short notice the brave little band would have been
making its way southward, but the necessity for flight
never came, and the work of preaching and teaching
went steadily on. Port Arthur is not very far from this
place, and news of the great battles and the fearful loss
of life filtered through or came from the homeland while
these brave soldiers of peace, forgiveness and love stood
to their post and comforted the hearts of the fear-strick-
en people.

The Presbyterian Church has a very strong station in
Pyeng Yang. The homes, school building, industrial
building, theological institute, and other buildings making quite a village in itself. They have eighteen missionaries here, teachers, preachers, evangelists. This in-
cludes only the men and women who are in the regular
work, and not the children, of whom there is a fine
bunch, as bright boys and girls as I have ever seen.
These missionaries, with native workers, go out from
here through a wide territory preaching the gospel and

distributing the Scriptures and Christian literature. The mother church of Presbyterianism for this region, seating fifteen hundred people, with a membership of about that number, has been a fruitful branch, setting up congregations, sending workers and members to organize other churches until now in about twenty years, she has more than forty churches organized in winning souls to Christ.

Not long ago they had a few days' convention of women for Bible study and prayer in this city, and six hundred Korean women walked in from all the surrounding country some of them feeble with old age, many of them coming from considerable distance, bringing their Bibles with them, paying their own board while they remained, searching the Scriptures and delighting in the instructions in the things of God. That was a sight to gladden the heart of Christ; to look upon six hundred women coming slowly over the plains from town, village, and hamlet, all facing to one common center; all with at least a portion of the holy Scriptures, often stopping for a rest and reading and praying by the way, coming up to learn of him who can take our sins away.

It was my privilege to preach in this great Presbyterian Church, Sabbath afternoon. The large building was full of people, and I had a fine interpreter. My theme was *salvation for all, free for all, present for all, conscious for all, and from all sin.* I never preached to a more attentive audience. At the close nine persons came forward to give themselves to Christ. At the opening of the service fifty persons were baptized by the Korean pastor, a cultured and deeply spiritual man.

This church often has fifteen hundred persons present

at the twice a week prayer meeting. Last year they contributed $1,500 to the running expenses of their church.

The M. E. Church has a fine work in Pyeng Yang. On Sabbath morning I preached in the great Methodist Church. It has a seating capacity, so they told me, of two thousand, but this requires crowding. Our congregation seemed to fill the place, but the brethren said we had only about fifteen hundred persons present. We had a gracious service, and a number came forward to profess faith in Christ.

The Methodist Church has a fine new hospital just completed, where many poor, suffering creatures are receiving tender care, and from which they may go out helped or healed. The physical suffering in heathen countries, because of sin, ignorance, neglect, filth and cruelty, is something frightful. The Methodists and Presbyterians have two large schools; one for young men and one for young women, affiliated together. The students and teachers come from the two churches, and seem to live and labor together in great harmony and good will. Bro. Noble is the superintendent of the Methodist work, and has a wonderful record of many years of hard, painstaking and most successful work in this region. The Japanese Methodist Church has a good church edifice in this city, and quite a considerable membership. They have a Japanese pastor and manage their own affairs.

Going up one of the principal business streets one Sabbath afternoon to the Presbyterian Church, my attention was called to the fact that a number of stores and shops were closed. "Our converts," said the minister, "when they come to Christ, close their stores on the Sabbath day." I heard many interesting stories here about evangelistic work, and the leading and blessing of the Lord. "That big Korean, standing at the door, was one of the most wicked men of this city; he is now one of the most devoted." "Old black Joe is our sexton; he gets black from the coal making the fires under the church; he is always happy. How he delights to ring the bell for services; he was one of the worst drunkards in the town, and used to beat his wife in the most cruel way, but is wonderfully changed now since he found Jesus." "The man walking in front of us came to church one night and was so powerfully convicted that he stood up to confess his sins, telling of his thefts and other misdoing. While talking he fell over stiff as a poker and lay for a long time; the people thought he was dying, but he came around all right, was soon converted and has been a most devout man." "One night," said a missionary, "a young man about eighteen years of age, got up to make public confession of his sins, and startled the congregation by telling how that some years before, his mother died leaving him a little baby brother to care for. The child was sick and cried all the time, so one night he took a chunk of wood and struck it on the head, killing it, and made the neighbors believe the child had died. After telling of his awful crime the young man fell over as if dead, and lay for a long time, apparently unconscious, but came to, and in time was powerfully converted, and has been a most devout Christian."

During the three days in Pyeng Yang, I preached seven times to several thousand people. Monday afternoon Bro. Piercy and myself, bade our new friends good-bye, and started on our return journey for Seoul, where we arrived after dark, and were kindly received

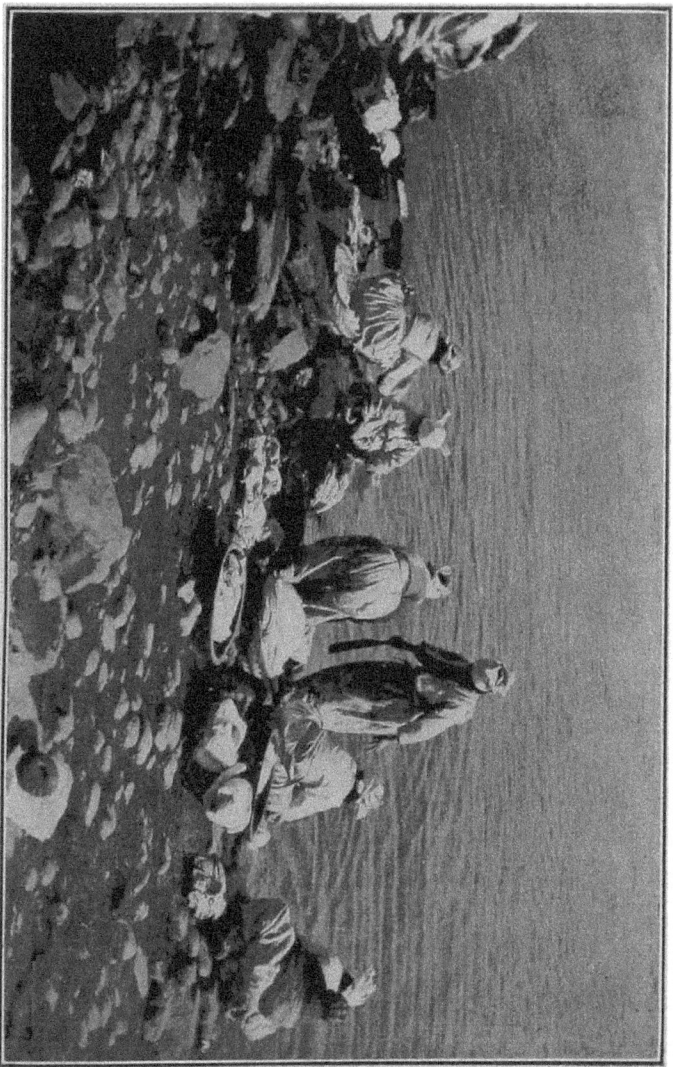

Korean Women washing at the river bank.

by our friends. The next day we attended to some business in the city in the morning, and in the afternoon gathered with a party of friends at the home of Mr. Hugh Miller, Rev. F. G. Vesey and wife coming over with their two fine boys, one of them a babe in arms. Mr. Miller is, I believe, a Presbyterian while Bro. Vesey is a Congregationalist, he and his wife being from London, England. These men represent the British and Foreign Bible Society in Korea, and are doing a wonderful work in spreading the Scriptures among the people. The Miller's also have two fine boys, and at their request, I baptized the four of them, fine little Britons. May God bless them. It was one of the sweetest privileges of all the long journey; this baptizing of children seems to link you on to them and their parents with a golden link of friendship that puts sweetness and meaning into life.

After supper at the Miller home, I preached to an audience of missionaries that well-nigh filled the chapel at the Methodist Girls' School. "The Coming of the Lord and the Wedding Garment" was the theme and I had close attention and a very kind reception. Bishop Harris, who had just come up from Japan to hold the Korean Conference, was present and prayed a wonderful prayer. His head and beard are white as snow, with as pure looking face as you could desire to look into.

Wednesday morning a party of friends came out to the depot to see us off, and after a most hearty, Christian farewell, we boarded the train and pulled out for Fusan, the point from which we sail for Japan. We got a better view of the country coming down than we had going up, and were much pleased with the beauti-

ful fields, without a weed or sprig of grass to be seen in
the carefully cultivated growing crops.

Korea is an agricultural country; the people, with
rather crude farming implements, get good results.
They know how to fertilize, irrigate and terrace up the
hillsides, and gather the crops in with careful economy.
They raise considerable grain for export and, although
the people are very poor, we encountered only two beggars during the several weeks we spent in the three most
populous cities of Korea.

There are rich gold mining regions in the country.
These mines are worked almost entirely by foreigners;
that is, they are owned by foreigners, mostly Americans
and English. The Korean is said to make a fine man as
a laborer in the mines. He is strong and steady at his
job, respectful and kindly in his disposition. He is
larger and a whiter man than either the Chinaman or
Japanese, and as dignified as the North American Indian. They have fine cattle in the country and it would
seem to be a fine climate for sheep raising, but we saw
no sheep. But little manufacturing is done in the country for export. The people make practically everything they need for their own use, and are very skillful
in brass work, also in the manufacture of furniture, but
they have sought little outside market for their trade in
these articles.

I suppose there never lived a more peaceable people
than the Koreans; they have had neither the power nor
the disposition to interfere with the affairs of other
nations. They would have loved to have been left
alone in peace among their beautiful hills and sunny
valleys, but all unexpectedly the highway of war between Japan and Russia lay through their peaceful

land, and all at once their far away secluded spot, became one of the centers of attraction, the stage upon
which one of the tragedies of human history is being enacted, with the scenes shifting so rapidly that the nations watch the rise and fall of the curtains with keenest
interest.

The Korean people are turning to the Lord as no
other people have ever done. The churches should deal
with this situation with a wide-open hand and loving
heart. The situation and the opportunity demand the
most spiritual and aggressive men in the church. It is a
crime against God and humanity for a missionary to be
a commonplace Christian. One may necessarily be a
commonplace man, but no one need be a commonplace
Christian. It is our privilege to be cleansed from all sin,
filled with the Spirit and burning with love for souls. If
the Korean people are led to Christ and instructed in
the things of salvation by such people, they will be a
very high order of Christians. It is of the greatest importance that the standard set be a high one—that of
the New Testament.

If I were in command of the forces in Korea, I would
set my heart on two things: church buildings in which
to worship, and a well-trained, Spirit-filled ministry to
preach the word to the people. The people of the villages are ready to do all they can in the way of building, but after they have done that, they should have
help and their churches should be large enough for the
great increase that is coming, comfortable and attractive enough to impress the outsiders, and strong enough
to stand for a century or longer. Blessed is the man
that dots Korea over with churches. No business can
be carried on successfully, without a place in which to

transact it; especially is this true of the great business of salvation.

The Korean's interest in religion, his fondness for the Bible, his humble earnestness in prayer, and the simplicity of his faith, are most remarkable and gratifying. Devil possession is supposed to exist among them to a considerable extent. Persons seem to be possessed of evil spirit, at least that is the Korean view of the condition of certain persons. I am told that the Christians often pray for these people until they are entirely delivered and clothed in their right minds, becoming happy and earnest Christians.

It was almost dark and raining when we arrived in Fusan. We hurried on board our little ship and got stowed away in time for supper, but the supper did not remain with me scarcely ten minutes; our ship was bobbing up and down like a cork as we came out of the harbor and finding my supper was not disposed to make the voyage, gladly left it behind and went forward in peace. We had a very good trip over, with restful sleep. By daylight the beautiful hills of Japan, arrayed in living green, were towering up in the distance from the water's edge, the rocky cliffs lifting themselves high above the dashing billows of the sea.

A sad and longing farewell to Korea. In my heart there is a hope that I shall see thee again. If not I shall expect to meet at Jesus' feet many souls to whom we were permitted to tell the glad, good news that our Christ is able to save all men from all sin.

Graduates from the Kindergarten in Japan.

CHAPTER XXIX.

SALVATION SCENES IN JAPAN.

We made the voyage from Shanghai, to Nagasaki Japan, on a Japanese ship, all the way in a heavy gale, a cold wind blowing from the north. The great waves beat against us with fury, almost every one on board seemed to be seasick. It was too cold to go on deck, and so we kept to our bunks, and wished for land.

One could scarcely imagine a more beautiful harbor than that at Nagasaki. The hills rise up on either side, terraced from base to crest with low stone walls, which hold a breadth of ten to thirty feet of rich earth, growing green with wheat, rice, or barley. Hillsides, so steep and rocky, that at home a sheep would hardly find grazing upon them, in Japan, are thus terraced and cultivated pouring down a great harvest of grain into the lap of indefatigable industry.

Just over to our left, as we come into the harbor, is a shipyard with a multitude of hammers ringing on the steel sides of a huge vessel upon the ways, fast approaching the day of her launching. Back of the shipyard the tall smokestacks of a factory are pouring great pillars of smoke into the air. In front of us lies the city of one hundred thousand population. In the narrow strip of land between the water and the hills, and clinging to the hillsides with huge, stone walls to support the foundation, are the houses and shops of the people, and high upon top of the hills are the towers of schools and beautiful homes nestling in great groves of tropical trees, where flowers bloom almost the whole year round.

A dozen coal barges surround us as soon as we come to anchor and directly they are alongside, made fast with cables, while several hundred Japanese, most of them women, are busy passing up little baskets of coal and dumping them into the bunkers. Steam tugs and rowboats of all sorts are gathering about us calling for passengers. The ship remains here through the day, and the passengers are going on shore for a look at the city. Bro. Piercy and myself got our baggage into a boat and got out of the melee and made for the shore, missing the friends who had come out to meet us, but we soon found our way to the M. E. Church Girls' School, which is situated on the hilltop in a beautiful grove of trees, overlooking the city and the bay. We were kindly received by Miss Young, president of the school, Miss Ashbaugh, who was for some time a much beloved teacher in Asbury College and Miss Melton, whom I had frequently met at Mountain Lake Park, and other holiness conventions. Other missionary teachers in the school were Miss Thomas and Miss Cody. There are also a number of Japanese women teaching in various departments of the school. At the time of our visit, most of the students were away on vacation, but enough were present to give us a high estimate both of the student body and the work being done by the school. I was pleased to find that these school-girls could sing beautifully. A few generations of Christians, the practice of the vocal cords, and the growth of the spirit of praise, and the Japanese will make sweet singers. These young women are sweet singers now.

There was a district convention of the Y. M. C. A., of forty delegates, just meeting in Nagasaki, with a large attendance from the city. It was arranged that I should preach each afternoon to the missionaries and other English-speaking people, and at night in the Y. M. C. A. hall to the convention through an interpreter. The attendance was very good, and there was much interest. First and last all the members of the convention were forward for prayer. A number of sinners held up their hands in the audience indicating a desire to become Christians, and requesting the prayers of the Christians. Several came forward for prayer, among them the night watchman at the college, who claimed to be converted and was very happy.

On Sabbath morning I preached at the Methodist Church to a large audience, made an altar call and many came; several strong-looking men sobbed out most earnest prayers. Of course I could not understand their language, but their whole manner spoke deep earnestness. They tell me it is a rare thing for Japanese to weep, but these men wept. The way to hold revivals among these eastern peoples in all countries we have visited, is to preach earnestly against sinning, to call sins by name, and point out the ruin in them, offer Christ as a Savior, explain how God so loved the world that he gave his Son, and exhort the people to come to the altar; when there, instruct and pray with them, trusting the Holy Ghost to enlighten, convict and save. He will fulfill his office.

Nagasaki, like every other field I have seen, is dead ripe for a revival; all that is necessary is to preach, sing and pray, get the people to decide and pray them through. Nowhere on earth is it a question of divine willingness or power, but of consecrated, Spirit-filled men and women, who will preach the word faithfully, trust God and keep pressing the battle for souls. At home and abroad there is a class of good people who are disposed to spend too much time trying to arrange to fix things so that they may get ready, to prepare the way for the gospel. This is a great mistake. *Preach the gospel, and let it prepare the way for every good thing.*

After the close of the Y. M. C. A. Convention, I preached afternoons to the missionaries, and at night in the Opera House to the English-speaking people of the city. The missionaries felt that the meetings did great good. A tragic story could be written of an army of young men who come from England and America to do business in the East. They come out from under the restraints of home and church; they did not know the rampant power of the carnal nature in them until they came to a land where there is almost nothing to restrain that nature, and there is so much to feed and pamper it. There are three graves up there on the hillside now, of fine young men who committed suicide. Their sins had kindled such a fire of torment within them, that they tore their lost souls out of their wrecked bodies and flung them away into eternal darkness. Numbers of them have died long before their time, debauched by women and wine, and some sort of a story has been fixed up to send back to the loved ones at home. All the way from Port Said, Egypt, to Yokohama, Japan, the silent,, desolate graves of young men, who came out full of hope for success and wealth, tell the sad story of blighted lives and blasted character—sad reminders that *"the wages of sin is death."*

There is a great work for such men as Chapman, Torry and Sunday in the great seaport cities of the Orient. Every year there ought to be a month of gospel evangelism uniting all churches and missionaries in a revival effort in Bombay, Madras, Calcutta, Rangoon, Singapore, Manila, Hongkong, Shanghai, Nagasaki, Seoul, and Yokohama; this circuit being followed up by men of world-wide reputation, who would draw the crowds. There is none better than our own George Stuart, who would introduce a new moral and spiritual era into the East, and be invaluable to the cause of missions. These meetings of powerful appeal to the lost, should be followed up by pentecostal conventions, leading the people into full salvation and establishing great spiritual churches in these strongholds, which not only wield a powerful influence over the men who go out from the West, but over the native population as well. Such a movement would result in the salvation of many young men who would enter the mission work, and the whole effect for good in the oriental countries would be incalculable. It woudl be the dawning of a new era in the Eastern world.

Rev. Ira Jones and wife, two old Asbury students, now stationed at Fukuoka, came down to Nagasaki to attend our meetings, and insisted that we should stop off for a few services at their city, which we were glad to do. So leaving Nagasaki Monday morning, we stopped at Fukuoka that afternoon, and I preached to an interesting congregation of Japanese at night. The pastor of the church has the reputation of being a man of fine intelligence and deep piety. I was impressed with the large number of fine looking young men present at the meeting, and was told forty or fifty of them had come into the church within the past year. There were hopeful indications of a revival in this church, and it was the purpose of the pastor to begin a series of meetings a few evenings later. I here met with a number of earnest missionaries to whom I preached in the afternoon on Tuesday. Among them were three fine young Baptist preachers, graduates of our Baptist Seminary in Louisville. Here, also, I had the pleasure of meeting Mrs. Miller and her husband. Mrs. Miller was Miss Daisy Sutton, who attended school and also taught in Asbury College. Rev. Mr. Miller, who is a graduate of the Lutheran College at Salem, Va., impressed me as being a high order of man. We also met several very devout Low Church Episcopal missionaries in this group of consecrated young people, deeply in love with Japan and expecting great things from God.

Some twenty years ago, I assisted Dr. Sam Steele in meetings in old McKendree Church, Nashville, Tenn. At that time there was a young Kentucky giant attending Vanderbilt University. He was one of the most powerful men physically, as well as one of the best students in the University. He had just been crippled in a football game and at the time of our meeting, had one of his limbs bound up in a cast of some kind and could only walk with crutches or by putting his arms around the neck of his fellow-students. He became deeply interested in the meetings and many a night came down one of the broad aisles of beautiful old McKendree with each arm around a schoolfellow's neck, his crippled limb sticking out in front of him. He became deeply interested in the experience of perfect love, sought full salvation and was blessedly sanctified. Later on he graduated; entered the ministry, was sent to the mission field and I had not seen him since the meetings at McKendree, until our train pulled into the station at Kobe, and there he was to meet me—Rev. S. E. Hager. How happy I was to look into his strong, ruddy face. He is still the athlete, but a little heavier than in the days at the University, fully saved. He is presiding elder, evangelist, teacher in the college, financial agent, lover of souls and one of the best Japanese scholars of his age in these islands, and one of the best missionaries in any church in the Orient. It was like going home to go to his house. He married a fine Tennessee woman and they had five interesting children.

Bro. Hager being my old friend, did not want to work me too hard, so on Friday, the day of our arrival, he only preached me twice. Saturday I must preach three times; twice at the Methodist Church and once at the Congregational Church to a convention of Christian women There were said to be six hundred Japanese women present. I am sure it would have made the hearts of the missionary women on our side glad to have seen this gathering of their sisters in Japan They had the appearance of being highly cultured and deeply·pious. The theme for consideration was prayer for the baptism with the Holy Ghost It pleased me to preach to them on that subject. It was a wonderful sight to look upon them from the pulpit—this audience of Christian women so neat, and yet so modest in dress and manner, so courteous to each other and with every outward mark of real devotion within, met here to pray for the outpouring of the Holy Spirit, which was announced in large letters on a long scroll hanging on the wall at the pulpit.

Many people were at the altar of prayer in the two services in the Methodist Church on Saturday. I was told that the Japanese people were very cold and that I need not expect them to weep and cry out at the altar as I had seen it in other countries, but I have found them a most responsive people to preach to. They give the closest attention, see the point, get the truth and if the preacher warms up they warm up too. The revival spirit was on from the beginning and the seekers at the altar poured out their hearts in most earnest prayers, many of them weeping in their earnestness of soul.

There was a sanctified Japanese brother who had come in to attend the meetings, who prayed with an agony of earnestness, with a face white with the soul struggle for the salvation of the people, the perspiration breaking out upon his forehead, that I have rarely seen surpassed. The faith and zeal of Bro. Hager and several other missionaries who held up my hands, made it easy and a great joy to preach. One of the Presbyterian ministers led the singing for the meetings and put his whole soul and body into it, in Japanese of course, and the singing was a fine feature of the meetings. This same minister had the joy of seing several young men of his flock in whom he was deeply interested, greatly blessed at the altar.

On Sabbath day I preached three times at the Methodist Church the Lord giving victory at each meeting, and late in the afternoon I preached at the English-speaking Church to a good congregation of

Japanese Girls.

missionaries and other foreigners. The Lord gave his blessing.

Monday, the last day of our four days' meetings, I preached in the morning in the chapel of the Kwansie Gakuin, or Anglo-Japanese College. This is a splendid plant. The new brick college chapel is one of the most beautiful houses of worship I have seen in the East. The auditorium is large and handsome and was filled from front to back seat with one of the finest looking bodies of students I have seen in all of my journeyings.

This school has a great dormitory which would look well on the campus of Vanderbilt University. I had a good time preaching to the students and at the close made a proposition which revealed the fact that a large per cent. of them were Christians; on another proposition, not less than thirty or forty arose indicating their desire to become Christians. I was delighted with this school, situation, grounds, buildings, professors, students and the spirit of the place. The atmosphere of a Christian college rested upon the beautiful plant.

Dr. J. C. C. Newton, who is much beloved, has poured out heart'and brain here. He is now absent in the homeland to recuperate his health. The Lambuths and Dr. Wainright put toil and prayer into this place and it has all brought forth fruit.

In the afternoon we had a meeting in the church in which the Holy Spirit graciously melted and blessed our hearts. Brother Piercy and myself went to supper with Rev. C. B. Moseley. We were in Wesley Hall together and this is the first sight I have seen of him since we parted there. He has wrought faithfully here for many years. He is principal of *Palmore Institute* and resides in the house in which the beloved Dr.

Lambuth lived and died. He has a charming family of a wife and five or six children—children that make your heart glad.

At six o'clock I preached to his High School; many of the boys stood for prayer and Brother Moseley announced that all who desired to go to the revival meetings at the church might do so and about one-fourth of them slipped out and hurried to the church. We went at once to the church and the Lord gave us a good time with all the altar space packed with earnest seeking souls. These have been four great days; I preached thirteen times but only once in English. I had to stand and listen to twelve of my sermons preached by my interpreter paragraph after paragraph, so preaching and hearing, I went through twenty-five sermons in the four days. Each day of the four Bro. Hager was up a little after dawn, on his wheel and away to the church where he was met by the devoted Japanese pastor and a few other earnest souls and they waited at the throne of grace and they waited not in vain. The God of the universe answered prayer. The last meeting closed late and Bro. Moseley walked up the hill with us and we said good-bye to each other under the stars, and my feet were heavy as I pulled up the stairs and reflected that there is no tenderer, truer friendship on earth than that which Methodist preachers feel for each other. How tender and true the love of the brethren, when that love is sanctified in Christ.

While conducting the meetings in Kobe, I was entertained in the home of Brother Hager, occupying the room in which our beloved Bishop Ward spent three weeks of his last illness. A short time before his death he was removed to another one of the mission homes

because Brother Hager was compelled to be absent a
few days attending the annual conference. He hastened back as soon as possible and united with the other
misionaries in giving the sinking Bishop every needed
attention.

When Bishop Ward landed in Japan his condition
was hopeless; in fact, had he remained at home and
had perfect rest, the supposition is that his malady was
so advanced that death would have been inevitable. It
was inexpressibly sad that he could not have spent his
last days in his own home, and among those who loved
him so devotedly; but his death on the great battle-field
of the Orient, was not without significance and was a
benediction to those who gathered about him.

Brother Hager talked to me much of the quiet dignity and beautiful patience of the distinguished suffer-
er. His trouble was a small tumor on the brain, in all
probability produced by overwork and hard study. At
times he suffered great pain, and frequently, for short
periods towards the last, was delirious, but even in
those moments not a word of complaint or out of harmony with high and pure character escaped his lips.
It was at one of these moments that the attendant physician said, "If there is any dross in him, this will bring it
to the surface, but there is none there."

On one occasion, as Brother Hager sat by his bedside, as the shades of night were falling, he heard the
Bishop saying in a low, tender voice, the prayer he had
lisped as a child at his mother's knee:

"Now I lay me down to sleep,
I pray the Lord my soul to keep,
If I should die before I wake,
I pray the Lord my soul to take.
All this I ask for Jesus' sake."

The trained nurse, an unconverted Japanese woman, who waited on him from the time he took sick until he passed away, begged for permission to sit by his remains through the night, which privilege was granted. She was frequently noticed shedding tears; shortly afterward she renounced idolatry, professed faith in Christ and was baptized.

The Southern Methodist missionaries in Korea and Japan greatly regretted Bishop Ward's death. On his former visit, he had shown such deep interest in their work, had inquired so carefully into all its details and had manifested such a spirit of Christian love for the missionaries, that they hoped for much from him and looked forward to his coming with great eagerness. Their disappointment and grief were pathetic.

Brother Hager said to me that his experience at the bedside of this sick and dying soldier of the cross, listening to his words of wisdom and looking at his spirit of humble resignation, was one of the greatest benedictions and blessings that had come into his life. Personally, I knew but little of Bishop Ward. I heard him speak on the subject of missions at several of our annual conferences and was impressed with the earnestness of the man. He never wasted a moment telling funny stories for the amusement of the brethren, in order to get their attention, but went straight to his subject with an intelligence and earnestness that claimed and held their attention from start to close, always making us feel that we should do more for the spread of the gospel.

How strange it seems to us poor, short-sighted creatures here that Bishops Tigert and Ward, men so young and strong, with the promise of such abundant and

Group of Missionaries and Native Christians at Nagasaki, Japan.

fruitful service, should have fallen just as they seemed to be girded up for splendid leadership in the hosts of the Lord. But be it so; no doubt in some higher realm, they go forward in a larger service, and while the hearts of those who loved them so devotedly have suffered great sorrow, they too, are comforted with the soothing whisper of him who wept on earth with those who mourned their dead. It seems significant that these two young leaders of the homeless, itinerant hosts, should themselves, have died away from home, one in the West, and the other on the far-flung battle lines of the Orient.

The war is going to be over by and by; the white banner of eternal peace will float high above all the field of strife, from which every foe shall have been swept away and the trumpet will sound a note so loud that those who have fallen in the conflict will hear and, rising up in triumph, will come marching with songs of praise and shouts of joy to gather about the King. One hour of that great, glad day would pay a man for ten thousand lives of toil, hardship and disappointment here. Fight on, ye soldiers of the cross; directly the dawn of that glad day of victory will be breaking upon the eternal hills of glory and we shall be forever with the Lord. Amen.

The Southern Methodists have acted wisely in their management of church affairs in Japan. They went into the union of Methodisms into one Japanese Methodist Church, but they retained certain control of church property and the entire handling of the moneys contributed by the church at home, until such time as they shall deem it wise to turn over everything to the management of the native brethren.

From Kobe, we went to Osaka, where we held meetings in the Free Methodist Church. The pastor and membership of this church impressed us profoundly with their deep piety. They were *Free Methodists*, true and zealous. Bro. Sasao, of Tokyo, came up and interpreted for us, and we had a most gracious time. The altar was filled at every service, and a great many souls professed either pardoning mercy or sanctifying power. From this place we went to the Cowman and Kilbourn, Oriental Mission in Tokyo.

We ran something more than half the distance from Osaka to Tokyo in daylight, and had a fine view of the beautiful country. The wheat and barley were in the head; vegetables were growing luxuriantly on every hand, and the farmers were busy putting in their rice crop.

Japan abounds in mountains, only a comparatively small part of the earth's surface is tillable. It is claimed that eighty-two per cent. of the acreage of the country is so mountainous that it is of little use for agriculture; but in many places we saw where the energetic farmer had terraced up the mountain sides and sown the narrow strips of earth with grain.

Some of the Japanese brethren at Tokyo came out to meet us as we approached the city. At the first city station where we changed cars for that part of the city where the mission we were to visit is located, quite a company of them met us with a hearty greeting, and when we got off at our destination not less than fifty of the Christians met us with a big banner bearing in large letters the word, *Hallelujah.* We found so happy and glad a people that although they were strangers in the flesh, we felt as if we were coming among old friends.

We were soon safely housed in comfortable quarters in the Oriental Mission.

For some years I have been seeing reports now and then from the Oriental Mission with headquarters at Tokyo, under the management of Cowman and Kilbourne. For some time I had been under promise to spend some days in meetings in their school located here at the headquarters of the mission. The meetings were so timed that the workers came in from all parts of the country for their annual conference, so that in addition to attending to their business they could also be in the revival meetings. The school had about forty students, all of them preparing for salvation work; and some fifty or sixty workers came in, besides many Japanese Christians of the city. First and last, quite a number of missionaries attended the meetings. The day services were held for Christians in the school building, but a number of the evening meetings were held in the city.

I preached four times in the largest Japanese Baptist Church in the city, and three times in the largest Japanese Methodist Church. The attendance at these services was large, the interest deep, and the seekers for the Lord many. There must sometimes have been as many as forty seekers at the altar at one time. Mos. of these were for pardon, but always some for sanctification. As the meetings went forward, tnere were some very bright, clear testimonies. The names and addresses of all those coming to the altar were taken, and the Christian workers propose to follow them up and instruct them in the way of the Lord more perfectly.

I could hardly conceive of a riper field for salvation

work than this great capital city of Japan. I was deeply impressed with the large number of bright young men who came out to the meetings and listened with closest attention to the gospel, and hastened at once to the altar of prayer.

The zeal with which the students of the *Oriental Mission School* worked in these meetings reminded me of our students of the best holiness colleges at home. They would sweep through the audience, bring in the seekers, and then get down with them, Bible in hand, and instruct them in the way of salvation.

The meetings in the school were strictly on holiness lines, sermons and talks to soul winners. The Lord blessed us, and many were at the altar with their various wants before the throne of grace.

The *Oriental Mission* is an independent holiness work. Bros. Cowman and Kilbourne were wholly sanctified business men of Chicago; about eight years ago, felt called of the Lord to this great field to plant and spread holiness as taught by Mr. Wesley and the early founders of Methodism. They have been signally blessed of the Lord; many souls have been converted and sanctified under their ministry, and they have gathered about them a band of most earnest and aggressive workers. Their great purpose and aim is to put native workers into the field, fully saved, clearly instructed and firmly grounded in the great fundamental truths of the Bible, as taught by the early Methodists. We have no holiness school at home more zealous for the doctrine of repentance, faith, regeneration, the remains of sin, entire sanctification, growth in grace, zealous service and the premillennial coming of the Lord, than these people. These brethren have been

Group Japanese Evangelists.

fortunate in securing the services and identifying with them two men of great zeal and intelligence, Bros. Narcata and Sasao. They have done and are doing a great work in the way of distributing the Scriptures and various gospels and many excellent tracts. They have translated and put into circulation some excellent holiness books. I was very grateful to find they had just brought out an edition of my little book on "The Baptism with the Holy Ghost" and was pleased to learn that it was having a rapid sale.

At the close of the meetings at the school, the students, workers, and friends gave Bro. Piercy and myself a most affectionate farewell, and a great company of them went with us to the depot, and waved us their Christian salutation as our car pulled away from the station. As far back as we could see, these dear children of the Father had their hands in the air. God grant that we may meet them in the clouds when the Master comes to catch away his bride.

After we closed our meetings in Tokyo, we were invited out to Aoyama Gakuin, the great school of the Methodist Episcopal Church in the suburbs, or residential part of the capital city. Dr. Chappell, dean of the school, asked us to spend a day and night resting in his quiet home, before going to Yokohama. Here we found one of the handsomest educational plants we have seen in all the missions of the Orient.

Some years ago, Rev. John Goucher, of Baltimore, Md., bought twenty-five acres of land here and gave it to the M. E. Church for school purposes. The land cost him $6,000; it is now supposed to be worth $500,000. Dr. Goucher has made large investments in the great mission fields of the East. In the various countries we visited, this and that property was pointed out to us with what had become a familiar saying, "Dr. Goucher gave us this."   One day I was talking with a highly-cultured Christian Indian who was at the head of a large school, and he said, "Dr. Goucher paid the expenses of my education," and so it has been throughout my journey.   I doubt if any man with means in this generation has made a wiser use of money than this modest, Christian gentleman.   It would be impossible to calculate with mere cold figures, the blessing that has come to the various mission fields because of his unostentatious liberality.

The whole place is alive with some five hundred young men and boys who are attending the school; on part of the campus is a young ladies' seminary, a home and industrial school, and all told there were about four hundred young ladies and girls in these two schools for women, making near nine hundred students in the place   The teachers for this large plant, make quite a colony of missionaries whom, I judge from what I saw of them, to be quite a high order of people.   Dr. Chappell had them assembled together in one of the large rooms, parlor and dining room being thrown together, while I rested and preached to them in the evening.   Mrs. Chappell had quite a company of choice spirits, men and women, who have been long on the field to take supper with us.

The next morning I made an address to the students of the male college and then hurried away to Yokohama, where I was to speak in the afternoon.   If the friends had not told me that I was resting, I would have thought I was going right on with the work, but it was a happy delusion and I got away feeling quite refresh-

ed. We shall not forget the kindly courtesy of Dr.
Chappell and his wife, who made us so welcome and
comfortable during our stay in their home. It was only
about twenty miles run down to Yokohama through
an interesting country which was most all the way
town or village. We were to dine at the home of Dr.
Draper who has been a long time in the work in Japan.
The Doctor was away but his wife, the accomplished
daughter of the deceased Bishop Haven, made us welcome and we had a delightful lunch, one of the sons
being present, the other children were all away in the
States studying in the same university from which their
parents graduated. Just here comes one of the hardships of the missionaries—separation from their children during the years while they must be in the homeland in school—those important years while character
is forming and the child needs the strong, tender hand
of the father and mother.

After the lunch at Dr. Draper's, we went to our
cheap, comfortable hotel on the bluff and at three
I was preaching to a goodly company in the wondrous
Bible Training School. That night I preached in
sock feet, in one of the large missions to a house packed with thoughtful people, shoes off sitting quietly on
the clean mats before me. I preached pardon for sinners and purity for believers and both classes were represented in the altar full that crowded to the place of
prayer. The following Sabbath evening I preached,
at the invitation of the pastor, to the Union Church congregation made up of ministers, merchants, officials and
travelers, with a Presbyterian pastor born in England,
educated in the States, married a wife who once re-
sided near Richmond, Ky. I preached to them on the

difference between a perfect heart, a perfect head, and a perfect service. It is a perfect heart that God requires. The head may blunder, the service may be poor, but if the heart is from sin set free and full of holy love and loyalty, God is satisfied. The benediction was pronounced and I walked out under the stars, just breaking from the blue, with my work done for the present in the Orient. I walked home a tired, worn man, full of gratitude for the gracious privileges of these strenuous months, with a strong faith that the gracious Spirit will bless the seed sown, and bring forth an abundant harvest.

Many a man may go around the world, preaching far greater sermons than I can preach, but no man can go around the world preaching a greater Christ than I have preached, for everywhere I have offered a Christ able to *save all men from all sin.*

Group of Southern Methodist Missionaries in Kobe.

CHAPTER XX

THE HIGHEST DUTY OF THE HOUR.

How to get the largest number of the best-equipped missionaries on the field where they are most needed, in the shortest time, at the least expense—that is the question. In answering this question, let us first ask and answer another one back of it.

What is the highest and first duty of the church to the heathen world at the present moment. *At the present moment,* mark you. We are not discussing what the church should have done one hundred, fifty, or even twenty-five years ago, neither will we undertake to tell what the church should do twenty-five years hence.

The highest duty of the church at this moment is to give the gospel of Jesus Christ, in the shortest time possible, to the entire heathen population of the earth. The church should now go into all the world and preach the gospel to every creature. Let the institutions of civilization take their place in the line of march but let the gospel lead.

Immense sums of missionary money have been spent on the foreign field for education and medical purpossess, while vast multitudes of people living in sight of the towers of these colleges, universities and hospitals, never heard of Christ and the great sacrifice He made for the lost souls of men. I am not to be understood as opposing education, or as underestimating the value of the medical work on the mission field, but it would be cruel for a life-saving crew to leave the struggling mass of passengers of a wrecked ship in the water, some of them sinking and drowning, while they held a convention on the shore debating the best method for the education and medical treatment of those who might be rescued after their slowly-laid plans were matured. The heathen are overboard, struggling in the great, sweeping waves of sin by the millions. The church should arise, gird herself and leap forward to the immediate rescue of the perishing. The gospel is the power of God unto salvation; let us go and faithfully preach it and trust the Holy Ghost to supply the power that will save the people. A saved people will look after the education of their children and healing of their bodies. In fact, whatever may have been the needs of the past, the various governments of the earth are beginning to look after the education and medical care of their people.

Take Japan, for instance; she is well advanced in medical science; the Japanese physician has already demonstrated his efficiency. The Japanese educational system compares favorably with that of so-called Christain nations. I do not mean to suggest that Japan is giving her people a Christian education; many of our great schools in America are not doing that; in fact, not a few of them are antagonistic to evangelical religion, but Japan makes her boast that within ten years there will not be a boy or girl in her isles who cannot read and write. After that she might organize a society for the promotion of the knowledge of A, B, C's in the vast illiterate districts of our own country.

If Japanese army surgeons had have had charge of our medical and hospital department during the Spanish and Philippine war, we would have had a much smaller death rate than we did have. Their success with the sick and wounded during the war with Russia, justifies such a conclusion.

Japan's greatest need is the Spirit-filled evangelists to mightily proclaim the gospel of salvation from sin. For the present, I could not agree with any sort of a proposition for building schools or hospitals in Japan with missionary money, except training schools for Christian workers. Of course, if some philanthropist desires to build a Christian school or hospital in Japan, he has a right to do so, and it would be a good work and a great field for usefulness, and I would be the last one to object, but the missionary money collected from the churches ought to be devoted to the immediate spread of the gospel to all the world. It is the duty of the British government to educate the people of India. There are many government schools there which are doing good work. The liquor and tobacco bill of the British Isles for one twelve-month would build schoolhouses all over India, put a school book in the hand of every child, and supply a teacher to guide it. There are many medical colleges and public hospitals in India; let the British government prove its fitness to govern India by supplying the people with schools, physicians, and the necessary public charities, *and let the church take the gospel of Christ to the people.*

Bring India to Christ, and she will rise up and educate herself. The Mohammedans and Hindus of India build their temples and support their priests; convert them to Christ and they will be ready to support all the institutions of the church. *Give them the gospel,* and the blessing of Christian civilization will naturally follow as the legitimate fruits. Salvation the cause, the happy home, the beautiful church, the comfortable hospital, the orphanage, the asylum, the library and every good thing the effect. Sow China down with gospel seed and Christianity will spring up and bring with it all the institutions for the enlightenment of men and the amelioration of their sufferings.

It would have been bad generalship to have stopped the United States troops on the coast when they landed in Cuba and spent years of time and millions of money building fortifications and military schools. On landing they hastened forward and swept the island of the foe, afterward they built barracks, and fortifications. The highest duty resting upon the church at this hour, is to sweep the world with the gospel, to tell the story of the love of God, the gift of Christ, His sufferings, death and resurrection, the full salvation there is in Him from all sin and His coming to receive His redeemed to Himself, and the importance of seeking in Him deliverance from evil and that holiness, without which no man shall see the Lord. This is the message of the church to a lost world. There are Christian schools in the foreign mission fields, built and kept up at large cost, accomplishing incalcuable good. Let them be multiplied an hundred fold. Gather the young people into them, win them to Christ, and educate them. Mark you, no one shall accuse me of saying the mission schools have not been a great blessing to heathen lands; I would not hint such a thing, but I do contend that the *duty of the hour* is EVANGELIZATION.

Let the church arise now and carry the good news to all men. Let her raise the money and enlist a vast army of consecrated souls and march throughout every heathen land, stir up every city, visit every village, seek out

Japanese Bible Woman.

every hut, climb up to every tree-dweller, take by the hand and look into the face of every heathen man, woman, and child who has not heard the good news and tell them of the Christ mighty to save.

Let every mission school become a center of evangelization, a place of revival power and salvation. Those missionaries in charge of schools who are tinctured with higher criticism, who do not believe in revivals of religion, and do not know how to lead souls to Christ, ought to be retired to the rear. There is no use dodging, explaining or excusing; the gospel is the power of God unto salvation everywhere and among all classes of men. We must not forget that the Holy Ghost is omnipresent, ready and mighty to use the faithfully-preached gospel.

No, I would not close one school or hospital, but would marshall an evangelistic host to sweep over the heathen world with the gospel. I would arouse the whole church and concentrate thought, money and prayer to this one greatest need of the hour—the immediate preaching of the gospel to the entire population of the earth.

Mission training schools for native workers would be a great factor in such a forward movement. Not schools for literary and scientific training so much, but schools for prayer, studying the word of God, establishing character and instruction in the best methods of soul winning.

The Christian world is guilty of long delay in the greatest work committed to men by Jesus Christ—that of carrying the gospel to all men. This generation must arise and spread the glad tidings through all the earth, or stand guilty before God in the presence of millions of neglected heathen in the day of judgment.

CHAPTER XXXI.

THE TOBACCO FIEND.

In my tour around the world, I was profoundly impressed with how little the Orientals know of the *real* South. When one comes to think over the matter, this ignorance of the great and good qualities of our southern people on the part of the Orientals is easily accounted for. For almost two generations the administration of our government has been in the hands of the men of the northeast and northwest.

The representatives of our nation in the Oriental countries, in fact in almost all countries of the world, have been eastern and northern men. The great ships that sail from our ports go largely from Boston, New York, Philadelphia, in the East, Seattle and San Francisco in the West, and by far the largest part of the travel from the United States is from the northeast and northwest. The consuls, diplomats, merchants, literary men, scientific travellers, army and naval officers, as well as men of large wealth and leisure who touch the Oriental life, are largely of the northern and eastern portion of our republic.

Almost all of the literature that goes into the Orient, books, newspapers, and magazines have printed on their fly leaf, "New York." The great bulk of the missionaries in the eastern world come out from the northern and western states.

However much it is to be regretted, it is nevertheless true, that for the last half century there has been strong prejudice between the great northern and southern sections of our country and in the nature of things, people going out from the North could hardly be expected to put themselves at pains to make a good impression on the Orientals for our southern people.

The Southern Methodist Church has no missionaries in Africa, Egypt, Palestine, Arabia, Persia, India, Burmah, the Straits Settlements, Java, Borneo, or the Philippine Islands. Our missionaries in the Orient are in China, Japan, and Korea.

The reader will readily see that educated classes in pagan and heathen countries know but little of our great, glorious southland. They do know that we had human beings in slavery, that we had a most horrible and bloody war in freeing those slaves, that a large per cent of the population of the South can neither read nor write, and that it is a common thing, in that great section of the country, for fierce mobs of men to hang their fellow beings accused of crime without trial and in utter disregard of law or reason. This information comes to them highly colored through the northern press, so the reader will readily understand that the southerner, even at his best, is not so well understood in the Orient.

The great Prohibition movement, which has been sweeping through the South, has been a surprise and an eye-opener to the educated, thoughtful people of the Orient. I heard a number of expressions of approval and amazement over this great moral movement in our country. I was asked many questions about the matter with an expression that seemed to say: Can any good thing come out of the land of slavery, illiteracy, and lynching?

In a conversation with an old Indian judge, a man of education and large travel and wide information, I found he had no good word for the South.

Our Southern Methodist missionaries in the Orient hold a very high place in the esteem of the people, among the Methodists of the North, European people, and the native population. There is something in southern courtesy, sentiment, candor and kindness, that wins anywhere in the world.

I have made the foregoing statements to give emphasis to a humble protest against the Southern Methodist Church sending into the Oriental countries bishops who smoke or chew tobacco. We have had such bishops from time to time representing us in those great countries and smoking publicly and privately, a thing practically unknown among missionaries or native Christians. This conduct on the part of certain southern bishops has caused much surprise and much unfavorable comment, It is unfair to our great southern country to have it represented in these far away and populous parts of the world by a great church ecclesiastic with a cigar in his mouth. It is unfair to our people who contribute the money to bear the expenses of the chief pastors on such journeys. It is unfair to our faithful missionaries who hold up the Southern Methodist banner among this people. It is unfair to our native converts who ought to have kept before them the very highest standards of Christian conduct. The whole church ought to protest against such procedure.

I say these things with a kindly regard in my heart for my brethren in high places even though they may indulge in the unhealthful and disgusting tobacco habit; but the day has come when a love of the church, and the glory and majesty of Jesus Christ our great Redeemer, should cause them to rise above their mere appetites and carnal habits.

CHAPTER XXXII.

THE HAND OF GOD IN HISTORY.

The British Isles were lifted out of the ocean in a high northern latitude, but with the Gulf Stream running about them so as to make them not only habitable, but giving them the climatic conditions which are favorable to the growth of a race of men capable of the highest development both of mind and body.

It was not an accident that a stormy stretch of sea swept between these Isles and Europe. God ordained it so. They were sufficiently separated from Europe to make them the home and resting place of the Protestant faith, to save them from the blight of Romanism and the mental and moral degradation which has prevailed in Southern Europe; yet near enough to Europe to wield a powerful influence over the destinies of her various nations.

The early wars between the inhabitants of the British Isles were in their way a schooling for the times to come when these sturdy Britons should sail away to the ends of the earth and help to establish law and order, to become a mighty force in the civilization and evangelization of the world.

Had the British Isles been larger, their inhabitants would have found room for the occupation of their energies at home and Britain would never have become the "Mistress of the Seas." Had she held in subjection the American colonies, she would have exhausted her resources of physical and mental strength on this great continent and her drumbeat might never have been heard around the world.

The fact that she failed to hold this western continent, gave her time for the stretching of her vast empire through the mighty eastern countries.

No true philosopher should regret the throwing of the tea overboard in Boston harbor. God had builded this great continent and fenced it in with a wide waste of ocean waves. He saw to it that the Pacific Ocean should be much wider than the Atlantic. Our Atlantic seaboard should be the front door of immigration. First our population must come in from the British Isles and from Europe. It was the divine purpose to gather the best seed corn from the best civilizations of the world and plant it in this great new country.

God permitted the Revolutionary War and the years of prejudice which followed, that we might be sufficiently divorced from the mother country to break ourselves entirely away from fixed customs and old ideals which would have encumbered and hindered our progress. He wanted a larger and better man than had yet been developed or that could be developed under conditions which existed in the lands of kings, emperors, and popes.

This continent was to be the home of a great democracy. Here He would produce an atmosphere of freedom, equality, and good fellowship among men which would enable man to grow into larger proportions.

He permitted various nations to colonize here, but it was evidently the divine order that the Anglo-Saxon predominate. He had had better raising, he was Protestant, he was a believer in equality, he believed in an open Bible, and had something of the democratic spirit within him.

The war of 1776, the prejudices that arose, weaned our forefathers away from the mother country and threw them upon their own resources, it bred into our people a spirit of independence and contempt for royal blood, titled nobility, and aristocracy.

All of this went into the making of a new order of man, the man God wanted and must have in the carrying forward of the great work of the world's uplift. Up out of the flight from the mother country for liberty of conscience, for freedom of soul to worship God in simplicity and truth, to struggle with severe climate and dense forests and stubborn soil and wild beasts and savage men, and the seven years' war for civil liberty, God evolved the Democrat. The new man who believed in freedom and equality.

On this anvil of the new continent, with the sledge hammer of rapidly passing events, of struggle, war, and conflict, he hammered the men of various isles and nations together into this new man, this better, stronger man than He had yet been able to produce, and behold! *an American!*

Having lost the American colonies, the British government turned her attention and devoted her splendid energies to the development of the East.

Comparatively few Americans realize the blood and treasure that the British have poured out in carrying modern civilization, with the school, hospital, court, and the gospel of Jesus Christ into the Oriental countries.

I do not believe that the true philosopher can regret that the United States should have hoisted her flag over the Philippine Islands. That the cost has been heavy in gold and blood I readily admit, but gold was minted to be spent and shed blood is the price of advancement in the salvation of the world.

It seems to me that the time has come when Great Britain and the United States should stand very close together in their sympathies and efforts for the betterment of the races of men. If I were a diplomat I would certainly advocate a close alliance for peace or for war between the English-speaking peoples. We are now coming to the times when old prejudices should be forgotten and cast away and the Anglo-Saxon race should stand shoulder to shoulder to preserve the peace of the world and to move forward for the overthrow of those cruelties that arise out of pagan and barbarian civilization, and for the advancement of modern civilization with its educative and Christianizing influences.

The enemy of harmony and peace between the American and British peoples is the enemy of the highest progress which makes for the betterment of the condition of the entire human race.

These thoughts pressed themselves upon me on land and sea as I made the circuit of the globe and I place them here for the contemplation of my fellow beings who love God and who would unite hand and heart for the blessing and welfare of all their fellows.

Yoke the sturdy tenacious Briton and the free, aggressive American together and they will triumphantly pull their burden of responsibility up to the hilltop of victory. We are of one blood, we speak the same language, we read with reverential and obedient faith the same Bible; we worship the one God, trust in the same crucified and risen Christ, and we MUST stand together for the peace and salvation of the world.

"Reading Philip Martin's collection, *The President Next Door*, is like listening to music, but his words are the notes. And like a good album, you play both sides in one sitting to get the full effect, or in this case, one nice afternoon's read. There are delta blues stomps, historical ballads, catchy ditties, mournful country hymns and ol' time rock and roll. His verses about the South taste authentic, peppered with characters we know and love, from our kinfolk to local heroes like Billy Bob Thornton, Miller Williams, Maya Angelou and a certain neighborhood fellow who once lived in the White House. Philip's noted journalistic background brings minutia and details to his poems, which make them bright and alive like a sharply picked mandolin. Listen with your eyes and enjoy."

—Jay Russell, director of *My Dog Skip*, *The Water Horse*, and *Ladder 49*

"Philip Martin's distinctively varied voice engages the reader intellectually and viscerally in this collection of poems and song lyrics. His extraordinary gift, shown page after page, is the ability to capture the fugitive essence of any subject he approaches. Martin's precisely tuned and freshly turned phrases enlarge the reader's understanding of what has come before. In pieces as different as the poem-and-song pairing devoted to Frank Lloyd Wright's client-cuckold-friend Edwin Cheney or the meditation on a youthful reporter's police-beat assignment ("First Body") or the considerations of family relationships (father-son, husband-wife, human-animal), Philip Martin speaks with authority, humility, and ease. His words touch something universal and true."

—William B. Jones, *Classics Illustrated: A Cultural History*, 2nd Ed.